We Are Afghan Women

. . . . .

Voices of Hope

Introduction by
LAURA BUSH

GEORGE W. BUSH
INSTITUTE

SCRIBNER
New York   London   Toronto   Sydney   New Delhi

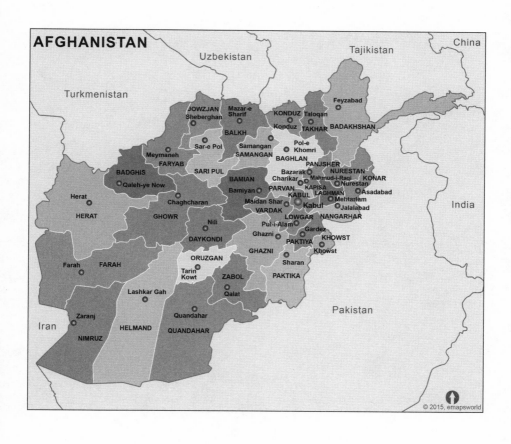

AFGHANISTAN

China

Uzbekistan

Tajikistan

Turkmenistan

Feyzabad

JOWZJAN
Sheberghan

Mazar-e
Sharif

KONDUZ Taloqan

BALKH

Konduz

TAKHAR

BADAKHSHAN

Sar-e Pol

Samangan

Pol-e
Khomri

Meymaneh

SAMANGAN

BAGHLAN

FARYAB

BADGHIS

SARI PUL

Bazarak

PANJSHER

NURESTAN

KONAR

Charikar

Mahmud-i-Raqi

Qaleh-ye Now

BAMIAN

PARVAN

KAPISA

Nurestan

Asadabad

Herat

Bamiyan

KABUL

LAGHMAN

Chaghcharan

Maidan Shar

Mehtarlam

HERAT

GHOWR

VARDAK

Kabul

Jalalabad

Nili

LOWGAR

NANGARHAR

DAYKONDI

Pul-i-Alam

Ghazni

Gardez

KHOWST

PAKTIYA

Khowst

ORUZGAN

GHAZNI

Farah

FARAH

Tarin
Kowt

ZABOL

Sharan

Lashkar Gah

Qalat

PAKTIKA

India

Pakistan

Zaranj

Quandahar

Iran

HELMAND

QUANDAHAR

NIMRUZ

© 2015, emapsworld

CONTENTS

. . . .

CONTENTS

CONTENTS

INTRODUCTION

. . . .

"I think Afghan women are capable of a lot and they do a lot, but they still are considered just secondhand humans. The moment you talk to men and you mention women's rights and equality and freedom, the response is 'What are women? What do they do? They're not capable of doing anything.' Most of them are not ready to hear that women are human beings."

—NASIMA RAHMANI, LAWYER, EDUCATOR, AND ACTIVIST

"My dream for the future of women in Afghanistan is to achieve 'bird-wing.' In Afghanistan, men are like birds that fly with one wing. Women need to fly right alongside the men, to be the 'other wing.'"

—MANIZHA WAFEQ, BUSINESS OWNER

. . . .

Like most Americans, my own recent history with Afghanistan begins on September 11, 2001. Before then, Afghanistan had received little sustained attention in the West. We knew it primarily as a cold war hotspot, and perhaps some of us as a centuries-old crossing point on the ancient Silk Road linking China, India, and Europe. Growing up in Midland, Texas, when my sixth-grade teacher, Mr. Bain, told us to write a country report, I decided that I wanted to pick a nation completely exotic and remote from anything I had ever seen, so I traced my finger halfway around a map of the world and chose Afghanistan. But after I wrote out my report in my best handwriting in a green notebook, I did not expect ever again to encounter this landlocked nation, which had enticed the likes of Alexander the Great and Genghis Khan, as well as the nineteenth-century British Crown and Russian tsars.

Then, more than four decades later, America and the world awoke to the barbaric Taliban regime in Afghanistan.

As I learned more about what had happened to this nation, what I discovered left me heartbroken. In September 1996, after the Taliban reached the capital of Kabul and captured it in a day, they imposed a form of gender apartheid never before seen in the modern world. A hallmark of the Taliban's rule was the brutal repression of women. Women were shut up in their homes. Women were forbidden from attending school, forbidden from working. They were even forbidden from showing their faces in public. Male drivers had their rearview mirrors removed so they would not have to bear the indignity of inadvertently gazing upon a woman.

The Taliban's religious police patrolled the streets, beating women who might venture out without a male guardian, or women who were not dressed "properly" or who dared to laugh out loud. Women were beaten if they wore shoes that made too much noise. They had their fingernails ripped off for the "crime" of wearing nail polish. Year after year, women and girls were stripped of their identity and dignity, until as one woman who lived through those days explains, "I would no longer think of myself as a human."

I was horrified by the extreme cruelty directed at Afghan women and appalled by the conditions in which they lived. By 2001, some 70 percent of Afghan people were malnourished, one in four children would not live past age five, and women often died in childbirth. Old age was forty-five. Children were deeply scarred. A UNICEF report stated that nearly three-quarters of the children living in Kabul had lost a family member during the preceding years of conflict, and half of the children in the city had watched someone being killed by a rocket or artillery attack. Corpses and dismembered body parts lay on the streets.

This devastation was not simply the result of five years of Taliban rule. It arose from a culture of war and fear that stretched back twenty-two years, all the way to the Soviet invasion of the country in late December 1979. That invasion led to the creation of an Afghan insurgency, the mujahideen, which was bent on defeating their Soviet invaders. When the Soviets withdrew their last troops in February 1989, those same mujahideen forces and factions turned on one another, resulting in a violent civil war. All of this occurred before the coming of the Taliban.

The human cost was devastating: at the height of the chaos during the Soviet occupation, more than six million refugees had fled across Afghanistan's borders and as many as two million had become displaced persons inside their own nation. It is estimated that in the 1980s, roughly half of the world's refugees were Afghan. The prolonged war left a staggering number of dead and wounded—best estimates are 1.5 million dead, more than 10 percent of the population at the time, and another four million or more who were disabled, maimed, or injured. Cities, villages, basic infrastructure, such as vital irrigation systems, and farmland and livestock had been destroyed. The nation once renowned for its fruit orchards, for its grapes and pomegranates, was stripped bare. In the frigid winters, people burned whatever they could find to stay warm. Among the survivors of these decades of conflict are millions of children and millions of young adults who have never known peace.

The struggle against the remaining Taliban insurgents, al Qaeda forces, and offshoots of the international terror group ISIS, the self-dubbed Islamic State, continues to this day. And so does the struggle to free Afghanistan's women from a life in the shadows, so that they may regain their rights and their lives.

Afghanistan from the air looks like no other place in the world. Much of it is carved into mountains and valleys, each region having been fortified by nature long before people began erecting walls and towers of their own. Afghanistan was a valuable stopping point along the Silk Road to and from China, but these ancient pathways did not translate into modern infrastructure. By the 1930s, the neighboring nations of Iran, what would later become Pakistan, and India had burgeoning networks of railways. Afghanistan had one track about five miles long that became operational for several years around 1920. Its three railroad locomotives, purchased from Germany, were ultimately placed in a museum. Roads faired only slightly better—many were built in the 1960s by the Americans and the Soviets. Even now, Afghanistan has less than ten thousand miles of paved roads, and the most recent figures place the number of registered cars at less than one million.

Progress came slowly on other fronts as well. While American women gained the right to vote in 1920, it wasn't until 1965 that Afghan women were allowed to vote in National Assembly elections, just six years after their government abolished the requirement that all women be veiled. By the early 1970s, a woman had been appointed to the cabinet as minister of public health, while in some areas of the country close to 40 percent of women held paying jobs, as teachers, doctors, and business owners. Increasingly, women also had the freedom to choose their own husbands. They played sports, watched movies, and in some larger cities wore current fashions.

But starting in 1971, the country suffered three years of severe drought, followed by a famine in which as many as eighty thousand people died. The existing Afghan government found itself under siege and was toppled by a coup. A pro-communist faction took power in 1978. Then in 1979, the Soviet Union, looking at Afghanistan's rich mineral resources and the turmoil on its border, decided to invade. Women's advances would be among the many casualties of that conflict.

At the end of 2001, the story changed again. By December, the United States and its military allies had removed the Taliban from power and disrupted al Qaeda terror cells, which were behind the horrific attacks of September 11. Women came out from hiding, out from under their burqas. They began to rebuild their homes and their nation.

Today, Afghanistan is a study in contrasts. It has one of the youngest populations in the world, with a median age of eighteen years, and more than 60 percent of its population is under the age of twenty-five. Yet its landscape is still covered with wood and mud-brick buildings. I made three trips to Afghanistan as First Lady of the United States, and each time, as I gazed down, I had the sense that I was flying over the outlines of an ancient civilization or the footprint that it had left behind.

On the ground, the conditions are equally disparate. The same landscape that is covered in winter snow is suddenly, barely a season later, engulfed in blinding dust storms. In places like the city of Jalalabad, the temperature can dip well below freezing and then rise to 120 degrees Fahrenheit—"screaming hot or freezing cold" is how some Americans put it. The harsh climate has weathered the people and buildings in much the same way, roughening their exteriors and adding deep lines. In the places touched by war, contrasts abound. Next to bombed-out Russian tanks and deadly fields peppered with land mines, beautiful flowers open and bloom each spring.

The Afghan people are as varied as their landscape. The Afghan

National Anthem mentions fourteen ethnic groups; the four largest—
Pashtun, Tajik, Hazara, and Uzbek—together comprise roughly 84
percent of the population. The Pashtuns are the largest group, and
Afghanistan has traditionally been governed by Pashtuns. The kings
who formed the Afghan empire in the mid-1700s and later in the
1800s were Pashtuns. Afghanistan has two official languages, Dari
and Pashto, with Dari having slightly more speakers and readers.
Dari is closer to Persian or Farsi, spoken in neighboring Iran, while
Pashto, the traditional language of the Pashtun people, is based on a
modified Arabic alphabet.

Today, the latest chapters in Afghanistan's history are being written. Peace has been elusive. After their overthrow, the Taliban and
its allies regrouped into insurgent forces, posing a new challenge. I
am humbled to see the faces, read the names, and meet families of
the many Americans who have given everything for freedom. We
remain a free and secure nation because of their devotion and their
families' sacrifice.

It is not only our sacrifice. Troops from forty-two countries have
served as part of an international security force overseen by NATO,
which has included forces from all twenty-eight NATO countries.
Afghanistan has rebuilt its own military from scratch, with its troops
fighting alongside international forces or undertaking missions on
their own.

American and international contributions to Afghanistan have
been substantial. The sacrifices have been many, and so has the gen-
erosity. American military doctors have worked in clinics to treat the
medical needs of ordinary Afghans. American soldiers and airmen
have collected shoes for Afghan children who would otherwise be
barefoot. American military lawyers have traveled the country to
help build an impartial justice system. Donors, from governments to
individuals and the private sector, have built schools and roads, pur-

chased textbooks, restored buildings, and even preserved Afghan traditional songs. Despite the challenges that remain, we should not lose sight of how much has been given, how much has been accomplished, and how much has changed for the better.

We see tremendous gains in education, where international donors have given more than $1.9 billion for Afghanistan's "Back to School" campaign. Under the Taliban, barely 5,000 girls attended school and only about 900,000 boys. Today, best estimates are that more than 2.5 million girls are in school and 8 million boys. More than 120,000 girls have graduated from secondary school and 15,000 girls have graduated from college. Thirty-seven percent of girls ages twelve to sixteen are literate. Thirty-six percent of teachers are women. These are numbers that will transform this nation.

One of the model programs for Afghanistan is the American University of Afghanistan, AUAF, a co-educational school in Kabul that replicates American Universities around the world, offering a Western model of education. AUAF opened ten years ago in a war-torn building, with fifty-three students. Only one of those students was a woman. Eight years later, in 2014, a female student, Onaba Payab, was named the graduating class valedictorian. Today, more than 50 percent of the incoming class is female. Onaba is pursuing a master's degree in public health and is working to support women's economic and educational rights. Her success is exactly the dream that I, along with many others, had when I traveled to Kabul to help launch AUAF.

Afghan women are making gains in the workplace. Nationwide, women own more than three thousand businesses. The reach has extended to the economically disadvantaged. ARZU, a rug company operating in rural Bamiyan province, has pioneered a new employment model. To weave with ARZU, women receive health services and literacy training and they pledge to send their children to school.

Today, all two thousand female ARZU weavers are literate and earn more than the average per capita income in Afghanistan.

These successes have a ripple effect across the larger community. Decades of research shows that women reinvest 90 percent of their income in three key areas: educating their children, accessing healthcare for their family, and growing their local economy. In Afghanistan, women's economic participation improves family dynamics by giving them a voice and respect in their own households, and it has a profound impact on health and educational opportunities for their children.

My first public effort on behalf of Afghanistan's women was delivering the November 17, 2001, weekly presidential radio address. I spoke about the Taliban's "degradation" of women and children. "The plight of women and children in Afghanistan is a matter of deliberate human cruelty, carried out by those who seek to intimidate and control," I said. Sadly, in parts of Afghanistan, those words remain true today; too many women and children still lead lives blighted by fear, violence, and intimidation. On the afternoon I recorded that radio address, when I put on the headphones and bent over the microphone, I thought about the millions of Afghan women who had been hidden away from the world and had the world hidden from them.

I am fortunate to have been able to help. I can speak out. I can support relief efforts. I have met with Afghan women who are teachers, lawyers, judges, human rights workers, and parliamentarians. I host conferences. I give speeches and publish op-eds. I have traveled to Kabul to help with the opening of the American University of Afghanistan and the creation of the Women's Teacher Training Institute to train female teachers from rural provinces. I have met with women studying to become police officers. I support scholarship programs and present diplomas. I serve as an honorary co-chair of the U.S.-Afghan Women's Council, a unique public-private partnership to improve the education, health, economic, and leadership status of Afghan women and children.

And I can ensure that the inspiring and beautiful voices of Afghan women will be heard.

This is a book of women's voices. The words spoken in these pages come from women of varying ages and experiences. All have become leaders in their communities or their professions. Each woman is her own success story, and each has her own remarkable story to tell. A few live abroad, some spent years in exile or as refugees before they were able to return. But each is committed to her homeland. Some have had the benefit of years of education, others have had their education interrupted, and a few had no formal learning until later in life. A few come from a world of relative privilege, others from poverty. They had fathers who were farmers or bicycle repairmen or traders or doctors or army officers or fighters with the mujahideen. More than a few had mothers who worked. They farmed, tended to animals, cleaned, or tailored, sometimes for pay, sometimes for barter. But all were working to support their households and families.

Many of the women who share their stories in these pages have witnessed painful death and unfathomable suffering. They have endured threats and violence; their homes have been looted and burned. One was locked inside her house by her husband every morning, forbidden to leave, forbidden to have visitors. Yet each of them has refused to give up or give in.

As I read their stories, I am struck by their courage, their resilience, and their hope. They hope for a better future, and theirs is not a naive hope. As one young Afghan woman says, "I have the option to be optimistic or pessimistic and my choice is to be optimistic."

Each woman believes in the importance of education for her children, daughters as well as sons. They agree on the desperate need for better "security," the catchall phrase meaning an end to violence. They know that the epidemic of brutal domestic and societal violence against women must stop.

These women wish for peace, personal peace and national peace for the men and women of Afghanistan.

Some of these women (and a number of Afghan men as well) have been galvanized by a single barbaric act that took place in March 2015: the brazen public murder of a twenty-seven-year-old woman named Farkhunda, who had just completed a degree in religious studies and was preparing to start work as a teacher. On March 19, 2015, Farkhunda got into a disagreement with a religious figure at a famous mosque, known as the Shrine of the King of Two Swords, in Kabul's old city. She was complaining about the practice of mullahs selling "good luck" charms or amulets to women who visit the shrine. She had argued that such charms only feed superstitions and run counter to traditional practices in Islam.

As Farkhunda spoke out, the shrine attendant accused her of burning the Koran, a grave sin in Islam. He shouted his accusation, she made her denial, but it did not matter. His charge led hundreds of angry men to the mosque. The mob surrounded Farkhunda. Then the mob turned savage. Farkhunda was thrown from a roof, dragged and run over by a car, and repeatedly beaten with sticks and stones. Video shows her bloodied, battered face as she tried to plead with the mass of attackers. In one final depraved act, her body was set on fire and dumped in the Kabul River. Witnesses said that the local police attempted to stop the crowd, but they were overwhelmed. They backed off and ultimately did not intervene. After Farkhunda's death, women carried her casket to her burial, insisting that no man should touch her body. (In strict Islamic tradition, women are not permitted at funerals or to carry the casket or to say burial prayers over the dead.)

Weeks and months later, Farkhunda's brutal death is still deeply personal to many Afghans and to many of the women sharing their stories here. They hope her death will be a turning point for Afghanistan.

How can we help change the lives of women in Afghanistan? The women in these pages have their own thoughtful answers. Their list is rich and varied: Some believe in economic empowerment. Some want to see an approach that uses religious interpretations and education to try to modernize long-standing customs. Others advocate for secular education, sports, better communication skills, microfinance, childcare, more exposure to the outside world, storytelling, and mentoring. They share their views on cultural issues like arranged marriages, on wearing a burqa, on whether it is better to teach basic skills or basic human rights. They speak of the importance of supporting each other through formal associations and networks, or simply by extending a hand. Women who come together in small groups to learn basic skills like embroidery find camaraderie that they did not have when they were kept isolated inside their homes.

Every woman in this book has her own perspective and understanding of the events that have shaped her life and the life of her nation. Some recall the Afghanistan of the 1960s and into the 1970s as a kind of paradise, while others openly question whether Afghanistan was in fact ever really a paradise for women.

The successes for Afghan women are real, but so are the challenges. The women sharing their stories capture both in vivid, poignant, and powerful detail. They know they face risks for speaking so openly, but they want the world to listen. When we listen, we support these women. As American University of Afghanistan's valedictorian, Onaba Payab, told me in September 2015 in Dallas, "This is a reminder that we are not alone in those tough places, that there are people who care about us."

* * *

This is a book of Afghan stories, but they are also universal stories. Many women will recognize their own struggles against discrimination in education or in the workplace. We see the women who confront domestic abuse and violence, serious and devastating problems not only in Afghanistan but here at home in the United States. We will find inspiration in the stories of women who stood up to the naysayers who told them their business ideas would fail, and the women who would not accept problems but solved them. We will recognize the power of perseverance in the young woman who spent hours at night studying to have the chance for a better education. We will share in the desire that mothers and fathers everywhere have for their own children to lead better lives.

To me, these stories refute the notion that anyone can ever be thought of as "a secondhand human"—the words of a rug weaver from Bamiyan province. Instead, these stories confirm the words of a traditional Afghan proverb: that we all can "bloom where you are planted."

Mrs. Laura Bush
Dallas, Texas

Living

Shopping at the bazaar

Two generations

Beekeeping

Harvesting vegetables

Washing utensils at the well

"A good year is determined by its spring" (traditional Afghan proverb). More than 15 million women call Afghanistan their home, and more than 10 million of those women are under twenty-five years of age. Roughly three-quarters of Afghanistan's population lives outside of major cities.

LIVING

. . . .

Imagine a world in which a woman keeps bees in secret, in which she doubles the number of her hives each year. She is not supposed to leave her house without permission, she is not supposed to work, and she is certainly not supposed to work as a beekeeper, a job reserved for men. But she does. And when she watches her bees take flight, she dreams of her own freedom and freedom for all Afghan women.

The stories told by the eight women featured here lift the veil on Afghan life, before the Taliban and after, and also further back, to the time before the Soviet invasion and then its aftermath. They speak of the price of decades of war, of their struggles to survive and find a place in the world, and how, despite everything, they have found their worth as women. They include older women, women in midlife, and young women, although in Afghanistan even those terms have different meanings, because in much of the country, the average life expectancy for a woman hovers around fifty-two years.

Afghanistan is a place where some women may go to college, where they may become lawyers, even judges and government ministers, but it is also a place where traditions and customs are so firmly embedded into the everyday culture that a young professional woman finds it "controversial" to admit she married for love. In some of the larger ethnic and tribal communities, the taking of a young woman's hand in marriage involves literally taking her hand. Groups of young women are gathered in a small room where they sit covered in burqas. Then a young man enters and each woman puts out one of her hands. No words are exchanged. They simply show their hands, and the man walks around

3

looking until he stops and selects one of the women to be his wife. They are married after just looking at one hand.

Understanding the complexity of Afghanistan and the life and history of its people, particularly its women, is central to beginning to understand the country. Here, a group of women of varying ages and backgrounds share their story and their nation's story in their own words.

Zainularab Miri is at that indeterminate age for Afghan women. Not yet fifty, she has become an elder in part by having survived in a place where the expectation is to die young.

Unlike many younger women in Afghanistan's provinces, Zainularab Miri does not draw her headscarf down over her hairline or wrap it tight above her brows. Instead, it drapes casually, resting loosely around her head. Today, her headscarf is black, like her hair, but lightly beaded, so that when the light catches it at just the right angle, it sparkles. She is quick to laugh, quick to follow a joke through layers of translation, from English to Dari, and then to reply with another humorous line, words that remain funny as they cross back over from Dari to English. Her face has the look of having been warmed and made ruddy by the sun, unlike many other Afghan women, whose porcelain cheeks, foreheads, and chins speak to years spent being covered, not simply behind veils, but also behind doors and inside of rooms.

· · · · · · · · · ·

I was born in Kabul, into a very modern, open-minded family. My father was a member of a council of elders, the council of wise men from his village, but he wanted all of his children to accumulate wisdom, daughters as well as sons. He and my mother gave me all the same chances that my brothers had. Everything my brothers did, I did too. If they ran around playing soccer, I ran around playing soccer. If they learned to play chess, I learned to play chess. I was never a stereotypical Afghan girl, playing only with dolls or sent off to wash clothes. Most importantly, I went to school. I attended a well-regarded elementary school. In high school, I concentrated on studying Dari, my native language, and even some English.

Although my family was very progressive, Afghanistan is a very traditional society. Historically, men have frowned on women working outside of the home. It has been considered an affront to the man that he cannot support his wife himself or be a father who cannot support his daughters. But I wanted a profession, and for a woman, one of the best ones was teaching, so in college I studied education and child development. I got married as I began my career. At first, I taught Dari to eleventh and twelfth graders, but after I had my first baby, I started teaching Dari to first graders because the elementary school was closer to my home and I wanted to be closer to my babies. That was nearly thirty years ago.

I had been a schoolgirl during the years of the Soviet invasion and occupation. I had been a teacher during the fight to drive the Soviet troops from Afghanistan's soil. My children were born in the time of the mujahideen and the civil war. But when the Soviet forces left, peace did not come. The mujahideen fought among themselves. Then a new group appeared. They called themselves "Taliban," to signify that they were students of Islamic knowledge. They were the holy ones; they would return order and Islam to Afghanistan, they said. In September 1995, after they had already captured Kandahar and other places, the Taliban captured Herat province—an important trading province with Afghanistan's third-largest city. We knew then that they were coming for Kabul.

One year later, in late September 1996, the Taliban had overthrown the Afghan president and now controlled Kabul. But we had already gone. My father was not native to Kabul. He had been born in Ghazni province, in the eastern part of Afghanistan, slightly south of Kabul. It is a mostly round-shaped province with a long tail that reaches almost all the way down to the Pakistani border. It is a province of valleys and snow-covered mountains, and its name comes from an ancient Persian word meaning "treasure." We would all go back to Ghazni in the summers to get out of the dry, dusty heat of Kabul. My father still had some land there and that is where we went.

The Taliban had their eyes on Kabul, on keeping Kabul in line. Ghazni was already a traditional province: people were religious, women were covered. They did not need to infiltrate our lives in Ghazni and so we felt safer. Even though women were banned from going out of the house or from working, I kept teaching. I had four hundred students. Seven of us, all women, had agreed to help the girls who were not allowed to go to school. Families of these girls would provide us with rooms and even sleeping spaces inside their homes. We seven women would then leave our own families and go door to door. We would teach for one day or sometimes for a few days in these hidden rooms, always with the curtains closed, so no light could come in and no outside eyes could see us. Everyone would sit on the floor, and in hushed voices we would teach the girls by taking turns. Each teacher had one subject. Mine was Dari, another woman taught math, and so on. Each person in those rooms, each person in those houses was risking their lives. If the Taliban found out, we would have surely faced death. This secret school went on for four years, when the Taliban had complete control.

But I did not just teach.

I was very lucky to have married a man who is just as open-minded as my father. As I moved around teaching, I realized that there were five men in our area of Ghazni who kept bees. In Afghanistan, bee-keeping is traditionally a male job. But that only made me more passionate to learn the business. As when I played soccer or chess as a girl, just like my brothers, I wanted to be like these men. I wanted to keep bees. I started by buying two hives from a friend of my family's, and as part of the bargain, I asked him to teach me what he knew. I, the teacher of Dari, became a student of bees.

Once I had my two hives, I wanted to expand. I was paid as much money for my nectar and honey as the male beekeepers were. No one thought to segregate my honey or pay me less because I was a woman. And each year, I added more hives and more bees. The Taliban did not know. They did not know that I was working, and that every year I was determined to double my cases of bees.

I did not find it hard at all to learn how to keep bees. Interestingly, for a beekeeper, even a woman beekeeper, the part that's the most challenging is making the queen bee. Without a good queen, the hive cannot be productive. The queen is what gives life to the hive, laying as many as fifteen hundred eggs in a peak day. Sometimes all the bees in the hive are her offspring. You cannot let the queen get too old or the hive will stop producing, but if you are going to have a good queen, you have to introduce her in just the right way, at just the right time. Picking the right queen, introducing the right queen, that is very hard to learn.

In a colony, the queen is the one bee that will never leave the hive. She spends her entire life inside the honeycombs. She can never escape the walls around her, never take flight. My honeybees could spread their wings and move from flower to flower or plant to plant, drinking in the sweetness. They could come and go as they pleased. I wonder if that is part of what makes honey so sweet, if it is the taste of that feeling of freedom, of flight.

As women in Afghanistan, during those Taliban years, many of us felt like the queen bee, trapped in our own hive. The bees build their honeycombs in the darkness. We too survived by working in darkness, behind curtains, under the cover of cloth; even my beekeeper suit hid who I was. But the darkness was appropriate, because the Taliban period was a very dark time for women.

When the Taliban fell, however, we found that we had our own honey. The girls who had been in seventh or eighth grade when the Taliban took hold were now in twelfth grade. Those years had not become a void in their young lives. They had continued with their education. Like the bees, they couldn't leave the hive, but when it was over, their learning was our honey, the residue of all their hard work.

Each season, watching my bees leave and fly off and then return laden with sweet nectar for honey fired in me a passion to be able to move about freely. But not just for me, for as many women as I could find. I believe that in order to change a country, first you must work on the women.

After the Taliban fell, Zainularab brought her beekeeping business out of hiding. In 2005, when the Afghan Women's Business Federation (AWBF) started, she was the first woman from Ghazni to sign up. She started traveling, to Italy to meet beekeepers, to Germany for leadership training, to the United States for a special business institute in Arizona where she studied management and marketing. When she returned to Afghanistan, with the help of her American mentor, she applied for a grant to start forty women as beekeepers, providing each woman with two hives and honey-making equipment.

Today, Zainularab is the head of the Ghazni Province Foundation of Women Beekeepers. She is also the secretary for the Afghan Beekeepers Society, making her a member of the beekeepers' council of elders. A few years ago, she sold all her hives, a total of three hundred, to build a house for herself and her husband and to pay for their three children to continue their education. Her son has a master's degree in computer science, her two daughters have studied in Sweden and India. But almost as soon as she sold her hives, she missed her bees, so she bought two new ones. Now she has thirty hives. And she has another new project.

I BELIEVE THAT IN ORDER TO CHANGE A COUNTRY, FIRST YOU MUST WORK ON THE WOMEN.

Afghanistan is a very male-dominated and traditional society. The men rule. It is still very chauvinistic. So we have created a circle of women. We call it "the Circle of the Chador," or Circle of the Scarf. We are five women trying to teach other women leadership in our province. We teach them things like how to network and how to stand up for their turf. We want them to have influence in this society, to have their opinions count. We start by telling the women that they know how to run their houses. That means they have leadership qualities. If you can lead in your house—or your hive—I tell them, then you can lead in society.

One of our major goals for the future is to create leadership and decision-making positions for women in government. Even when women go door-to-door and campaign, it is the men who get all the credit for any election win. The women who knocked on the doors and convinced the people to vote do not get credit. But now men need to hear them out.

One half of every society is women. If that 50 percent is voiceless, then that particular society becomes sick. Together, men and women are like the two wings of a bird. If one wing is hurt, the bird cannot fly. Society needs the bird to have both wings.

Khatereh Soltani is nineteen years old. She is part of Zainularab Miri's Circle of the Chador, and considers Zainularab to be her role model. She is wrapped in a black chador, a full-body cloak, from which only the face is visible, with a full black headscarf. The fabric cuts off her forehead right above her eyebrows. Her face is pale and freshly scrubbed, without a trace of makeup. Underneath, she is every bit as serious as her appearance. When she smiles, it is quick, as if she barely has the time. Khatereh has already trained as a midwife. Now she is studying law. Unlike most Afghan girls her age, she is not married. But someday soon, she knows that her father and her brothers will choose a husband for her. The girl, she explains, has no say.

. . . .

I want to become self-sufficient and independent. Most young women are not allowed to work outside of the house. When they do work, they need to have a woman like Zainularab. My parents and my sisters support my education, but my brothers are not as open-minded.

What young women need most of all is security. Right now, there is no sense of security. The minute you leave your house, you don't know if you are coming back in one piece. Every time, you wonder if today is the day that you will die or be maimed. Politically and socially, there is no kind of safe space to live and thrive in. You might be studying, but you do not know if one day your brothers will simply decide that there is something wrong with that, and will come and pull you off the street as you are walking.

We need to change the minds of the women and the men. When a woman cannot leave the house, she won't even be aware of her own rights. In each home, there is a lack of knowledge. As five women who have joined together to create the Circle of the Chador, we are trying to bring awareness. Women don't know that they have rights; they don't know that they can have a support system in the outside world. But to get that, they need access to education at home and abroad.

Some people really believe that the Taliban and the DAESH [ISIS in Afghanistan] are the true Muslims. They don't think for themselves; it is dictated for them. It is going to be a very long and hard struggle against these extremist groups.

The best way to win someone's mind is by giving them awareness of their rights and the better culture they can create by knowing their rights. A promise of a better future is what will make them want to come our way.

"I am old," Belquis Gavagan says. She is sitting in a spare Washington, D.C., office inside the gleaming building where she now works. Belquis makes herself a cup of tea, but does not drink it. Instead, it grows cold on her desk. Out her window is a view of the Potomac and a bit of Arlington National Cemetery lies beyond. She has easily witnessed as much death as the men and women who forever rest on that hill. She never expected to one day reside in the United States after arriving here as a refugee.

She tells her story matter-of-factly, but beneath it there is deep emotion. It is as if she has lived with these memories for so long that she is now beyond tears.

· · · · · · · · · ·

I was seven years old on the day the Russian troops entered Kabul. I remember what seemed like hundreds of helicopters flying around my house. I couldn't make sense of what was going on, but I was so excited to see so many helicopters in the sky. I didn't understand how things would change.

My father was an engineer and he worked for a construction company in Kuwait, so he was gone for much of my early childhood. At that time, it was just my mother, my sister, who was one year younger, and me. Many evenings, the three of us would walk to a hill that was close to our home. From on the top of the hill, you could see the entire city. It was so beautiful. I would take my books and my notebooks and do my homework on top of that hill. But when the Russians came things changed. They quickly understood that they too could see all of Kabul from the top of that hill. They established a military base around it. For a few months we didn't go back, until I insisted that we go. My mother gave in and the three of us set off, but before we could even reach the hillside, the Russian soldiers met us and said sternly, "No, you cannot come close." So we turned back, but after we got home—which was only a ten-minute walk—I slipped out of the house and went back by myself.

I was walking up when a Russian soldier pulled me by my hair. At that moment, I was so scared. He said something in Russian that I couldn't understand. And I tried to run away and fell. I was crying. I ran back home and was bleeding from falling down. And my mother got very mad at me. I was hurting from where I fell, from what had happened, and I kept thinking in my seven-year-old mind, "These invaders, they must go out of our place and country," because that place was so special to me. And I kept thinking about taking revenge.

The next day when I was on my way to school, I saw a Russian tank on the main street. I took a rock in my hand and I threw it at the tank. A soldier came out of the tank and started chasing me. But I was little so I could run faster than him. I took off and then I hid in a shop. There were very few shops at the time near our school, but there were a few, and the shopkeeper hid me under a table. That's how I got away with it, and I felt a sense of satisfaction. In a way, I'm embarrassed now. I look at all these kids in Palestine throwing stones and getting in trouble. But back then, on that morning, throwing that rock was at least something that I could do.

I was born in Kabul, but my parents were from Paktia, although they lived most of their adult lives in Kabul. My father actually got his undergraduate degree from George Washington University in the United States. In the old days, the prime minister's office was involved in selecting Afghan students to go abroad and study. My father had the highest scores in his high school. Somehow that information made it to the prime minister's desk. The prime minister's office decided first that my father should go to the Afghan National Army school. My father didn't want to, but he was forced. Forced to the point that security officers came and took him out of his house in the village to go to the school. He tried to escape, and he was punished. Eventually he gave in, but then they allowed him to go to school in the United States instead of the army. His marriage with my mother was arranged, as was the custom of the time. But it clicked and they fell in love with each other. My mother was fifteen years younger than my father, which was also not uncommon. My father passed away here in the United States in 2013 and my mother now lives here.

Everything changed when the Russians took over, even my school. We had a lot of communism and Marxism taught to us in school. At least once a week if not more, we were also forced to go and march in the streets. The bus would come and park in front of our classroom and we had no way to escape. As we rode to one of the main streets in Kabul, then they would tell us what slogans we had to shout that week. I remember that some of them were chants like "Death to America. Death to Thatcher." I didn't even know who Margaret Thatcher [the British prime minister from 1979 to 1990] was.

Living in Kabul, at first I knew very little about the mujahideen. To me they were brutal, savage people who killed other people. At least, that was my understanding from the propaganda from the Russian-backed government. But then we had relatives who would come in from the village where my parents had been born, and they would tell us the terrible things that the Russian soldiers and their

Afghan government supporters were doing to them. So I started to have conflicting views about what's good and not good.

I was young, but I remember how in most cases those who supported the mujahideen had no choice. The mujahideen would come to their houses at night, knock on the door, and say, "Hey, cook for me—bake for me and wash my clothes." And they could not say no. Then the next day, the government would retaliate. One story that has stayed in my mind was of a guy who was tied to the back of a truck—he was dragged around the village by the government truck, his body breaking over the road. Eventually he died.

I also remember how the Russian troops searched people's houses at night. At midnight they would appear, kick in the doors, and ransack people's houses. I remember them searching our house many times. We would be asleep and they would knock at the door with their boots. And then they would open the doors to our rooms and walk on our beds with their dirty shoes. They never found anything in our house except a lot of English books and magazines. My father collected issues of *National Geographic*. We also had an English typewriter, and we got in trouble for that. They took my uncle, my father's brother, and detained him for several days. His crime was having that English typewriter. After that, we started hiding our books and magazines. Oh, and one other thing was that they would come at night, crazy drunk, and knock at people's doors. When the people inside opened the door, the soldiers would start yelling basically "wife needed" or "woman needed." That was when some of our neighbors started sending their daughters to Pakistan to stay with relatives

> THEY NEVER FOUND ANYTHING IN OUR HOUSE EXCEPT A LOT OF ENGLISH BOOKS AND MAGAZINES. MY FATHER COLLECTED ISSUES OF *NATIONAL GEOGRAPHIC*. WE ALSO HAD AN ENGLISH TYPEWRITER, AND WE GOT IN TROUBLE FOR THAT.

because they were afraid that they would be raped if they stayed at home.

So that was my childhood.

The Russians were withdrawing from Afghanistan when I went to university in the fall of 1988. They left behind an Afghan government with an Afghan ruler, but it was a government that they supported. I was in law school when I decided to do something different aside from completing my education. So in addition to studying law and political science, I began studying nursing. A big international aid group had just opened their offices in Kabul, and they were training people and recruiting for a new hospital.

Then, in 1992, the mujahideen came.

I remember the day that they entered Kabul. It was April 28, 1992. The hospital that the aid group had built was for the war wounded. And that's where I was working as a nurse. We were treating wounded from all sides—government, civilians, and also mujahideen. Most government people were treated in a military hospital or government hospitals, but because many of our surgeons and staff were foreigners, the standard of care was much higher and some government officers were trying to get to our hospital for treatment.

The day before, in that last week of April, we received a phone call in the hospital. One of the mujahideen factions said they had some wounded that they wanted treated at the hospital—they told us to send an ambulance and get their wounded. The head nurse, Nurse Walker, was an Australian woman. She called me into her office and told me to talk to this person because she couldn't speak Dari. So I got on the phone, and he said, our location is in this place and we have wounded and send an ambulance. And then I heard Nurse Walker saying, "Okay, we're going to send an ambulance but someone has to go with the driver and the triage nurse to translate," and I said, "I'll go." So Jon, the other nurse—I forgot his last name, but he was from Iceland—Jon, myself, and the driver started out. But by the time we got out to the city outskirts the mujahideen were already positioned in those areas. Our ambulance was stopped basically every few hundred meters because each of the factions had established their own check posts. We told them who we were and most knew us, but one post was very aggressive. They stopped the car and the first thing they asked was if either of the two guys were my *mahram*, an appropriate male guardian to accompany a woman as required by Islamic law. I said, "Hell, no. One is my driver and one is my colleague." And the fighters said, women are not allowed to be sitting next to men who are not their *mahrams*. I replied that I am also a nurse.

It got very nasty very fast. We decided from that day on that I would sit in the middle, in case someone attacked me, so the driver on one side and Jon on the other side could protect me. The next day we were supposed to go to Maidan Wardak, which is a province about half an hour from central Kabul. We had received notice that there was a wounded man in critical condition and we had to bring him to Kabul for treatment. I was supposed to go with Jon but the next morning I got so sick I couldn't get out of bed. So poor Jon, he went alone to the clinic. There was no Afghan with him because some Afghans were supposed to meet him. As soon as he parked the car he was met with rains of bullets. The snipers were already there, waiting for him. He died instantly.

That happened in the morning and by two o'clock I felt a little better so I went to the hospital. By the time I got there, Jon's body had been brought back, and it was very emotional. He wasn't even supposed to be in Kabul. His duty station was Herat province, and he was in Kabul filling in for someone else.

By the next day the mujahideen were in Kabul, and the first changes we noticed were that we had to wear headscarves. I mean no one told the women to do that but we all did it. And then once we did it, the mujahideen decided what size our scarf had to be because a small scarf was not good enough.

After they had taken the city, the fighters also started firing all their guns in the air, and we had hundreds of people falling down dead because of all those celebratory bullets. I don't know what was going through their heads. They had fought for years and years and still couldn't figure out that when you shoot your gun into the air, the bullet comes back down eventually?

That was April. It was around July and August when the actual factional fighting started. It was constant fighting. There were a number of factions and splinter factions, but the ones directly and actively involved in the interfactional fighting were Jamiat-e-Islami, Itihad-e-Islami, Hezb-e-Islami, Wahdat-e-Islami, Harakat-e-Islami, and Junbesh-e-Islami. And then of course they all switched sides so many times. The Jamiat faction would switch and fight with Itihad and then they would both attack the Junbesh faction or the Hezb-e-Islami. It went back and forth all the time. The most notorious and feared commanders were three men: Abdul Rab Rassoul Sayyaf of the Itihad-e-Islami, Gulbuddin Hekmatyar of Hezb-e-Islami, and Abdul Rashid Dostum, who had been a commander in the National Army, loyal to the Soviets. Dostum had as many as forty thousand men under arms and when he defected to the mujahideen, his soldiers became one of the most feared fighting forces. Throughout the mujahideen times in Kabul, Dostum and his people kept switching sides among the commanders aligned with different, leading factions. They raped women. They looted people's houses. I was always afraid of them.

Working in the hospital, we all witnessed so much brutality.

Basically human life meant nothing to any of those fighters in those groups. We had cases of rapes and gang rapes. We had cases of men being raped. We had so many wounded—they would bring them to the hospital.

By August all the expatriates had left and the Afghans took charge of the hospital. I became a head nurse. We had two head nurses because we worked different shifts. There was an Afghan guy and me. Sometimes we worked up to seventy-two hours at once. We would get fifty, a hundred wounded at a time and we didn't have the capacity to handle them. We couldn't give them beds inside so we just put them under the trees. We would move them as the sun moved so at least they were in the shade all the time.

We also had carpenters who would make coffins. Sometimes we had dead bodies and no one would claim them and they would stay for weeks on a stretcher. That would take a lot of space, so then we started putting each unclaimed body in a coffin and we would put that coffin over the other coffins, stacking them as high as we could. We also used to take pictures of those dead bodies and post them outside the hospital walls. And sometimes we would take the pictures around to the local mosques and other places to try to find their relatives. We also had an agreement with some imams in different mosques that if after a certain period of time no one had claimed the bodies, we would take them to the mosque and pay the burial cost to the imam.

WE JUST PUT THE WOUNDED UNDER THE TREES. WE WOULD MOVE THEM AS THE SUN MOVED SO AT LEAST THEY WERE IN THE SHADE ALL THE TIME.

The hospital itself was not secure. It came under attack several times. We had rockets landing in our operating room and in our emergency rooms and the wards where the children were. We had people who got wounded inside the hospital, relatives who came

to visit the wounded and were wounded themselves when the rockets went off.

The saddest of all were the hostages. Every mujahideen faction
took hostages. Five or six separate factions had encircled Kabul like a
giant ring. They controlled the different areas and points of entry so
closely that each side could see the other. One group would take hostages so they could exchange them with another group, then the other
side would take any Pashtun or Hazara or Tajik people as hostages to
exchange for their fighters who had been taken hostage. It was a very
nasty game that they were playing with each other, and the civilians paid
a very high price. The fighters would bring the injured and wounded
hostages to us for treatment, but as soon as they were well enough to
be removed from their beds, we had to hand them back over to their
hostage takers. Sometimes we would treat the wounded and then we
would also engage in negotiating between the different factions to try to
get them released.

Those were the mujahideen times.

I did not get along with the leader of one of the factions. I didn't
really get along with any of the fighters, but this man in particular used
to come to the hospital to visit his wounded fighters and whenever he
came, he had his own rules. He would come in with armed bodyguards.
But we had a policy that no one could bring guns into the hospital, so
when I opposed him bringing in his own armed guards, he did not
like that. He took it personally. I didn't know that he had spies among
the hospital guards and support staff, but he did. They were basically
watching me and all my moves.

One time I helped a hostage escape from the hospital. I thought I
had been smart about it and that no one figured out what happened.
But one morning a fighter came to my office first thing. He was very
nervous, and he said, "You must leave now." I said, "What do you
mean? My shift just started." He said, "They're going to arrest you."

And I couldn't make sense of what he was saying. He was working for the intelligence department of the Hezb-e-Wahdat, the faction in control of the area where the hospital was located. And he felt that he needed to tell me because I had donated blood for him and his family members. Then he said, "Baaba"—meaning Ali Mazari, another one of the notorious warlords, who was the head of the faction—"has issued a letter saying that you must be arrested within twenty-four hours and taken to prison." I said, "I don't believe you—I haven't done anything wrong. I have basically sacrificed my life working in this front line." I was stubborn, and so he put his life at risk and went and got a copy of the letter.

It was—remember in the old days how they had carbon paper?—so he showed me a carbon copy. I couldn't believe it. I became so emotional. I sat there and cried. I called the international aid group's main office in Kabul and said, I need a vehicle, come and pick me up. Before I left, I did say good-bye to my staff. I have this picture in my mind of some of them crying. But I said my good-byes and told them it was time for me to move on. I went home later that day. My mother was surprised that I was home because I was supposed to be at work for twenty-four hours or so. And I explained what had happened.

For almost five years I had forced myself not to show emotions; I had forced myself to be strong. I didn't cry for years and years. And all of a sudden, after that morning, I just couldn't stop crying. And then I started having nightmares of all the terrible things that I had seen.

Once I was out of the hospital, the mujahideen forgot about me, and I started looking for another job in downtown Kabul. I found a position first with CARE International and then I moved from there to another aid organization, working in administration. By then it was 1996, the year the Taliban seized control of most of Afghanistan. I remember the day the Taliban took Kabul—that was September 26, 1996. A day or two before, I, along with a group of international aid workers, went to the minister of foreign affairs for a meeting, and the minister briefed us on the security situation and all that. He basically said that the government was in control of everything, that there was no way the Taliban would take Kabul. After, I went to him and said, "Tell me what you really think, Afghan to Afghan." He said he was offended that I didn't believe him. He said, "We defeated the Russians. We did this and that. There is no way the Taliban will take Kabul." I said, "Okay." But deep inside I knew that the Taliban would take Kabul.

They were so close—they were at Surobi, which is about a half-hour drive away. The next day I went to the office. At ten o'clock in the morning the female staff came to me and said they wanted to go home. We could hear rockets coming in and going out, but there was no immediate threat to us. Still, I let them go. I called my driver and said take them home. Then around three p.m., I called my driver again and said I wanted to go for a drive around the city. He said, "What?" And I said, "I want to go for a drive." He told me, "No, it's not safe." And I said, "I'm the boss. I'm telling you, start your car and we're going to go for a drive." So he did. I don't know why I did it but something, my sixth sense maybe, was telling me that it would be the last time I would be able to go out freely in Kabul. We went from one corner of the city to another corner. Then we drove back to the office and I packed all of my personal belongings that were in my drawers and my driver dropped me off at home. By the time we got to my house, around 5:30 in the afternoon, there were rumors that the Taliban were already in the city. By seven p.m. it was confirmed that the Taliban had taken the city.

In the old days, there was a Russian munitions center at the nearby army base. After the Russians left, the National Army stored ammunition there—and a rocket hit. Bullets were flying everywhere. Kabul's sky was lit up blue and red and every other color because of all the explosions and the bullets shooting up in the air above us. My mother came to me and said let's go to the basement. But all I wanted to do was cry and think of my next move. As soon as she closed my bedroom door, I got so scared. So I took my blanket and my pillows and crawled under my bed. And within seconds a bullet hit the window, burst through, and landed on top of my bed. It was that fast.

The next morning we turned on the radio. The state-run Afghanistan radio station had been renamed Radio Sharia and a male voice was reciting verse after verse of the Koran. Eventually there was a voice that said, "We have taken the city." They said schools for girls would be closed, and "sisters," meaning all women, were instructed and advised to stay home until further notice. And that was it.

I stayed in Kabul for two more weeks. I had two or three options. One option was to do what the Taliban said—stay home—be useless basically. Another option was to go to the north, by Panjshir, and join the mujahideen. And the third option was to go to Pakistan. I decided to do the third: I went to Pakistan.

I wasn't very lucky, because usually you could go from Kabul to Jalalabad and then to Peshawar in Pakistan. Under the best conditions, the trip would take about seven hours because the road conditions were so bad at the time. But the Taliban had blocked the road going to Jalalabad so we had to go a different route, first to Logar, then to Paktia, and then to Khost. I didn't make my decision to leave until the night before, on October 7. We were having dinner and I told my father that I wanted to go to Pakistan. My father replied that the Taliban wouldn't last long and asked if I really wanted to go to all the trouble? I said that I wanted to go to "all that trouble even if it was only for one day." He told me to "wait, because I need to inform my office and get leave and then go with you." I said that I was going tomorrow and that was it. And then my uncle, my father's brother, said he could go with me, that he didn't have anything else to do. One of my female cousins from the provinces who had been visiting us was also now stuck in Kabul. She wanted to go back to her home. I said, "Let's go together."

My mother immediately went to the neighbor's house and borrowed a burqa, the full body veil that also completely covers a woman's head and face, except for a thin mesh slit for the eyes to peer out of, for me. I said, "No, I'm not wearing a burqa." To me wearing a burqa meant obeying the Taliban, and I didn't want to do that. She begged me. She cried. I said, "No, I'm not doing that." So I wore a big scarf. It was almost the size of a bedsheet. I was completely covered and so was my cousin, who did the same thing. The next morning, the three of us took a taxi to the main bus stop. We drove down the street where my office was, and then we drove by where Dr. Najibullah, the last Afghan ruler, had been hanged by the Taliban just a few weeks before. Now there was a thick rope hanging there on that spot. It was very chilling.

So we went to the bus stop, and we were waiting for the other passengers because we were very early. I thought if we left early we would avoid the Taliban, but I was wrong.

My cousin and I didn't know all those Taliban rules because they were not announced publicly, yet everyone else just seemed to know. For example, women were not allowed to sit immediately in the backseat of a car or a bus because the driver might see them in the rearview mirror. After a time, anyone with a woman in the car covered the rearview mirror, so the woman could not be seen by accident. But I didn't know about where to sit, so I sat in the back, behind the driver's seat. I was sitting by the window, and my cousin was sitting next to me. My uncle had gone into a shop to buy some snacks for the long trip and we were the only two women in the minibus. And I just couldn't stop crying because I had survived a civil war. I witnessed so many things and now I was leaving my family behind.

I was just crying quietly, weeping, when someone shouted at me. It was almost like waking up from a dream. It was a young kid, probably fourteen or fifteen years old. He had an AK-47 on his shoulder. He barely had a beard because he was so young. He started shouting at me, yelling and calling me names. He called me a whore. He called me anything you can think of. And I didn't know what to do, what to say, except to keep crying. And because I had my scarf covering my face—he couldn't see my face—I didn't know what to do. Do I expose my face and talk to him or what? And then my uncle came and asked, "What's wrong?" The boy asked, "Are you with this woman?" My uncle answered, "Yes, I am."

This boy said, "Shame on you. Are you Muslim? Why are they not wearing a burqa?" And then my uncle, being an older man, argued with him. He said, "But you can't see their faces. What's the problem?" But the boy just kept saying, "Aren't you Muslim? They're supposed to be wearing a burqa. If you're their *mahram* you should be with them at all times." But my uncle would not give up. He said, "Where in the Koran does it say that women should wear a burqa?" And then the guy got really agitated and said, "Who are you to lecture me on the Koran?" And then he raised his gun and pointed it and was about to pull the trigger. Suddenly the driver came running up and some of the other passengers had arrived. They all said, "Oh, forgive him—he's old—he doesn't know what he's talking about." At that moment, I felt so devastated for my uncle. He was a very dignified, honorable person who had taught in schools. And here he was being trashed by a kid with a gun.

Then a tall Taliban man joined this boy and said, "What's going on?" The other people explained, and this man said, "Okay, because you're an older guy we forgive you. But these women must sit in the luggage compartment." My uncle had tears in his eyes. He came to me and said, "Let's go back home. I won't make you sit in with the luggage." And I said, "You know what, I'm going to do it because if I don't do it now I have to do it another time and I'm prepared for it." So we did it. My cousin and I sat in the luggage compartment at the back of the minibus. It was so small. There was luggage and every kind of package there. Within a few minutes my legs were numb. I couldn't feel anything. And then we could hear the passengers talking, "Oh, these women, they must be so uncomfortable in there." And I would burst into tears.

We rode for a couple of hours and then the bus broke. But once we were outside Kabul, I think the Taliban were more relaxed. They stopped the bus, but when they went inside, they just looked around and didn't say anything about people reading books or anything like that. Once the bus broke all the other passengers decided to find other means of transportation. But I said, "No, we're going to stay with this bus. I'm not in a hurry."

After the driver and the contractor fixed the engine it was just my uncle, my cousin, and me, so we sat in the seats. When we reached the first city, we stopped at another uncle's house, and everyone was shocked that my cousin and I were not wearing burqas, coming from Kabul. In the villages, many women did not wear burqas. At that time, it was a city thing. The villages were already more traditional and more religious; it was in the cities that the Taliban needed to gain control. Here, the Taliban had already come and then gone.

The next day my uncle said let's wait one more day here because it's close to Kabul. If something happens, we can just go back to Kabul. But I said, "No, let's go to Khost," which was the next city on our roundabout way to Peshawar, Pakistan. In Khost, all the women also begged me to wear the burqa. But I said I'm not wearing a burqa. The next day, we left again and we rode for hours and hours on the back roads until we got to the border. By the end, my butt was so sore and every joint in my body hurt.

Inside Pakistan, we stayed with relatives in a refugee camp for two days. But my uncle had to go back, and I decided to go into the city of Peshawar. I was very lucky because the organization that I worked for in Kabul located a position for me in Pakistan. Within a week I had a job. I found an apartment. I borrowed a mattress from one person and sheets from another person and a pillow from a third person. That's refugee life.

But the rest of my family was still in Kabul. Once every two weeks or so, I would send a letter to my family and they would send a letter to me; someone had to smuggle the letters across the border between the cities. Slowly they started sending me small packages with household items like pots and pans and dishes. I had three brothers and three sisters who were still living in Kabul. My oldest brother was barely eleven years old. Soon, the Taliban started forcing boys to be their fighters, boys my brothers' ages, nine, ten, or eleven. And my parents became very worried that they would probably take my oldest brother. So they sent him to Pakistan to live with me. I immediately enrolled him in school. And soon after, they also sent my fourteen-year-old sister to Peshawar.

My youngest sister was only nine years old and in grade three or four. She was very smart. But now she couldn't go to school, she couldn't even leave the house. And she became very depressed. In one of her letters she said she hated God for creating her as a

woman. She said she couldn't go to
school because she was a woman. It was
a very emotional letter—and she wrote
to me that she wished she were dead.
As soon as I read her letter, I raced
to find one of my friends at the BBC
[British Broadcasting Company]. The

MY YOUNGEST SISTER
WAS VERY SMART. IN
ONE OF HER LETTERS SHE
SAID SHE HATED GOD
FOR CREATING HER AS A
WOMAN

phone lines were not working in Kabul, so I would send a message
to my friends in the BBC organization, because they still had people
in Kabul, and ask them to get a message to my father so I could talk
to him.

Right away, I told my father to send my youngest sister to live
with me. So I had two sisters and a brother who lived with me in Pakistan for a couple of years. I became a single parent. It was very tough,
very challenging for us at times. I did everything I could. I sent them
to school for you name it, English classes, French classes, everything
that they might have wanted to do in Kabul that they couldn't. My
parents didn't want to move to Pakistan with me because of my third
sister, the sister who was one year younger than me. She was the one
who used to climb with me to the top of the hill near our home and
look down over all of Kabul in the evenings. When she was fourteen,
while the Russians were still in Kabul, a rocket hit her school. She
wasn't injured by the shrapnel, but she hit her head on the ground
and she was affected mentally. Her condition gradually deteriorated
until she was in a totally vegetative state, and she stayed that way for
many years. Moving her around was such a nightmare. During the
Taliban years, my parents did try to take her to a doctor once but she
couldn't wear a burqa. The Taliban stopped the car they were in and
tried to drag her out and beat her because she wasn't wearing a burqa.
So from that day on my parents decided just to stay put—not to go
anywhere from the house.

*   *   *

In Pakistan, my work was to advocate for women's rights. I tried to raise awareness of the plight of Afghan women at every opportu-nity, inside Pakistan and outside. We used to travel a lot to Europe, to Asian countries. But by doing that I also became known to the Taliban who were in Peshawar. There were lots of Taliban in Pesha-war by then. They started harassing me. My office decided to seek assistance from Pakistan's ISI [Inter-Services Intelligence, the state security apparatus] because they had a unit that was responsible for the safety and security of foreigners and NGOs [nongovernmental organizations, usually private aid groups]. They were very nice in the beginning. They gave me a phone line in my apartment. But they also started harassing me, because I was a young, single woman, liv-ing alone with three teenagers. It was a different type of harassment than what I faced from the Taliban. When the Taliban operatives threatened me over the phone that the ISI had provided, saying they would harm my brother if I didn't stop my work, I knew I could not stay in Pakistan.

My supervisor asked for refugee resettlement for me. That was how I came to the United States. My first home in the U.S. was in St. Louis, Missouri. I was coming from Pakistan, and it was Janu-ary in St. Louis, so you can imagine how cold it was. But I found the people very nice. My siblings could go to school. They had their challenges adapting to a new lifestyle and education and all that and so did I. The first few months were all about figuring out what to do and learning about places. But then all of a sudden it hits you, "Wow, I have left so much behind." It's a lot to think about. It was overwhelming at times.

But I liked the fact that we had freedom of movement. Even in Pakistan I couldn't move around. And in the United States the

Afghan expatriate communities were very helpful. But it was also interesting that many of the families I came to know were often looking for wives for their sons, and I had two young sisters who had not been spoiled yet. So they were all over us mostly because of that.

In December 1999, I was working two part-time jobs, going to Saint Louis University, and taking care of my teenage siblings. Life was not easy. And I was also concerned about my family back in Kabul.

One day I got home and there was a message on my answering machine from a woman from the White House who wanted me to return her call. I thought it was a mistake. Who would call me from the White House? So I ignored it. And the next day there was another message. I ignored it. And the third time I thought, Let me call. So I called and they had called because they wanted to invite me to an event at the White House for International Human Rights Day.

President Clinton's cultural advisor asked if there was anything he or the president should be aware of before the formal public meeting. I said, "Well, my parents still live in Kabul, so I don't want any culturally inappropriate hugging or kissing or anything like that. The Taliban will be upset if I am seen having contact with a man." Then I met with President Clinton one-on-one to talk about the women's rights situation, and he had a sense of humor. He said, "So is there anything else I can be aware of—can we shake hands?" And I said, "Yes, we can shake hands."

At the actual event, I think Hillary spoke first. I spoke about what was going on in Afghanistan, about the situation for women. And after the presentation, I think it was Jesse Jackson who came up on the stage, and he immediately shook my hand and gave me a hug. And guess what, just at that moment someone in the press took a picture. That picture made it all the way to Kabul. The Taliban saw it and my father was detained and beaten. Before he was released, my father also had to renounce me and refuse to have anything to do with me. Just because of that one picture.

Not long after, I was offered a job in Washington, D.C., so I moved my siblings to Virginia. And then a year later, I sponsored my parents and my two brothers to come to the States. My sister had passed away in Kabul.

Now my siblings, who I used to call my kids, are all grown up. They're all married. My sister has a one-year-old daughter, and my brother has a one-year-old daughter. And my other sister is also married. They all have completed their education. One of my sisters is studying for her doctoral degree in public health. My brother has a degree in political science. My other sister is in business management. And they are all pretty much independent. They don't need me anymore. After they grew up, I got married. A lot of my life has been the opposite of what I ever imagined.

I continued working in women's rights advocacy. And then 9/11 happened. My parents and my two younger siblings were living with me in Virginia. I had called in sick that day and stayed home. Two days before, Ahmad Shah Massoud, the commander of the Northern Alliance, the last group fighting against the Taliban, had been assassinated. One of my friends who was living in the UK called me and said, "Did you hear? Now no one will stop the Taliban."

I was very worried. I was at home, watching TV in the living room. When the images of the Twin Towers came on, I thought it was a movie or something. I couldn't make sense of what was happening. Then I turned on the volume and said, "Oh my gosh." My parents were still sleeping. And I screamed and my father asked, "What's happening?" I said we are under attack. When my youngest brother came from school, he was all shaky, and he said, "Are the Taliban going to come after us here?" And I said, "No, they won't." But everything changed from that day on.

The first time I went back to Kabul, on January 2, 2002, it was very emotional. There were no direct flights from anywhere except humanitarian flights from Peshawar and Islamabad. From Islamabad I took the UN flight to Bagram Air Base because the Kabul civilian airport was not open yet. When I got to the city, everything looked so familiar but at the same time very different. Now there was so much poverty and everything was so dusty. Ninety-seven percent of the women were still in burqas. I went to see some former colleagues and friends. I remember the lane was so narrow that the car couldn't take me all the way to the front of one house. So I had to walk a few hundred steps. And the boys outside who saw me without a burqa were screaming and yelling, "Oh, this woman is going to hell. She doesn't have a burqa."

Part of the reason I was there was to assess the situation for young women. I talked with women from different sectors—education, legal professionals, health—and the stories they were telling me were so sad and so long. I had scheduled my meetings close together; my schedule was very tight. But I realized after the first day that I needed more time because those women had so many stories they wanted to tell me.

So much has happened since then.

I think the mujahideen paved the way for the Taliban. All those restrictions imposed by the Taliban were introduced on different levels by mujahideen. The Taliban just took them to a higher level— Afghanistan was never a paradise for women to begin with. There was a huge gap between men and women, and still is unfortunately.

The pictures of women in the sixties and seventies wearing Western fashions like short skirts and high heels that you see were such a small slice of society. Afghanistan was and still is a strongly patriarchal society. Women in most cases are seen as inferior to men, they are seen as people who need protection because they cannot take care of themselves. They are considered to be very hypersexual and the belief is that you cannot trust them. That mentality is still there. What some of our American and other friends are wrong about is that they see the pictures from the sixties and seventies, and they think that's how Afghanistan was. And then all of a sudden the Taliban came.

But the reality is more complex. Afghanistan's very first girls' school wasn't established in Kabul until 1921. Just fifty girls were enrolled, and those were only the girls who belonged to the elite and privileged families. By 1926 there were three hundred girls studying. And by 1929, there were eight hundred girls in schools, but only in Kabul. All of this reform for women was instituted by King Amanullah, who wanted to modernize Afghanistan. But he didn't just establish reforms for women. The king also imposed a dress code on men: if they worked for the government, they had to wear a suit and tie and cut off their beards. Men who wore turbans in Kabul would sometimes be ridiculed. There are stories of men who came to Kabul and had to rent suits in order to be allowed to enter movie theaters. That didn't go over well with the traditional, conservative Afghans, who were very poor at the time and had no exposure to the outside world. All they knew about the proper way of being a Muslim was to be conservative, to be covered, to basically stick to a very strict interpretation of Islamic laws. King Amanullah's biggest failure was that he did not pave the way for his reforms to be implemented. In 1929, he was overthrown by Habibullah Kalakani, who came to power using Islam as a way to topple the existing regime. When Habibullah Kalakani took control, there were girls studying in Turkey and some other countries, and they were called back to Afghanistan. The girls' schools inside Afghanistan were closed.

Habibullah Kalakani's regime only lasted nine months, but over the next twenty-nine or so years the government didn't dare to reform or promote women's rights in a meaningful way. Then in 1959, Prime Minister Daoud encouraged women to not be veiled all the time. And he also encouraged education. The 1964 constitution was what recognized women's rights to education and employment and allowed women to vote. And then, of course, fifteen years later, in 1979, the Russians came.

> WHAT SOME OF OUR AMERICAN AND OTHER FRIENDS ARE WRONG ABOUT IS THAT THEY SEE THE PICTURES FROM THE SIXTIES AND SEVENTIES, AND THEY THINK THAT'S HOW AFGHANISTAN WAS. AND THEN ALL OF A SUDDEN THE TALIBAN CAME.

Before the Russians, women in the other major cities of Balkh and Herat had gradually begun to follow the path of Kabul women. They got an education, they began to dress in a less conservative style. But the difference in opinions and lifestyle between these urban women and the rural women in the provinces was vast. I remember when I went to school, the Kabulis looked down on people who came from the provinces. They were the first to state that these provincial people were ignorant peasants. And that is probably one of the main reasons why the Taliban just hated educated Afghans. They treated them with disrespect because they were taking revenge for how badly they and their families had once been treated by the educated Afghans themselves.

Sometimes I think that we have unfair expectations. Women's problems did not start with the Taliban or even with the mujahideen. To erase centuries of discrimination and injustice it takes generations. I think the fatigue and frustration that you see is because we expect that everything will go back to being like we imagine it was in the sixties and seventies. But even there, some studies suggest that the number of women living in the urban areas in the 1960s and 1970s was only about ten thousand people out of an overall population of about eleven million, in a country where roughly half of the population is women. So you're talking about a very tiny percentage of the population that was educated and culturally progressive at that time.

I think we also need to go back and analyze historic attitudes toward women in Afghanistan. Although Afghans claim that they have a very strong culture, I don't think that's necessarily completely true. Because Afghanistan is literally a crossroads between east and west, it has been influenced by so many other cultures for centuries. There are still Afghans who practice or believe in the teachings that were brought over by Alexander the Great when he conquered the area in about 330 BC. The Greek philosopher Aristotle was loved by many Afghans, but in his teachings and his books, he viewed women as inferior to men. He said that women were not full persons, that they were physically and intellectually and in every sense inferior to men, and that they were basically the property of men. His point was that men were designed to rule and women to be ruled. Even now a large number of Afghans, men and women, still believe in what Aristotle said or in what the Greeks said. Even Islam could not erase that.

The true values and teachings of Islam are different from what's practiced in Afghanistan. This conflation of culture, tradition, practices, and religion in Afghanistan is part of what makes the country so confusing to so many foreigners. Even Afghans themselves sometimes cannot differentiate between what is a long-standing custom and cultural or tribal practice and what is a religious teaching. Everything is wrapped together in one package.

I think education and going back to understand the history is important. It's happening right now but it's very slow. Afghanistan, as a nation, also has to be careful about shaping people's image of the history that they are so proud of without even knowing what exactly they are proud of. I remember when I was in grade five or six, we were sitting in our history class and

> THIS CONFLATION OF CULTURE, TRADITION, PRACTICES, AND RELIGION IN AFGHANISTAN IS PART OF WHAT MAKES THE COUNTRY SO CONFUSING TO SO MANY FOREIGNERS. EVEN AFGHANS THEMSELVES SOMETIMES CANNOT DIFFERENTIATE BETWEEN WHAT IS A LONG-STANDING CUSTOM AND CULTURAL OR TRIBAL PRACTICE AND WHAT IS A RELIGIOUS TEACHING.

reading about Genghis Khan, the Mongol warrior, and what a horrible leader he was because he destroyed Afghanistan. Then a chapter later, we were reading about Mahmud of Ghazni, who is a hero for many Afghans, but who did exactly the same thing in India as Genghis Khan did in Afghanistan. I remember asking my teacher, "So what's the difference between Genghis Khan and Mahmud of Ghazni?" And I got into trouble for asking that and I had to pay the price. I was punished for even questioning or comparing Mahmud of Ghazni, who Afghans are supposed to admire, with Genghis Khan.

I'm happy that the younger generation is now trying to change this. They are questioning in public what they are told. Over time that will create change. But also don't forget that the educated segment of the population is still very small. So providing the same opportunity to the rural population is the key to bringing sustainable changes. That requires a lot of time and effort and resources. You can't impose change on people. The Russians failed in part because they tried to impose change on Afghans. Some of their policies, like more education or better treatment of women, were very positive, but because they imposed them, there was a backlash.

Today the two most important issues are education and economic empowerment. There are now very small programs supporting women entrepreneurs in different provinces. I was working with one where we were providing some vocational training. Six months after the project we contacted the women beneficiaries to find out if their lives have changed. Surprisingly, the vast majority of them said that they are no longer victims of domestic violence, which is a huge problem in Afghanistan. Up to 87 percent of women have been subjected to some form of abuse, but after vocational training, these women are respected in their households because they are earning an income. By working, they know their rights and they know other people's rights—that's important.

You also cannot separate men from women and talk about improving just the women's situations. Without support from the men in their families and their societies, I don't think you can bring positive and long-lasting change to women's lives in Afghanistan because men are their sons, their brothers, their fathers, their husbands, their neighbors. So they have to be involved and engaged and consulted.

I think the media has a very important role to play in changing attitudes. Unfortunately, they haven't been all that successful and innovative. There has to be a very honest conversation with the big media players to see what their responsibilities are, how they should portray women. And inside Afghanistan, exposure to the rest of the world is important. I have talked to so many male colleagues and they say that they are different than they were ten years ago because of their exposure to different cultures, to information, knowledge, and so on.

But we also can't count on the fact that some Afghans are now exposed to the outside world and expect that will change everything. On the one hand, it's great that college scholarships are provided to Afghans in different countries, especially in the United States. But they don't always have the desired effect. A few years ago, Georgetown University gave a scholarship to a guy from Kandahar, a Taliban stronghold. He had lived with and grown up under the Taliban. He came to the United States as a student and had so much trouble adapting to life here that he quit his studies. He would sit in the classrooms and tell the women around him to cover up and say to them don't wear shorts or mini-skirts. After class, he would just lock himself in his room and study because he didn't want to be exposed to women. With individuals like that, instead of doing them and their communities a favor, well-meaning people in the West are basically doing more harm because these people only take what they consider the negative values and traits back to their communities. They return home and tell everyone in their community, "This is how those infidels live and if you send your daughters to America or other countries to study, they will be doing the same thing."

So everyone has to think in advance about what are the potential consequences. If you want to educate people from Kandahar and Helmand, yes, do that. I'm all for it. But send them to Kabul first. Then have them go to India or Malaysia, rather than bringing someone from those places directly to the United States. I have worked with mullahs who have gone to Italy and European countries, and they went back to Afghanistan more conservative than they were before. It is, after all, a complex country. Afghans say that they are unique. I don't think they're as unique as they may think, but in many ways, culturally, they still are.

Inside Afghanistan, the standard of education also needs to change. It's great that we have millions of kids going to school, but there has been very little focus on the quality of the education they are getting. Most Afghan kids are in school for two to four hours each day. The luckiest get four hours because there are very few schools, so each school has two or three shifts. Many of the teachers are also not well paid, so a lot of them work second or third jobs in order to be teachers. And the violence that has become part of Afghans' daily life and culture is also in the schools. There are still teachers who physically punish kids in school, hit them and beat them. That needs to stop. Peace building should become part of the curriculum in all the schools throughout Afghanistan. If we had invested enough in quality education fourteen years ago we would be in much better shape now. But we didn't, unfortunately.

Think about it—some of the men who attacked Farkhunda and killed her brutally outside of the Islamic shrine in central Kabul were probably educated men, they had been to school. I think it's time, especially after three decades of war, that something like social and emotional education is included in the school curriculum. We can't just teach students subjects, we also need to help them learn values and basic humanity.

We particularly need to do this because we haven't paid enough attention to the psychological impact of war and violence on both men and women. I mean, I know as a woman—as a human being—that Afghan women are treated badly in general. But women are also part of that same population that supported all the wars and all the violent conflict, so don't expect all the women to just be the victims and all the men just to be the violent perpetrators. Women also play a role in perpetuating violence, especially violence against other women. Mothers-in-law beat their daughters-in-law or treat them like slaves. Some women also believe discriminatory behavior is part of life. There are women—even educated women—who believe that they are inferior to men.

I don't want to be completely pessimistic. The fact that now there are men who come out on the streets to defend women's rights—that's a big shift. I think people are slowly breaking the taboos. After Farkhunda was killed, women carried her casket—that has not happened before in the region, so change is coming. But it's slow, and the deteriorating security in Afghanistan is further slowing that process.

In the rest of the world, we live a very fast-paced life. We want everything to happen in front of our eyes. We don't think about the future. We don't invest in the future, unfortunately. And that needs to change. I'm sure other nations have gone through this societal change probably hundreds of years ago. I mean look at European countries, Greece, for example. I think it will happen in Afghanistan. We just have to be patient and not give up. Because once you give up you have to start from scratch all over again.

Like many Afghans, Shamsi and Khadija only go by one name. Today, they are both rug weavers with ARZU, a nonprofit that works to support traditional Afghan rug weaving and improve the lives of its artisans. But they only came to rug weaving after decades of struggles, first surviving the Soviet invasion in their rural villages in Bamiyan province, then the mujahideen civil wars, and finally the coming of the Taliban. Forced to flee into the mountains as refugees, they eventually made it to the UN refugee tent cities inside Pakistan. Since returning home, weaving has given these women a chance to escape poverty, to no longer be considered, in Khadija's words, "useless humans."

· · · · · · · · · ·

My name is Shamsi. I am forty-five years old and was born in the Jajikan village of the Yakawlang district of Bamiyan province. I had two sisters and one brother. My father was a farmer and used to work on our small land. My mother would work in the field too. We had six cows and my mother would keep them. I was about six years old when my mother died delivering a baby, and I think it was the first disaster in my life.

After two years, my father got married again, this time to a woman who had a nervous illness. She was an angry person and would annoy us. She would not make us new clothes. This was at the same time the Soviets invaded. Our village elders told us that foreign forces had invaded the country. By the time they reached the Yakawlang district, we all had left the village and gone to hide in the mountains. After two days someone came and told us that "If you are farmers then they do not kill you, but if you have any guns then you should give them to the Russians."

One day we heard a strange noise, like a deep voice, and when we went out of the house, we saw something like birds in the sky. I had never seen a plane and it was my first time. After that, the Soviet planes would fly always in the sky.

After some years we heard that their forces had left the county, and it was about that time that I got married. I was around eighteen years old. One day when my husband wanted to go out for work, some armed people arrested him and took him to their base. They had told him that he should join them and fight with another armed group who were in Panjaw district. They would say that "We are mujahideen and you must do what we say."

The mujahideen would go to each village and stay there for a week or more and force people to join them and force the women to cook for them and wash their clothes. There were several armed groups that fought against each other. Many people would be killed or wounded in the wars. After one year there was too much trouble. We left that village and went to the Deh Sorkh village across the border in Iran, where my husband's family was living.

I had four kids when the Taliban came to Bamiyan. The first time they came, the people of Bamiyan fought against them and defeated them. But when they came for the second time to Bamiyan, they destroyed everything and killed many people. We were very scared of them and left the village for one month. We went to the mountains and stayed there. When the situation was better we went back to our home, but the Taliban had burned all our belongings. We stayed about four months in our burned home, but we could not go anywhere and the men always had to escape from the Taliban.

After four months we had to leave our home and immigrate to Pakistan. When we reached there, some UN agencies helped us and gave us some food and clothes with a tent. We lived about two years in the tent and after that my husband found a job and rented a house for us. I had a neighbor who was a rug weaver, so I decided to learn rug weaving. After six months working with them as an apprentice and with no fees, I became a rug weaver and I could teach my kids. We started to weave rugs so we could earn some money.

When the situation got better in Afghanistan and the Taliban were defeated, we returned back to Bamiyan, but we did not go back to our region because we knew that there was nothing left.

My husband went to the Shash Pul region and made a tent. After some time the governor came to Shash Pul village and gave the refugees a piece of land to make houses for themselves. After one year we could build one room on the land and live there.

I was one of the first families to join the ARZU rug-weaving program. With the rug money, we bought many things for our home such as carpets, dishes, new clothes, and even jewelry. The life is good now. When I start a rug, I start to make a plan for the money that I get from the rug, so I first think that it should be a good rug. I always have tried to make the best rugs. I have seven children and I can send all of them to school. My bigger son became a teacher last year and my daughter is in grade eleven at high school.

I want to support them to finish their education, and then they can make a better life and future.

. . . .

My name is Khadija and I am thirty-seven years old. I grew up in a poor rural family. We did not have agricultural land and my father had to work for others. My mother also would work with him on the farm. At that time the people did not pay cash for work; instead, when someone would work, they would give him some flour or wheat or oil.

When the Soviets invaded Afghanistan, I was very small and I did not understand what was happening. I just remember that when the Soviet convoys would pass along the road, we would all run away and go to homes and hide under the blankets. I lost my older sister in a bombing. She was only twelve years old. When the mujahideen defeated the Soviets, we were happy, but it did not last too long and the civil war between the armed groups began.

One day a group of armed men came to our village and gathered all the men and took them for fighting. Every day we had to cook for them and they did not pay for our food.

During the mujahideen wars, I got married. We went to our new home at night, because it was not safe to go there during the day. My father died seven days after I married, but I could not go to his funeral or home after his death because it was not safe. I am still sad thinking of that.

When the Taliban came to Bamiyan, I had two small kids; my son was four and my daughter was only two years old. We heard that the Taliban kill all the men and take the women and girls for themselves, so we were very scared and left our home at night. We put a blanket and some food on a donkey and went to the mountains. After a week we returned back to our home, but the Taliban had taken our belongings and burned the home.

My husband borrowed some money and we eventually were able to become refugees in Pakistan. We already had relatives in the Haji camp district, but they told us that we needed to work. My husband let me learn rug weaving. I earned money to help support my children. After five years we returned to Bamiyan. We hoped to start a new life on our small land and home, but when we went to the village, we saw a burned house and when we went into our home, we found some hungry dogs there. So we had to leave again and start over. Today, I am a rug weaver with ARZU.

WHEN I WAS JOBLESS I THOUGHT THAT A WOMAN IS A USELESS HUMAN, BUT NOW I AM PROUD TO BE MYSELF. I KNOW THAT I HAVE A LOT OF ABILITIES LIKE A MAN AND THIS MAKES ME HOPEFUL FOR MY LIFE.

When I was jobless I thought that a woman is a useless human, but now I am proud to be myself. I know that I have a lot of abilities like a man and this makes me hopeful for my life.

No one knows with certainty the exact size of Afghanistan's current population. Recent estimates place the figure at more than thirty-one million, but that is partly guesswork—the last official national census was conducted in 1979. The Afghan diaspora is somewhat better counted. At the height of the violence, conflicts inside Afghanistan produced in excess of six million refugees. More than 2.5 million refugees still remain in neighboring Pakistan and Iran. But increasingly, tens of thousands of Afghans have migrated to the West. A few have found ways to make Afghanistan the focus of their professional work. Hodei Sultan is an international development expert and part of the Afghan diaspora who frequently returns to the nation of her birth for her work.

· · · · · · · · · ·

I am thirty years old, born in Kabul, raised there until my parents fled and lived in Zimbabwe from 1992 through 1999 before coming to the United States. We have an entire generation in Afghanistan that has never known peace.

In June 2013, I was conducting a five-day training session for a group of university students and we were discussing the topic of resilience. I had just asked the students in the room to recall a very traumatic incident that had happened to them when an explosion went off right next door. A large car bomb had been detonated as a vehicle convoy carrying an Afghan lawmaker passed very near the Afghanistan Independent Human Rights Commission [AIHRC] headquarters. The *New York Times* reported that the blast could be heard all across the city. I later learned that three people died.

Immediately following this incident, I was shaken up. I spent the evening thinking about the topic we were discussing and how the students responded to this incident and their astounding level of resilience in the face of conflict. I recalled how calmly the students got up, walked into the hallway, made a phone call or texted to make sure their family members were okay, and then came to the classroom and sat down composed. I asked them if they wanted to continue or break for the day. And most responded, "We're fine. We can continue. It's up to you." It was a complete contrast, their reaction and my reaction. The next day, I asked each student to reflect on what had happened and how they had responded. One participant said, "We never take each day for granted. We make sure we say good-bye to our families because we know that we may not all be at the same dinner table that night."

I hear those thoughts and fears again and again in different forms. I was talking with an Afghan woman who said, "For me, I don't care who in your country [meaning the U.S.] is in power or how many troops you have here. I have three children. I'm not leaving this country. But I want to have the peace of mind that I can kiss my children good-bye and send them off to school and they will come back home safe. I want to know that my daughters won't be homebound, but can go out into the world and make a difference." This exemplifies that the Afghan War that has gone on for decades can be simply boiled down to basic human needs: the need for security, the need for education, the need for social and economic survival.

There is a Taliban saying, "Americans have the watches, but we have the time." In the beginning, after the Taliban fell, everyone accepted insecurity in the provinces, but Kabul was relatively safe. Today, you don't feel safe in Kabul. Before we used to talk about the Taliban spring offensive, now it is an all-year offensive. And many extremist elements have infiltrated Kabul.

We are supposed to have reintegration and millions have been spent on reintegrating the Taliban into general Afghan society, but no one seems to know if negotiations with the Taliban are achieving what they were meant to. I was told the story of two midlevel Taliban fighters that were willing to be reconciled and leave the Taliban. These Taliban fighters were brought to Kabul and promised a place to stay and jobs. But when they got to the city, there were no jobs for them and no place for them to stay. After waiting for two months and with no new prospects, no way to earn a livelihood, they returned to their communities. Their rationale for returning was that at least with the Taliban, they were getting paid and they could feed their families. This in itself is dangerous because on the one hand we are talking about reconciling and reintegrating the Taliban, but on the other hand it sounds like there is not a concrete strategy to achieve this goal.

Also, what do we mean when we refer to the Taliban? It is very apparent now that the Taliban are splintered, and while there are those that are willing to negotiate, they do not necessarily reflect the wishes of the hardliners. And the hardliners are the ones who can truly make a difference in reducing this cycle of violent conflict. If these issues are not addressed, I wonder when we will ever again truly know peace.

Razia Jan had an idyllic childhood growing up in Afghanistan—before war, before restrictions. She was studying abroad when the Russians invaded. It was three decades before she was able to set foot again in her homeland. Hers is a refugee story, but most of all it is the story of Afghanistan, of Afghan life before and life after. She recalls the great changes that she experienced as a young girl coming of age in the 1960s, versus what it is like to be a young girl there in the early twenty-first century, when it seems that much of the country has changed and even drifted back in time. She speaks with great understanding and great longing.

. . . .

I was born in Afghanistan, in one of the provinces, and we lived in a house that was really my grandfather's. It was built on about five acres of land, and he also owned orchards and farms, which made him a landlord. The whole family lived together: my grandfather, my parents, and my uncle and his family. Each family had their own small area to live, but we all grew up together. Every summer, the cousins, uncles, and aunts would come to spend holidays with us. Growing up, my experience was great because I could go to school—no one ever stopped me or my sister or my cousins from going to school. We had the privilege of getting educated. And I never wore a burqa; we never even covered our faces. I could wear a skirt. I could ride a bike. Right now in most of the country, a woman can't even walk outside without a male companion and wearing a burqa, the full-body veil. It's such a difficult world today.

After I finished high school, I went to Lesley College in Massachusetts. I even took some classes at Harvard. That was in the early

1970s. At that time, there were lots of opportunities. Women were allowed to go abroad and learn. If you wanted to be a seamstress, you could go to Paris and study fashion. My cousins did that. And a lot of girls went to universities in Britain and the United States. Back then, really, we had the same opportunity as any young man. But when the Russians invaded, that kept me away from Afghanistan for more than thirty years. I couldn't go back. After 9/11, the first thing I did was to return to Afghanistan. It was the only thing I was thinking: now I can go back and help.

It's almost impossible to compare my really pleasant childhood to almost forty years later, when I landed in Afghanistan in January 2002 and saw the destruction. In those years, the people changed completely. They have seen so much war, have spent so many years being refugees, that I think their mentality is very different. I think it will take about thirty or forty years for them to really be a country that could have pleasure and to become something maybe similar to what we grew up in. But right now it's a very different world.

It all started with the Russian invasion. That started the creation of the largest single refugee population in the world—six million refugees. It's just beyond belief. Everybody had to leave their homes because the women were raped and the men were being killed. It all started there, and then after that the tribes and the mujahideen started to fight among themselves in a civil war, and then of course the Taliban came and that was the beginning of the end.

At first, some people embraced the Taliban because after all the chaos, they kind of changed the whole system. But once they got settled, they ruled by fear. What they did was worse than the Russians or anybody because they took away the rights of the women—and also of the men. People couldn't even listen to music. And every Friday, after prayers, they would gather the men into a big stadium. Then they would bring in these poor women that had worn red socks or gone outside without a guardian, women who just went out to do shopping because they were widows and had to feed their children, and they brought them into this stadium, in front of the crowd, as if it were a soccer match, and they stoned them and they shot them. It was terrorizing for everyone.

At the same time, education was completely stopped. The Taliban burned most of the schools; they burned the books. Even in the women's college, the teachers' college, they burned all the books. They even destroyed or closed boys' schools. The only education boys could have was a religious education in a madrasa. Everything else was forbidden.

In my book, these men behaved more like animals. In fact, they are worse than animals, because if an animal gets hurt the other animals come and try to help, they lick the wound, they bring food, or do something. But here, many of these people didn't have any respect for human life, especially for a woman's life. It's nothing to do with Islam. It's nothing to do with anything. This is just how they grew up—they believe if they do things that are truly inhuman it will give them strength.

Everyone who stayed in Afghanistan suffered. Everyone. Now it's our history, it's part of us, and I don't know how long it's going to take to really make it better.

People have only just started to live their lives again, and they're still not sure really what tomorrow brings. Today, too many people are very scared. Too many people are still very poor; they don't have food to put on their tables for their families. And then there are a very few people who are very rich, who are warlords, or who take bribes. To get anything done, it seems you have to bribe people, starting from the top and working down. We have tremendous corruption and we still don't have law and order. The day Afghanistan will get better is the day people start saying: I am satisfied with what I have, give the opportunity to someone who needs it more. Right now, everybody says give it to me. We have too many people who only think of themselves, who will only put themselves first.

When I first went back to Kabul in January 2002, I wanted to see the home that my cousins, my family, had in Kabul, and I literally couldn't find it. Everything was so destroyed, it seemed like every building had been bombed. You really couldn't see any landmarks; the streets were all dirt. People looked so terrorized and afraid and scared. In the beginning, I felt terrorized myself. I was also really, really hurt to see the people and how the whole country, all of Afghanistan, all of Kabul was completely destroyed, devastated, and suffering.

When I finally did find the block where our family house had been, it was demolished. Before, the area had been full of beautiful gardens, rose gardens, which were my most favorite flower and a favorite in Kabul, as well as orchards of plums and cherries and almonds and peach trees. It was so beautiful and now, nothing was left. It was completely gone.

If a house was still standing in Kabul, most of the time it had been taken over. Once a family left their house, another family moved in. So people came back after twenty years, and their house was no longer theirs. There was nothing they could do about it.

In the beginning, I worked on all kinds of aid projects. One of the earliest was Operation Shoefly, with a bunch of guys from the U.S. Air Force who were stationed at Bagram Air Base. Almost every child they saw in Afghanistan was walking barefoot because they didn't have shoes, especially the girls, so they really wanted shoes for the kids. I helped arrange for the collection of thirty thousand pairs of shoes for them, and they would take these shoes to different villages and donate them. They were a unit from Hawaii, and there were also some guys from the U.S. Army. Before their tour ended, I went with them on one of their last donation trips. They picked me up in Kabul, and on our way to Bagram, we stopped in one village. The military guys started handing out gifts to the boys and also to the girls. They'd give the boy a football, a piece of equipment like a hammer, or some clothing, and then they'd also give something to the girls, maybe a doll or a shirt or a blouse. But the moment these girls walked away, the boys would snatch whatever gift the girls had gotten. They would snatch it and hide it. I watched it all happen. And these girls couldn't say anything. Right there, I really wanted to do something for these girls and for Afghan women, because they are the ones that are suffering so much. That became my passion and dream—to give them a chance of feeling proud of themselves and their accomplishments.

I'm not a rich person, but I knew that I could help. In 2007, with the help of my Rotary Club, we raised enough funds to build the first free private girls' high school in an area that never had a girls' school. While building the school, I started working with an organization named ARZU. It's a rug-weaving company that employs women. But to weave with ARZU, the women have to agree to send their daughters and sons to school. ARZU also provided them with medical care. One of our central goals was to give women personal strength through their work. In certain parts of rural Afghanistan, women do everything. They do all the housework, they grow the vegetables, they care for the animals. Everything and anything—it's all women. The men hardly work. They may think they work, but it is the women who do everything, but receive no income. So for me to work with a company that could help give women power, help them to establish themselves, and become a person that the whole family looked upon with respect, that was very important.

Gradually, I began to have my own dream of a way to help in Afghanistan. As a Rotarian, I believe in community projects. At first, I really wanted to build a library for the teachers' college. In 2004, when I was in Kabul for an education conference, I saw that nobody had books. There were no books anywhere, all the students had were pieces of paper, and each person had to copy whatever they needed to read onto their pieces of paper. But then the University of Massachusetts gave the college a grant of about $8 million, so I thought my little money would not do much for them. Then I got a new idea: I should build a school for girls somewhere that had never had a girls' school. And that is what I did.

I found a site, a very historical piece of land, a place where decades before the Afghan king had built a boys' school for that group of villages. The villages never had a school before that.

When I first saw the site, the original school that had been built there was destroyed. Everyone threw their trash in what was left of the building. But it was still very important to me, because so many years ago, people had built this school for boys, and it would really be something for girls now to go to school in the same spot. The best thing for these girls would be to have such a historical place.

Another thing about the area was that it was home to many of the mujahideen. They were the ones who fought the Russians and then later these mujahideen fought against the Taliban. They are religious people, and the Taliban was never able to come in and destroy their homes and take over. There are thousands of graves near these villages. The graveyard on one side of the road is full of the Taliban fighters that were killed. The other side is what is considered the heroes graveyard for all the mujahideen. The local people are very protective of the area; they are very vigilant. If anybody, a stranger, enters these villages, they are questioned.

At the start of the construction there was a lot of opposition to the school because they had never had a school for girls and they couldn't even think of their daughters going to school. So I worked with the community, but it was very hard. I oversaw the building of the school myself, standing there on that site for six, seven months. And for all that time, people in the community were always saying, "Change your mind. Have it be a boys' school." And I said no, no. When the school was finished, we scheduled the opening. The vice president was coming, the minister of education was coming, and the day before the opening, four men came to see me. They were all very well dressed, very well groomed. It was evening and we were inside trying to set up the school, set up the classrooms, and my project manager came in and said there are some men here and they want to see you. So I came down—I don't know if my head was even covered. These men were standing in the courtyard and one of them told me that they had a worry. Just then, he put his finger toward my face and said, "Razia Jan, this is your last chance to change your mind and make it a boys' school because the backbone of Afghanistan are men."

I just put my finger right back in his face and said, "You know, the women of Afghanistan are the eyesight of Afghanistan and unfortunately you all are blind, and I want to give some sight to you all." Once I said that, they were really mad, and they turned around and left. In the past eight years, I never saw them again.

When we opened the school we had 108 girls up through the fourth grade. From the very beginning I told my teachers that the first thing these girls need to do is to learn to write their father's name, in the local language and also in English, and then take that piece of paper home with them to show their fathers. Even now, at the start of school, my kindergarten class learns to write their father's name in two languages and then the students take it home. And believe me, I have fathers coming literally crying and saying, "I can't write my own name. I put my thumb on paper to sign, and my daughter, she is just four years old, and right now, she can write my name."

In this part of Afghanistan, when I would ask a man how many children he has, he would often say "two sons," although he may also have six daughters. The girls and the women are like property to them, like objects. But now many say very proudly, "I have six daughters and two sons." I think having their daughters become educated has had a great impact on them. From the beginning, I also tried to work with these men and with the community in a way that would show that I didn't want to offend them. I'm very willing to listen to them. But I'm also very determined and I know what I want to do for the girls. And I think the men have come to understand that education is something that will really benefit these girls in the long run. And their entire families as well, because these girls go home and they teach their mothers or their older sisters who are not going to school at least how to write their names and how to add and subtract.

These girls are very hardworking, just to go to school. They get up at four o'clock in the morning to help their mothers clean, wash, whatever they need to do, and then they come to school and they spend seven hours at school. And the moment they return home, they start helping their mothers again. In a family that's the deal. In Western countries, our daughters, our sons, they don't do anything. We have to do everything for them. But in Afghanistan, girls are expected to work at home from the time they are very small.

And watching this and seeing their daughters devote themselves

I HAVE FATHERS COMING LITERALLY CRYING AND SAYING, "I CAN'T WRITE MY OWN NAME. I PUT MY THUMB ON PAPER TO SIGN, AND MY DAUGHTER, SHE IS JUST FOUR YEARS OLD, AND RIGHT NOW, SHE CAN WRITE MY NAME."

so much to school and learning, I think the fathers are realizing that these girls really do matter. I think right now to their fathers these girls matter a lot. That is a great pleasure for me, the happiness that I get from seeing these girls blossom and that they are recognized and hopefully that they can stand up for themselves and speak for themselves.

I also have a very specific philosophy for my school. The first day we opened, we had about eight teachers. And I told them that I want them to really respect these children, to love these children and not to be harsh. In most schools in Afghanistan, learning can be very harsh—if a child makes a mistake they are hit very hard. I told my teachers that no one could even raise their hand to a student, not ever, even though this is the way it is done in many other schools. Most of my teachers were themselves slapped around or beaten by their own teachers when they were growing up. But I told them that we have to love these girls; we cannot allow any teachers to mistreat any girl or hit them at all. These girls face a lot of problems at home, not only poverty, but pressure from their fathers or mothers, brothers, cousins, uncles, and grandfathers not to continue their education. That's one of the reasons why I set my school up to run eleven months a year.

Most schools give three months off, but if I did this and the girls stayed home for three months, it is very likely that their father and their brother will look at them, see them only helping their mother and reaching an age where they can be married off, and then the father or brother will say, "Hey, you've had enough education; you don't need to go back. You are too old now." But in my school, I give them ten days off in spring, ten days in summer, and ten days in winter. Everybody has a routine, and it's hard for the parents to tell them, "Hey, you've grown up and you can't go to school."

Instead, as the girls get older, they say, "Well, you have to wear a burqa," which is fine. And I've talked to these girls and the teachers have talked to these girls. We tell them, yes, wear the burqa, there's nothing wrong with it, it's the culture, and you have to do it. But why not get education and be with your friends while wearing the burqa? Wearing a burqa shouldn't be a reason for you not to come to school.

It's been more than eight years. We have close to five hundred girls going to school right now. We don't charge any money; we pay for everything through private donations and grants. They are all so beautiful, they are amazing little girls. And once they come to school they are just as happy as any child who's studying in the United States or any other country. They forget their hardships, or if they were hungry, or if at night they didn't have food, even though many of their families are living on less than a dollar a day. They come here and they spend five or six hours as a child, as a young woman. They can study, they can be friends with new girls, not only their relatives, which is what would happen if they stayed at home. The custom in Afghanistan is to marry these girls off when they are very young. It doesn't matter if the man is old; the families say they can't keep these girls at home. But now in my school, these girls are waiting to get married until after they finish high school. This is a tremendous change for these girls, and it's so positive, which really gives me hope. It's a small step but I think there is a very good chance that these girls will make something of themselves and be able to take care of themselves.

I also think that the daughters of these girls at my school will always go to school. Now that they have had a taste of education, I think no matter where they go or when they get married, they will always look for a way to send their own daughters to school. Maybe even a better education than they got, maybe even go on to higher education.

*　　　*　　　*

My next project is to build an institute or college for these girls, because they will not be allowed to go away from their village to attend school. There is no transportation and they can't afford it. It is hard enough for us to help the girls go to school in their same village. Most of the families are very conservative and they are not comfortable letting their daughters go away. So we are building the institute right next to our school, to be a place where they can get two years of teacher's training, two years of midwifery, or learn computer science or English as a second language. I hope and I pray that in maybe five years or ten years these girls will be allowed to go places and do the things they want to. But right now, under the circumstances, I think it is important for us to give them the opportunity to get a degree so they can have more skills, even if they only work in the village. If some of our girls become midwives, they can go to local homes and take care of the women. Some of these girls could also teach with us. We just have to start somewhere. I think it's possible for them to start working in the neighborhood and eventually, hopefully, our girls will be allowed to attend universities and colleges and maybe someday they might even study abroad. We have to give it time to see them really move forward.

And we have to remember where we are.

It's a miracle right now that there are over two million girls going to school. Because all over Afghanistan girls' schools have been destroyed and often the girls who were studying at them are just married off. Some girls who were going to school have even been poisoned. I'm really happy so far that our school has not been targeted. But still I worry every day, every second. God forbid anything should happen to these girls; I won't survive.

While some of these new schools might not be the best education, at least the girls are getting out of the house and going somewhere.

Even a little education is still some education and that will get them the self-respect that they deserve.

This used to be a great culture. This is a country that was like the Paris of the Middle East and the people had peace. Now everyone is just trying to survive. And there's so much uncertainty because of America pulling out. I hope at least they are not going to completely abandon Afghanistan.

I think education is the only thing that enables a person to understand themselves, be civilized, and know how to treat another person, know how to be kind, and how not to be destructive. When people are educated, they are more likely to respect each other and to respect each other's rights. Education is the only way that our people are going to learn and it's going to take a long time. But Afghanistan is a great country. It is a beautiful land, and I think one day it will be again what it used to be years ago.

"I was born in Afghanistan, but my family left the country during the civil war and moved to Pakistan when I was four years old." In a quarter century, Wazhma Furmuli has lived the equivalent of several lifetimes. At age fourteen, she finished high school as a refugee in Pakistan. By age sixteen, she was working in accounting and finance in post-Taliban Kabul. At age eighteen, she was holding down a job, attending night school, and studying English by the light of a gas lamp because her home had no electricity, staying up until four a.m. to review her grammar and vocabulary. She tested well enough to receive a scholarship from the Initiative To Educate Afghan Women and to attend Randolph College in the United States. Today, she works with PricewaterhouseCoopers (PwC). She could be mistaken for any other professional in a conservative office, until she begins telling her story, as she did one afternoon, from a windowless space in New York City.

. . . .

Growing up, I actually didn't remember very much about Afghanistan. The only part that I could remember was the last year, and that was all war. It was the days that we hid in our dark basement, shaking as each bomb fell, the days we didn't have electricity. It was the staccato sound of gunfire; it was the constant barking of street dogs. So it wasn't a beautiful Afghanistan that I remembered. What I remembered was a really broken country—nobody on the streets, people very scared.

I was raised mostly in Pakistan, because we lived in Pakistan for nearly twelve years. I went to school there and I also worked there for a couple of years. We moved back to Afghanistan in 2004 because it wasn't possible for me or my siblings to go to university in Pakistan. Two years before I graduated, all the refugee colleges and universities inside Pakistan were closed to Afghans. But Kabul University had reopened. It was kind of ironic that finally Afghanistan was a better place for education than Pakistan. For years, many Afghan families have chosen a far more difficult and expensive life away from home because they wanted their children to be educated above all else.

It took me a while to be excited to go back. A couple of days before we had left for Pakistan, a rocket had landed in front of our house. It exploded on the street and killed a lot of people who were standing in line outside a small, mud-brick bakery to buy bread for their breakfast. There wasn't enough food in Kabul, so people had to wait for a long time to get a piece of bread. Everyone in line was killed. My house was on that main street and we were all safe except for one of my sisters, who was sleeping close to the balcony. A piece of the rocket hit her leg. She was bleeding badly, but we couldn't take her to the hospital. We were very fortunate because my uncle was there. He was a doctor and knew how to help her. Several of my relatives had been living in our house because they thought our location was safe. The safe and unsafe places changed almost every day. We regularly moved from house to house because the location of the fighting was always changing.

At night, my uncles and dad wouldn't sleep because they had to guard the house and especially to guard the girls and the women. There were incidents where armed men would break into houses. After the rocket attack, my dad decided that we would leave. It usually takes around six to eight hours to drive from Kabul to Pakistan. But it took us almost two days to get there. About halfway to Pakistan, we were stopped and a bunch of armed men took my dad. Usually when someone was taken away, it meant they would be killed.

But somehow, they let my dad go free after an hour or so. We all thought he would be killed, even my dad.

I never wanted to go back to that Afghanistan. It wasn't even something where I was like, "OK, I do want to go back and see how it is."

During our twelve years in Pakistan, even during the Taliban, my dad would still visit family members who had stayed behind. But he never allowed us to come. He thought it wasn't like a proper place, and we wouldn't be safe. And everybody that came across the border to Pakistan, the stories that they told us, they weren't pretty stories.

Then, in 2002, my older sister went back to Kabul. She can speak very good English, and she got a job with an international organization. Every time she would visit us, she would tell us how different things were. She said that people are hopeful, people are back on the streets, and there are laws about going to school. When my sister painted this new picture of Afghanistan, I started getting excited. By 2004 I was looking forward to going back. I wanted to be part of a positive change. And I felt like I had a responsibility to go home.

But I was nervous too. I wondered about very small things. I wondered if there would be electricity or TV or proper houses or would the houses all be broken? Would I be able to walk outside on the street without worrying that something was going to happen to me?

Returning to Afghanistan was rough. I think it's still very rough there. The first few days it was exciting. We thought, We've moved back. We're going to have a better life. But after about two or three months, there was one day when I was so depressed that I started crying. I didn't have access to educational materials. I didn't have classes or books or anything. I wasn't going to school. I wasn't working. I was just at home. There was no electricity. There was no Internet. There was only one private TV station, TOLO television, that operated from about six o'clock to nine o'clock at night and that was it. Radio Television Afghanistan, RTA, the government TV and radio station, operated at random, the way it had during the war.

The main reason why I was very, very excited to be back was to go to university. I wanted to be a medical doctor. I had wanted to be a medical doctor the whole time that I was growing up in Pakistan. But the educational system in Afghanistan is very different from the United States. You have to take an entry test for the university, and every student in Afghanistan has to take the same test on the same day. There are questions on every single subject that you have studied in high school. Tens of thousands of people were sitting for the exam, but they only have a few thousand slots. And you can't choose your own major once you get admission; your major is largely decided by the exam board based on your grade. The higher your grade, the better major you're going to get. The better majors are really dependent on what people in Kabul think—and many of them think that the best major is to be a doctor, to go to medical school. And the next one will be engineering and the next one will be law and it just follows from there. Whichever one has more financial stability after you graduate—that's usually the top major.

When I went to file my application for the exam, one of the administrators asked my dad, "What does your daughter want to study?" And he said, "She wants to study medicine." And the administrator asked my dad, "Well, do you know how much it costs?" And my dad said, "What do you mean how much it costs? The university is free, it's a public university." And the administrator very frankly said, "Yeah, but in order to get a seat in that department in the university, you have to pay 250,000 AFs [a shorthand for the currency, Afghan Afghanis]."

So 250,000 AFs, at that time, was equal to about US$5,000, while the average income for a working adult in Afghanistan was about $270 a year. It was very disappointing. I felt like I had been sent into exile all over again. I still sat for the exam, but I didn't get into medical school. Instead, I was assigned to economics, but I had a friend who was already studying economics and accounting at the university, and she told me that they were learning single entry for accounting. I didn't even know single entry existed because today every transaction is recorded on a double-entry basis. But she said, "Yeah, well, we had a lesson about single entry and how single entry works."

It was basically as if all the professors who had left during the war were back, and they were teaching exactly as they had over two decades ago, without updating any of the knowledge that had been in use all that time. The materials they were teaching hadn't been updated in probably the last thirty years.

They also don't get paid enough. Their salaries are pretty low and they still need to feed their families. So for them it's a good excuse to say they don't get paid enough to go for additional training. Some even practice fraud in class. My friend said that one of her classmates wanted to get a high grade and the professor told her, give me a printer and the ink for the printer and you'll get a top grade. So by just getting the professor a printer and ink, she got a top grade. For me, that was disappointing and sad. At the same time you can look at it from the professor's perspective: the professor needs a printer and the government can't afford it, what is he going to do? He can't afford it on his salary, there's no added funding, so it's a very difficult situation for everyone.

Ultimately, I decided that going to university would be worse than not going. Why go waste time on something that you know you're not going to get anything out of it? Why not work instead and improve your work skills and wait until you have an opportunity for a better education?

I started volunteering for a nonprofit organization, and then I got a job. That's when things improved. I was sixteen years old—I was fourteen when I graduated high school.

More than a year later, I learned about a job opening at the new American University of Afghanistan. I had heard about the idea for this university years before, from my sister on one of her trips to Pakistan. She said people were talking about this school and were doing surveys to see if Afghans would be interested. She said it was very exciting, but because it was a private school, the tuition would be high. Not only would it be hard to get admission, but then you actually had to be able to afford to pay for it. But I started dreaming about one day going to this American university and having a really quality education. And my sister said not to worry, you never know what's going to happen.

I didn't get admitted as a student—the school wasn't really open yet, but it had received funding from the U.S. government and Laura Bush, the First Lady, had helped with its launch. Before it opened, I applied for a job to help them establish a finance department. I wanted to be right up front. I really wanted there to be an honest relationship between the finance department and the students. I didn't want there to be any corruption or graft. The school administrators had lots of questions about how to recruit students and how to set up a scholarship program. I got the job and I waited for their undergraduate programs to start so I could join.

In the meantime, there was a private school that had opened around 2006—it only taught accounting courses, and I started going there to learn more about accounting. I had a classmate in the school who is now my best friend. She's the one who told me about the Initiative To Educate Afghan Women [the Initiative], which offers scholarships for Afghan women at U.S. colleges and universities. She had applied the year before and was waiting to get a scholarship for the next year. She said to me, "Why don't you try it?" So I applied. I really liked how the program was very clean and clear. You don't get picked just because you know someone.

I submitted my application to Paula Nirschel, the program's founder. She sent me an email the next day. She said that she had read my application and she wanted to see all my other documents. I sent her those, and the day after that she told me she was coming to Kabul in the summer and would like to meet me. When I went for my interview, there were already many students waiting—so many girls for so few scholarships. And there were some people who actually knew each other. So they were talking to each other, and I was wondering if they were all relatives or friends. I felt really disappointed. I thought back to everything at Kabul University, and I thought I'm not going to get a scholarship.

I met with Mrs. Nirschel, and she told me that if I was selected to proceed to the next round of interviews, I would get a phone call the next day. I thought: I'll never get called. The next day, I was working on an first inventory project at the university. I left my cell phone in my desk drawer. When I came back, there were about fifteen missed calls. They had called me back for a second interview. They had called my accounting school; they had called all of my references, trying to get in touch with me.

I went back for a second round to talk about the things I had done. In addition to my classes and working at AUAF, together with a friend, I had started a very small business to support women, which

I did mostly on the weekends. We would buy materials to send to women in the provinces so they could make embroidered pieces, clothing and other things they would design. It was work they could do from home. They would send the finished pieces back to us, and we would have displays at the Intercontinental Hotel and other places that foreigners stayed and visited. We would sell the pieces and send the money back to the provinces.

I was offered a scholarship, but in order to receive it, I had to pass one more hurdle: I had to score in the top percentile on the Test of English as a Foreign Language [TOEFL]. There were about twenty students who had been asked by the Initiative to take the test and about seven scholarships available at that time. Even if you don't know a lot about math, those are not great odds. For the next few months, every free moment, I studied and tried to improve my English.

I would work during the day, go to my accounting classes in the evening, and get home at nine o'clock. We still didn't have electricity all night long, so I would turn on a gas light and study my English until about four o'clock in the morning. I studied right up until the TOEFL test day. They administered the test during the Muslim holy month of Ramadan, when Muslims are required to fast the entire day, from sunrise until sundown. And the test itself was nearly five hours. It was difficult to take such a long test when I couldn't drink or eat anything. But I sat for the test and so did my friend, who had first told me about the scholarship. Two months later, our scores were reported to the Initiative. It turned out that I had one of the highest scores.

I still remember the day I opened my email and read that I had been offered admission to Randolph College. I was at work. I sat there and reread that email again and again: the entire email, the main paragraph, the conclusion, the main paragraph again, the opening sentence, every part of it, piece by piece. I wanted to call out to everyone in my office, but in the next second I realized that being "the girl going to study in the U.S." might not be considered good news. I did not know whom I could trust. Instead, I quickly left the room and called my mom. Almost as soon as I got the words out of my mouth, we both burst into tears. We couldn't talk, we just cried over the wireless lines.

Although she was as hardworking as I was, my friend did not get a scholarship. It was very hard for me to tell her that I got in. In a way, it felt like I took the opportunity from her. Then everything else happened so fast. In less than a month, I had my visa and I was leaving for the United States.

I left for my education in the United States the same year that the American University of Afghanistan started its undergraduate classes. But every summer, I went back to Kabul, and I kept working with the school. My last summer in Kabul, I worked with the university's vice president and president to establish their budget and to find ways to match the funding they were receiving from the United States Agency for International Development [USAID] and also from other generous private donors. It was a very cool experience. I have very fond memories of the university. I still have very good friends there. And I have a lot of friends too who actually graduated or are still studying there. Every time I visit the school, I feel like it's one of the very successful projects that the United States is going to leave behind for Afghanistan.

I was nineteen years old when I moved to the United States. I guess there was some culture shock, but it was a different type of culture shock. I was very, very excited about that trip. People say, you were nineteen years old and you traveled by yourself to the United States and you were fine? But it wasn't like I was going from the United States to Afghanistan. I was leaving one country and going to another country where I knew there were so many opportunities. And I was thirsty for all those opportunities.

At the same time, working at the American University of Afghanistan I had been exposed to American culture. The university's faculty was mostly American; the vice president was the former vice president of the University of Massachusetts. And the TV shows, the movies, the entertainment from the United States sort of teach you what to expect. What was culture shock was going to the school itself—the whole education system was so different. It is still amazing to me how different it was. I think the biggest thing that I had to adjust to was the concept of asking questions and speaking up in the class.

Even back in Pakistan when I went to middle school and high school, I was penalized a couple of times for asking questions and speaking up or sharing an opinion that was different from that of my teachers. The teachers thought that I was asking those questions because I wanted to embarrass them. Or because I was being disrespectful of their ability or their knowledge, rather than simply trying to understand something. I remember when I was in eighth grade one of my teachers penalized me for asking questions; she didn't let me participate in the class for over a week. And when I was finally allowed to participate, for a long time my voice would tremble because I was so scared that I was going to participate too much, and the teacher was going to punish me.

In the United States, I went to Randolph College, a very small liberal arts college that used to be a women's college. The classes were small and the teachers were very focused on improvement and on having a relationship with each student. In some classes, about 20 percent of the grade was class participation. I was shocked. I couldn't believe that I had to participate in a class, and that if I participated, the teachers would actually appreciate me rather than penalize me. It took me a while to get used to it. But once I started, it was such a good feeling. Knowing that you can share whatever you think—it's a freedom by itself. I think a lot of people don't realize how special that is until they take it away from you.

It was also amazing to me how much the school focused on critical thinking, on thinking outside the box, on how much they taught tolerance to the students along with a liberal arts education. For a small school, the student body was very diverse. There were people from more than thirty countries. Having all those different ideas, learning from so many different points of view, those four years by themselves totally changed the way I thought about life. The way I think about everything, the way I think about myself, the way I think about my family, the war, and everything is so different. And I believe it was all because of the educational system that I found in the United States.

It's hard to explain just how different the education was and still is between the U.S. and Afghanistan. Let's assume you froze an education system at a college in the United States thirty years ago, and then revisit it today. That's essentially what happened in Afghanistan. The brains of the professors, the materials, the whole foundation of the university, everything was frozen for thirty years. But biology, chemistry, math—they have all changed. Even the social sciences, the way people look at human relations, the way people look at literature, those subjects have changed. And the world has changed, especially with globalization. There is so much more tolerance toward other people. I don't think those things have been adopted yet at Afghan universities. And I don't know how long it's going to take them to adopt it. This is not about money or how much financing they need to improve everything. They have the infrastructure at Kabul University. What we need is a whole new generation to change the system in Afghanistan.

During my middle and high school time, I never learned about any religion, history, or culture except Islamic ones. That's pretty narrow. I think the teachers were worried about exposing us to ideas and lifestyles that are considered to be contrary to Islam. But not to expose people to other options is probably not the best way to keep everyone Muslim. You might as well have them be really educated about everything from the beginning. I think that's where tolerance comes from also. I can't really expect people in Afghanistan to be tolerant toward all the differences in the world if they haven't been exposed to different points of view.

Personally, I think many people would be better Muslims, Christians, Hindus, or Buddhists if they are the ones who actually choose their own religion. Right now, it's more a cultural rite to be a Muslim if you live in a Muslim nation, just like it's the culture to be a Christian for a lot of people living in other countries. In many places, religion is treated almost the same way as race or anything else you're born with. You don't have a choice to change it, or even to understand or to question it.

I really think that not only for Afghanistan, but for all the countries in that region, the only solution is to improve the level and quality of education and offer more opportunities for a liberal arts education. A major reason why we have a lot of issues right now in that part of the world is because we don't teach our children how to think critically. We don't teach them to look at other opinions. Even if you teach that everything is black and white, it's not going to be black and white in the real world. But first, we have to teach our teachers. If teachers don't know that there's something called critical thinking, and that they need to teach critical thinking and embrace it in their students, nothing is going to improve.

I do believe that we can raise the level of education in Afghanistan. The good thing about education is that there is always a new group of students coming in. With new students, it's not like they only know one system and they're not going to accept a new system. They are new; they don't have a system. I also think it would really help to have an independent, third-party body to rate all the colleges and universities, including the state schools like Kabul University and the schools in the provinces. Students could choose which school to go to based on their rating. I also think the administrations would be forced to update how they operate.

When I came to the United States, Afghanistan was like an unknown country in the West—though September 11 changed some of that. Americans don't know much about Afghanistan. They don't know much about the people in the country or the lives that they have, and how the culture is really different from other countries. The picture of Afghanistan in the West has been all about war and terrorism. If someone wants to learn about the culture, there aren't a lot of resources available. All people here really seemed to have read were novels, like *The Kite Runner* or *A Thousand Splendid Suns*. Of course, nobody wants to go as a tourist to Afghanistan. And what the media portrays is the war side of the country. They focus on things that go wrong. They focus on all the failures.

The media doesn't talk about the improvements in the last ten years. They don't report on how the youth is improving or on how many more schools are open, on how many more people have graduated or how the conditions for women have changed. Yes, it's a country that's gone through war for a long time. It's a country that's fully dependent on foreign aid, but it's a country with a rich culture. It's a country where around 60 percent of the current population is under twenty-five years of age, so we're like a group of millennials who want to do better, who want to improve things, who don't want to have the same Afghanistan as ten years ago.

I don't think a lot of people in the West have that picture. And that's because there aren't a lot of Afghan people in the West either. So it's not really a misperception, it's just that you don't know what you don't know.

How Afghanistan sees the West is the same story but from a different side of it. A lot of people in Afghanistan are not educated, a lot don't have access to the Internet. Only a small percentage of people can read in English. And even if they want to read, they don't have access to books about other countries or from other countries. So their knowledge of the West is limited to what they see in the Afghan media, which just focuses on politics or pop culture. The perception of too many Afghan people is not to see that the people in the West are human, just like them. Yes, there are differences, but at the end of the day we're all alike in

> IT'S A COUNTRY THAT'S FULLY DEPENDENT ON FOREIGN AID, BUT IT'S A COUNTRY WITH A RICH CULTURE. IT'S A COUNTRY WHERE AROUND 60 PERCENT OF THE CURRENT POPULATION IS UNDER TWENTY-FIVE YEARS OF AGE, SO WE'RE LIKE A GROUP OF MILLENNIALS WHO WANT TO DO BETTER, WHO WANT TO IMPROVE THINGS, WHO DON'T WANT TO HAVE THE SAME AFGHANISTAN AS TEN YEARS AGO.

that we are all human. But that's not the perception that a lot of people have.

Once again, I really think this is the fault of our larger educational system. It's the lack of education, it's the way people have been brought up, it's the way they have been taught in the mosque or everywhere else. First, they think about their religion, and then they think about whether the other person is human or not—they don't see the person first and the religion second. If you are not Muslim, then you are somehow less of a person. Their view is also that they are Muslim, and the West is not Muslim. But a lot of this comes down to the fact that they haven't been exposed to other ideas and other cultures.

Even in my own family, when I got the scholarship to the United States, my parents and my sister and brothers were very, very supportive, but one of my uncles didn't want me to leave Afghanistan. My mom said to me, "Don't worry, you just go and I'll take care of it." My uncle was very upset. He told my mom, "Why did you let her go—she's so young—she's going to lose her religion—she's going to forget about her religion—she's going to forget about her culture—she will be very Westernized and she's not going to fit in the family and she'll bring shame to her family." I consider my family pretty open-minded and pretty educated compared to other families that I have seen, but that really was my uncle's perception. And my mom just said, "No, nothing's going to happen. She's going to be fine; she's mature enough."

When I came back home for the summer, I think it was my first week home and it was a weekend, so I was sleeping. And then I heard my uncle talking. I walked into the living room. He said, "When did you come home?" He was surprised to see me. I was wearing the same clothes that I always wore at home and he saw that nothing really had changed physically about me. We sat and talked for over an hour, and at the end he said, "I was wrong last year. I thought that you were going to change but I don't see anything that has changed in you except the way you talk and the way you think. It's so much more mature than last year."

And guess what? Now he's encouraging his daughter to pursue higher education in "Amrecka."

I think if more of our elders have that exposure, if they can see for themselves that education abroad or a good, critical-thinking education is not something to be afraid of, then more things will change. Think about it—if you change the education system, you're going to reach everyone. Because right now there are so many kids in school, that whole generation will be agents of change. I don't think they can alter their parents' strongly held views and beliefs, but I'm sure they can have some influence. Even through small things, such as having one conversation, you can make them aware that they can think differently, that ideas are not always black and white. I think those tiny things will eventually add up and become real change.

I don't have a hard time navigating between the United States and Afghanistan, but that's probably because I went from Afghanistan to the U.S. and not from the U.S. to Afghanistan. I think it would have been very challenging if I went to Afghanistan as an American woman, and not a Muslim, and had to work in a male-dominated society that has a very set view of what kind of person I am and my role.

One of the biggest cultural differences is simply being a woman in Afghanistan. I remember when I was taking accounting classes in Kabul. The school would hire teachers from India and Pakistan—and some of them were not very good. I was the first one to raise my hand and to go speak to the principal and ask, "Why are you not hiring the right professors? We come here in the evening and we are not getting an education." But I was one of just three girls in a classroom of eighty students. Everyone else was a guy. No one wanted to listen to me. But then we had to take our first course exam. The whole program was managed by the British, so the exams and questions were the same as what British students took and we had to take our exam at the same time as all the students in the UK. It was the first time that this exam had been given in Afghanistan. When the results came out, I had the highest score.

After that, the principal's attitude changed. He started to listen to me and to respect me. After a year, he asked me if I would work with him at school as an administrator. I had my scholarship so I didn't want that job. But that one year had changed his mind. That's a problem with the majority of Afghan men, they don't think women are capable. They don't think women should be outside the home. They think the place of women is at home, taking care of the children. Those basic obstacles make it really, really difficult to try to raise your voice and to become an active member of society.

Another problem is that as a woman in Afghanistan working outside the home, you have to be very careful of how you dress, how you talk, who you talk to, how late you work, really careful of everything. You will be judged by every one of your actions. If you are a woman who works, you can't be very friendly with people, especially guys, even if you are working on the same project with them. You can't laugh with people. If you laugh, they think you are only there to enjoy yourself. You have to have a serious face all the time or people will think you're not really working. They will think that you are there for other things. But guys, they can laugh, they can do anything.

There are a few people, particularly in the younger generation, who have worked with foreign NGOs or who have traveled outside of Afghanistan. I think they do respect women for working really hard and showing that they are equal to their male counterparts. I've had a couple of colleagues who told me that they very much appreciated what I was doing. But that is in the minority. In most jobs, that is not how they think about you if you are a woman.

And these prohibitions extend to every part of life. If you are a woman, you should not take the bus or public transportation by yourself. Even if you're with someone else on the bus, you're not supposed to laugh out loud or smile or joke when you're on the bus or out anywhere in public. But if guys do it, it's totally fine. And also, if you are a woman, you're not supposed to be out late in the evening. You're not supposed to do a lot of things, even something as simple as exercising. You won't see a woman exercising outside. My own brothers exercise. They will go outside every day. When I was in Kabul, I suggested that I should go outside and exercise too, and one of them said, "That's probably not a good idea. I think people are going to start staring at you and then create trouble for you and for us, so you might as well just exercise at home."

It's going to take a long time to change some of these attitudes. You can teach someone accounting or science or math. You can teach all that in school, but it's difficult to change how a person thinks about something once they are set in their views. Things can only change if people will teach their children differently.

It's going to take a very long time. We need more activists. We need more awareness.

But I also see how much my old life and my family's life and my friends' lives have changed for the good in the last ten, fifteen years. Even the government, for all its problems, is better. For the first time in our history, we had a peaceful transfer of power. It had never happened before. Even Pakistan doesn't have peaceful transfers of power, and they haven't had the years of war that we have. Almost every time in Pakistan, someone stages a coup to take over the government. So changing governments peacefully was a great accomplishment. I think the fact that so much of the Afghan population is so young will also make a huge difference.

Afghan people are really eager. They are tired of the lives they have had. Nobody wants to go through what has happened again. We don't want to be forced from our homeland another time. Coming back is like lying in your own bed after a long trip, it is familiar and sweet.

In terms of the future, I don't have a lot of options. I have the option to be optimistic or pessimistic and my choice is to be optimistic. Twelve years ago, if you had asked me if I would finish college, or if I would finish college in the United States, I probably would have said, "No, that's not possible." But it did happen. It happened for my siblings. It happened for a lot of my friends. And today I'm working for one of the biggest accounting firms in the world in one of the world's biggest cities. I'm serving one of the company's biggest global clients right now. If that can happen, I'm sure things will change in Afghanistan. All the people who go back, together they are going to change the future.

Most of my relatives, even my older sisters, had arranged marriages. There's still a huge part of the population that follows the custom, especially in the provinces. But I think that's going to be different in the future. Arranged marriages probably worked at one point, but I don't think that will be the way I will pursue my life. Choosing a partner that you're going to be happy with is probably the most important decision of your life. That's one of the things that having an education, being empowered, knowing who you are, what you are, and what you want in your life frees you to do—make choices.

Perhaps the most amazing story of choices is one of my older sisters. She was a medical student in Pakistan. Then the school closed, so she couldn't continue her education. She started working. Then she got married. It was an arranged marriage, and when she got married, my brother-in-law wasn't in favor of her working outside of the home, so my sister stayed at home for ten years. Before that, she had two different jobs, and was still hoping to return to medical school. Then, literally, her whole life was taken away from her. She had to stay at home for ten years. Every time she would visit us, I really held back. I didn't talk too much about my work and school life. My two other sisters and I all had jobs and school and everything. And I knew that my older sister really wanted the same thing for herself.

After ten years, after seeing how all of us had gone to school and gotten an education, she finally had the courage to start a different life. She managed to resolve it with her husband to a point that she has the freedom to work and study. I never thought my brother-in-law would do it but he finally let my sister go back to university. She's finishing her undergraduate degree and also teaching high school part-time. So she's outside the home all day long and loving her life. And she has a 4.0 GPA.

I had a conversation with my sister last weekend. We Skyped, and she asked if there was any way she could come to get her master's degree in the U.S. She said, "Can you tell me about the admissions process for U.S. schools?" And I said, "What did you just say?" I was shocked.

I asked, "What about your husband?" She said, "I think he will manage for a few years."

That's very impressive. People are changing.

$\mathcal{L}$earning

A damaged classroom

Getting the answer right

Taking a test

Composing an essay

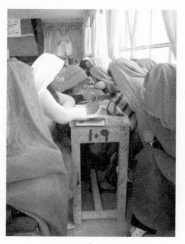

Studying

From literacy courses taught on mobile phones to women pursuing degrees in fields such as law and accounting, education is opening minds and possibilities for a new Afghanistan.

LEARNING

. . . .

In Afghanistan, education is truly a matter of life and death. Schools for girls have been burned to the ground, hundreds of teachers educating girls have been threatened or killed, and the girls themselves are targets, with thousands of students becoming victims. They have been severely sickened in gas attacks while sitting in their classrooms. In brazen attacks, men throw acid into the faces of teenage girls as they walk to school, blinding them and disfiguring them for life. Hand grenades are thrown into gatherings of school-age girls. Every day around the country, girls' schools even test the water in their buildings for signs of poison.

The collapse of women's education can be seen in one statistic: approximately 75 percent of adult Afghan women cannot read or write or do basic math. Under the Taliban, girls were forbidden to attend school. Fewer than five thousand were educated. There were no women studying in a university. Today, roughly 40 percent of Afghan girls attend elementary school, but only one in twenty girls will continue her education after completing the sixth grade. Co-ed education is very rare; most Afghan families, if they allow their daughters to attend school, require their daughters to attend all-girls schools close to their homes. Still, there have been important gains. More than 120,000 girls have graduated from secondary school and more than one-quarter of all university students are women.

Here are the stories of three women and one young man who are devoting themselves to girls' education. They include Dr. Sakena Yacoobi, who kept underground schools alive during the Taliban era and is working on new ways to educate the most vulnerable, through traditional classrooms as well as other means. As a teenage boy, Nang Attal stole chalk from his boys' school so that he might teach girls the basics of reading and writing in his mother's mud-brick kitchen. He speaks honestly of a tribal culture that too often sees women as little more than an expense or a commodity.

In Afghanistan, more than 50 percent of girls are married or engaged by age twelve, even though a recent law says that a man cannot legally obtain a marriage license until his bride is seventeen. Almost 80 percent of marriages are "arranged," with young girls being married off to far older men, sometimes as second or third or fourth wives to men in their sixties. Some girls are bartered into marriage to repay a debt or resolve a dispute. Others are sent off on the belief that they will no longer be targets for kidnapping or rape. And crushing poverty often forces parents to marry off their daughters simply to escape the cost of caring for them. "I am standing for girls' education," says Attal, adding, "Women are treated in a way that we have to change."

Energy seems to emanate from Dr. Sakena Yacoobi. It rolls off her as she moves from place to place or just sits and speaks, a combination of fervor, passion, and optimism. Even her words are fast. Listening to her sentences stream out one after another is a bit like watching a crowd of runners at the starting line, each jostling for position, anxious, eager to take off. Above all, Dr. Yacoobi is an evangelist for education. Phrases that might sound trite coming from others, she makes sound true. "If you have a good teacher in the classroom, no matter how poor the people, they will stay in the classroom," she says. And the ultimate goal is not simply to learn, but "to make a better human being." Born in Herat, Afghanistan's third-largest city and site of an ancient trading route near Iran, Dr. Yacoobi once dreamed of becoming a medical doctor. Instead, during the war among the mujahideen, she opened schools in Afghan refugee camps, eventually starting eighty underground schools for girls inside Afghanistan during the Taliban era. Today, her Afghan Institute of Learning is one of the largest Afghan nongovernmental organizations (NGOs). In spite of everything she has seen, Dr. Yacoobi says, "I believe that when we do something good, the outcome will be good too."

· · · · · · · · · ·

My mother had sixteen pregnancies, but only five of her children survived. So many times, I thought my mother was going to bleed to death in front of my eyes. As a girl, every day, leaving school, I would see the body of a child or a woman being taken to the graveyard. And I was afraid every day that something would happen to my mother, that it would be her body that they were carrying.

But it wasn't just the women and babies who died from childbirth or illness. At night, in my own house, I would hear the cries of women from the houses around me. I would ask my father what was happening and he would tell me not to worry, that it was just another family's dispute, or that it was nothing. But I knew, each time I heard the crying, I knew a woman was being beaten by a husband or a brother.

I was very lucky because I had a father who really encouraged me to stand on my own. His own father had died when he was five and he grew up an orphan, but by himself, he became a successful businessman. He made the decision that all his children, whether girl or boy, would go to school. By the time I was four years old, I was going to school at the mosque. By six, I had completed religious school and went off to regular school. I was dreaming of becoming a doctor. In Herat, where we lived, there was no university. The only university was in Kabul. My father was able to send me to the United States for my undergraduate studies. While I was enrolled in graduate school, the Soviet Union invaded Afghanistan. For me, time stopped. I could not reach my family. I did not know if my family was alive or dead. I waited months for any word.

The Soviet invasion devastated Afghanistan and my own family lost everything. They fled as refugees to Iran. As soon as I heard from them, I wanted to leave my education and go to them, but my father said no. Once I started teaching science and working as a public health consultant, I brought all the members of my family to the United States. I loved teaching in the U.S., I loved my students, but I also realized that they did not need me here. They had plenty of good people to teach them. Watching the news, hearing from refugees, there were tears in my eyes for my people. I knew that I could do so much more at home. With my family safe, I decided to go back, to go to a refugee camp in Pakistan.

*　　　*　　　*

When I arrived, the scene was horrible. Worse than anything I could imagine. People were everywhere. All of them had lost their homes, their property, their loved ones, their husbands, their children. I would see young girls and young widows with three, six, eight children. These girls and these mothers were just sleeping and crying in their tents. Everywhere I went, walking around, I saw people who were hungry, who were barely alive.

The tents were packed in very tight with each other. And nowhere was safe. In the middle of the night, Pakistani soldiers would come. They would enter any tent and do anything. And everyone in the camp was afraid to say anything because if they did, they would be kicked out of the camp. The only thing more terrible than the camp was being forced to leave. Inside the tents, people had nothing. They had a blanket and maybe a plastic floor covering to put on the ground. All the land where the refugees lived was so bad. The sanitation was terrible. There was almost no water. Women went to wash clothes on the side of a stream, and they had to carry water in buckets back to camp for miles from that same stream. Even worse was the bathroom. There was always a line. Men and women had to stand together, and in Afghan culture, that was very hard for the women. I looked around and I was heartbroken. In Herat, when I was growing up, we did not have beggars in the street or people without shelter. Now, thousands of Afghans were living like that. I looked around and I thought, what am I going to be able to do as one person? How can I possibly help these people?

I knew one thing, though. Education had changed my life. With education, I was able to help my own family. Once you have education, no one can ever take that away from you. If you have education, you can start over. The one thing my father had always wanted for me was to go after my own education. What, I thought, if I could educate these people in this camp?

The people in the camps were against education. Part of the problem was that when the Russians invaded, they came into the cities and towns and forced people to learn under the Soviet system. When I talked about teaching, many refugees said, "The Russians brought a new system of education and look what happened."

I knew I was not going to change their minds alone. I searched and searched, and I found one mullah. He was about eighty years old and anything that he said, the people followed. He was so respected. So I said to myself, I'm going to him. Everyone else told me it wouldn't work. For three months, I went each day to his house and we sat drinking tea. Finally, after three months, I told him that I wanted to start a school and I wanted him to be a teacher. I remember he looked at me and he said, "You crazy woman. I am a mullah, not a teacher." And I said, "I can teach you to be a teacher. You can read the Koran. You can be a teacher."

We put seven tents in his compound, and we opened our first school in 1992. And we taught the students. I trained his wife and his daughters and his daughters-in-law to be teachers for the girls. We showed everyone that girls can learn how to read and write. When students came to us, after four and a half months, they knew how to read and write. Soon I began writing teaching manuals and training more teachers. From seven tents, we moved to fifteen schools and twenty-one thousand students, sponsored by the International Refugee Committee. When the IRC ran out of money, I spent $20,000 of my own money to start the Afghan Institute of Learning. People in the camps trusted us with their kids. And we didn't just teach from a book. I wanted the students to learn critical thinking; I wanted them to be challenged and to learn how to be active, how to challenge what they heard and what they thought.

*　　　*　　　*

Around 1997, a group of men crossed over into Pakistan from Afghanistan. Although the Taliban was in power, people still crossed back and forth over the border. News traveled along with the people, and through word of mouth, these men had heard about our schools. They came to where I was in Peshawar and asked me to open a school inside Afghanistan. At first I said no. In the Taliban time, if people had a book and went outside and the Taliban saw them, they would be killed. That was it. I told the men that I was not going to risk my teachers or anyone else sending them into Afghanistan. "These people, teaching, they will be killed," I told them.

But they persisted. In a way, it was a bit like what I had done with the mullah. They wore me down. Finally, I said yes, but I had several conditions. The community for the school has to give me a place where the school can be held. It must be a place that is liked and respected. And I am not going to send one of my teachers from the camps in Pakistan. They also have to give me a teacher that comes from the community. And they have to provide protection for that teacher. In turn, I would provide the salary for the teacher, the books and materials, and the teacher training. And all of this had to be set down in a written agreement, we all had to sign a contract. It was going to be two-way, not one-way. They said yes. Together, we opened eighty schools inside people's houses in Kabul, Jalalabad, Herat, and other cities. And each community did it. They protected, they supported, they nourished some three thousand students at a time when there was almost no schooling all across Afghanistan.

Some of the young girls that attended these schools have grown up to become Fulbright Scholars, some are now young leaders in Afghanistan.

I get frustrated when people tell me that all the women of Afghanistan are submissive. I say, no, they are similar to all the women around the world. I also know my religion. If people want to challenge me, I can answer. My whole life is gender equality, children, and women's rights. So when people say that the Taliban is Islam in Afghanistan, I say that Islam is a beautiful religion, a peaceful religion, one that teaches us how to be kind and respectful to each other, and it gives freedom to women. Islam prevents child killing and girl killing. It was Muhammad himself who stopped that practice. Islam also allows men and women to be equal, side by side. Look back to the beginning. Muhammad's own daughter was an accountant, his granddaughter a great speaker.

What does Afghanistan need in order to heal? The Afghan people are smart, intelligent, loving people. We have a rich tradition, literature and architecture, but after nearly forty years of war, people have lost respect, forgiveness, and love. People do not trust anymore. I've put together several conferences on peace, love, and forgiveness. I gather people together and we read poems by the great Afghan poet Rumi, poems about fairness, justice, love, and how to be kind. We play traditional, classic Afghan music. Hearing the notes, listening to the words, people are crying. We are reintroducing ideas that they have forgotten. But I think people can forgive.

ISLAM ALSO ALLOWS MEN AND WOMEN TO BE EQUAL, SIDE BY SIDE. LOOK BACK TO THE BEGINNING. MUHAMMAD'S OWN DAUGHTER WAS AN ACCOUNTANT, HIS GRANDDAUGHTER A GREAT SPEAKER.

What we need too is a safe country. Afghanistan today is not safe. We need to build good citizenship and practice the rule of law. We need a good economy. Even our teachers don't make enough money. They have to do too many other jobs and they are too focused on that to earn a living, not on their teaching. One of my new projects is to create learning centers. They are not just educational schools, we help teach people how to open their own businesses like tailor shops or beauty shops. They learn about income generation. We have mobile health units with nurses and doctors, because many young women don't know how to breast-feed, to feed and dress their babies. We have hygiene education. Local people tell us that mortality rates have significantly fallen in the places where we have the health service clinics. We have workshops on democracy, education, and child rights. And I want each center to become self-sufficient and do its own management. Many of the centers have been able to do that. In these centers, women can take literacy classes. We have a mobile phone app that lets women learn to read. I have an eighty-year-old woman, probably a great-grandmother. She is learning to read with the mobile phone app and she wants to go all the way to high school and get her degree.

No matter what happens, I don't allow myself to be discouraged. I'm a spiritual person. I believe God is protecting me. I sit and I pray, and that brings me back. I have an orphanage with four hundred children. When things are difficult, I go to visit them and get down on the floor and play with the children for even five or ten minutes. In those minutes when I am with them, the whole world is off my shoulders.

People ask me, do you have any children? I tell them I have thousands and thousands of children.

Nang Attal is a man. But he is devoting himself to girls' education. He's been working with girls and teaching girls since he was thirteen. He started teaching in his mother's kitchen, writing lessons on the kitchen wall using a bit of charred wood—wood that he usually gathered in the mornings before walking to his own school. Attal grew up in the Khawat Valley, about sixty miles from Kabul, in a tribal region. Both his parents were illiterate, but Attal graduated from Kabul Education University and was awarded a prestigious Fulbright scholarship to study in the United States. He has been a visiting researcher at the University of California, Berkeley, and earned a master's at Golden Gate University. In 2014, he received a United Nations Youth Courage Award for his work on behalf of Afghan girls and young women.

· · · · · · · · · ·

For a long time, I didn't know when I was born. I didn't know the exact year or the exact day. I didn't know because no one recorded my birth. That's pretty typical for illiterate parents, and both of my parents were illiterate. When I finally needed to know my birthday, I started asking. My mom remembered that I had been born in the spring, and she remembered a few children who had been born a month or two after me. So I asked those children and their parents, and finally, based on that, I figured out a date. And that day is now my birthday. But it is sad to be a child and not to know when you were born.

I grew up in the countryside about sixty miles south of Kabul in Wardak province. It's a very rural area. Our villages didn't have electricity and even now people in my village don't have electricity. They have some solar power but not electricity. In our village, most people were poor. Two families owned about 80 percent of the crops and gardens, the rest of the people owned the remaining land and gardens, and about 5 percent of the villagers owned very little or almost nothing. I grew up in that last 5 percent. We had a small piece of land and a garden, but we did not own the crops that we grew, due to an Islamic Sharia concept called *ijarah*, which is practiced in our area. In the simplest explanation, *ijarah* will not allow anything that might be consumed to be leased; instead it is treated as a loan. My family was only able to pay off most of this "loan" in 2013. So, we were extremely poor. Normally we had to work for others or my dad would go to other parts of the country to work as a seasonal laborer.

My parents were hardworking but uneducated. My dad had been a kind of mujahideen fighter against the Soviets, so he didn't have a chance to go to school, or his school was disrupted. Or maybe he was not that interested in education. My mom had basic oral religious education from her dad because her dad was a religious kind of priest. But she could not read and write. Now, since her children have gone to school, she can read some very basic things. She learned along with us.

Our house sits up in the hills. It's made of mud, all mud walls, and inside there are three rooms. One is the living room; one is a kind of kitchen—a traditional Afghan kitchen; and one room is a place where you put your shoes, your clothes, and things like that. The whole family, five brothers and first one and then two sisters, mostly lived in one room.

We lived differently depending on the season. In the summer, I had to wake up early in the morning to bring the water from the well and carry it in buckets on my shoulders. The well was about fifty or one hundred meters away. So I would bring water and then boil the water over the firewood and make tea in the morning. The tea responsibility in our house was on me. After that I would have a quick breakfast and leave to walk to school. Our school was around five miles away. So I had to walk an hour and a half just to get there, and I had to wake up very early. School would be done around noon and then I would walk back and get home around 1:30 or 2:00. And we'd have a quick kind of lunch and then I would go down to work in the garden or be busy with my dad.

Some days after school we would also sneak off and go swimming in the river. We were always careful that our dad wouldn't see us because he didn't allow us to swim. He was cautious—he would say that the current was strong and we were children. But most days, we were busy until early evening with the crops. Wheat, potatoes, and beans are the main crops, along with some vegetables. We had fruit trees, red cherries, black cherries, and also grapes. But these are not huge gardens like in the United States. We had just a few trees, maybe two or three for a variety of fruits.

When we came back to the house, I would also help my mom cook the food, particularly the bread. To bake the bread, she needed a lot of firewood. In the evening I would bring more water back to the house. After dinner, we would sit down and do our homework for school. But when I would go down to the crops after lunch, or when I would take the cow out for feeding, or go to feed the chickens, most of the time I took a book. I would read and study while I looked after the cow.

In the winter, we didn't have school. If the weather was okay, I would get up very early in the morning, maybe three or four o'clock, and go into the mountains to bring some bushes and sticks for firewood. It's hard to find firewood at that time of the year and you have to try hard to find a lot of it. I would also have to go very early in order to reach a part of the mountain that didn't have snow. And I had to carry all the wood strapped to my back. Hopefully I would be back around one or two o'clock for lunch. I did that until I went away to university. I'll probably do it again when I go back to the village.

In the winter, there are also a lot of religious studies. We would go to mosque to study. After 2002, we also had an English learning center in the village, so we would go and study English there and then come back around dinnertime. At dinner, everyone would gather and I and my older brothers would try to teach our younger siblings.

We also had to clean the snow off the roofs of the local buildings, especially the mosque. You do that every morning. And we would need to take firewood to the mosque as well. How often you take firewood, how many days you are responsible for heating the mosque, is based on the number of children you have. Since my dad had more children than some of the other families, we had to bring a lot of firewood to heat the mosque.

Our favorite game in the winter was traditional baseball, which is different from what you play in the United States. In the U.S., the other person is throwing the ball. But in our case you take the ball in one hand and take the bat in the other. You throw the ball up and then hit it with the bat. Usually we play with twelve people on a team; it doesn't always have to be twelve, but it has to be an equal number on both sides. You have two teams and the losing team has to get wood for the other team or something like that.

We mostly ate what we got from our own crops, like potatoes and beans and rice. Sometimes my dad would go to the bazaar or market in the district and he might bring back meat if he had money. My mom also raised chickens, so we could have eggs. If we had a guest, she might kill a chicken and we would have chicken. But it was not every day that we had eggs and certainly not chicken. My mom was very strict like that.

*　　　*　　　*

The earliest memory I have, though, is not of any of those things. The earliest I have is of the bombardment. It happened a few villages down from us. They bombarded a headquarters for the mujahideen on the top of the hill. The mujahideen kept some artillery and weapons on the top of the hill. In my mind, I can still see the smoke rising from the peak of the mountain and the faces of all the people who were so scared. It's a beautiful valley with mountains, but every time I passed that area, I would be reminded of the image of the smoke. In the winter, when we were going into the mountains to bring back bushes and firewood, I would never go close to that place. I had a bad feeling about it. And I never knew who bombed that place—whether it was the Soviet government or another group of mujahideen. I remember too my dad coming back with a gun, because he was a mujahideen fighter, although now my dad regrets that time. He doesn't like to speak about it. It was a bad period for him.

I remember the Taliban exactly. I was in grade four in elementary and I remember when they came because the first order they issued was that we should have turbans. My elementary school was a long walk, maybe three miles. And some of the walk was uphill and past land that had been mined by the Russians during the Soviet invasion. The school was very small and simple, with limited rooms. It could not accommodate all the students. So I pretty much studied my elementary education outside, sitting on the ground, and the teacher sitting with the blackboard. In the Taliban time, there were a lot of restrictions about what you should wear, and we had to walk to school and sit and study wearing our turbans.

But at the same time, I think those years were when the education system became better because the Taliban were a lot stricter.

Under the Taliban, the teachers were on time to school and they had an agenda. There were a lot of religious subjects. When I graduated from elementary school in grade six, I wanted to go to the district high school, which was around five miles away. But to attend the high school, I had to pass a special exam (the exam doesn't exist anymore). My parents did not allow me to sit for that exam; they did not want me to go on to high school. They said, "You don't need to go to the high school because it's far away. You won't pass the exams. You need to wait because you are very small and skinny." I was one of the smallest kids in the school by age and by height. But I wanted to go to high school.

On the day of the exam, I sneaked out of the house and took the exam and came back home. When I came back, my mom asked, "Where were you?" And I said I went to my grandma's house. She didn't say anything else; she didn't inquire about those things. A week later, I went back to see my results. There were all these guys with turbans crowding around the board. I'm the smallest kid and I'm trying to see and no one is giving way. I kept saying please, and I waited a really long time. Finally, people began to walk away. I made it to the list, and my name was third. I guess I scored the third highest of everyone taking the exam. I was so pleased and so happy.

That same day, they gave us all the books for high school. If you go to high school, they give you lots of books. And then I started thinking how can I carry all these books back to my home? It was so hard. I arrived home late in the afternoon. I remember my younger aunt, who has since passed away from a heart attack, happened to be at our house. She was sitting around the outdoor fireplace and when she saw me with all the books, she spoke up and supported and encouraged me. After that, everyone else was okay with what I had done. They said, It's up to you if you want to go or not, but it was fine with them.

*　　　*　　　*

At that point in my life, I was still very slim and skinny. They would call me the "skinny guy." That was my nickname in school, in town. If you asked someone for Attal, there was no Attal. If you asked for Nang, there was no Nang. But if you asked for the Skinny Guy, it was, "Oh, yeah, Skinny Guy. Oh, yeah, I know him." In all my life, I was referred to as Skinny Guy. Some of my relatives still call me Skinny Guy, even though I am grown.

Economically we were in a very bad situation and especially during the time of the Taliban, because the country was under sanctions. The farmers suffered a lot. We had drought and we lost a lot of our crops. Then, what goats or crops we had, we couldn't sell. We couldn't feed our cows and goats, so we lost the livestock as well. It was a very, very poor situation. And food was very rare.

In grade four or five, we were taking biology as a subject and when our teacher wanted to explain the human skeleton, he would ask me, "Hey, Skinny Guy, come over." And in front of the whole class, he would bend me from my shoulder and say, "This is an example of a human skeleton." He was the one who gave me the name "Skinny Guy." I really don't like him. But I was extremely thin, extremely weak, and had to walk all that way. I'm still physically suffering from those years.

Under the Taliban there was no girls' education and also earlier during the mujahideen time, there was no girls' education in the countryside. Since my mom knew basic oral religious education, she was teaching the girls from the immediate neighborhood religious prayers, things like that. For the Taliban, religious education was okay. But after I started going to high school, my mom asked me to teach the girls how to read and write. I said, "Yeah, I can do that." I had about five girls sitting in the kitchen to start and from there that number grew. My mom would teach them to say the religious prayers and after I would teach them how to read and write.

At first, I was writing on the wall with a piece of charred firewood. But that wasn't very effective. So we had to find a blackboard. That was a struggle. My mom asked one of the religious priests for a blackboard. He didn't have one, but his brother was, I think, a doctor. And by some chance, he was working in a nearby school. They had an old blackboard and he brought it to us. But once you find a blackboard in the countryside in a third-world country, then you have to find chalk. There was no chalk anywhere, so sometimes I would just steal some chalk from my boys' school and use it for the girls' school. All of this happened around 2002, right after the Taliban left power.

At some point in 2002, for the first time foreigners came to our village. I remember the scene because I saw three cars in our village. To us, three cars looked like we were watching a miracle. I wondered what was wrong and I ran down. A crowd had gathered; a lot of people were moving around. And as I got closer, I saw the group of foreigners, and there was a blond lady standing in the middle. Later I found out that she was German.

> ONCE YOU FIND A BLACKBOARD IN THE COUNTRYSIDE, YOU HAVE TO FIND CHALK. THERE WAS NO CHALK ANYWHERE, SO SOMETIMES I WOULD JUST STEAL SOME CHALK FROM MY BOYS' SCHOOL AND USE IT FOR THE GIRLS' SCHOOL.

At that time, I knew basic English, very basic phrases like "Hi, how are you? What is your name?" I pushed my way to the middle of the crowd and I just thought, this is the time for me to practice my English with her. And I said, "Hi, how are you?"

And for her, this was unbelievable. Here is this shepherd guy in the middle of an Afghan village speaking to me in English. And then she tried to take my picture from every angle she could. I told her that we have a girls' school here and asked her to help us and send us some books and stationery. We did get two boxes of stationery later. I don't know if she did it or some other organization, but we got that stationery and distributed it for the girls and it was a very happy day for them.

Gradually, the number of girls in our home school grew. I was going to school in the morning and in the afternoon teaching at my mom's school. Some of the girls I taught are now midwives, they went on and got more intensive education.

Later, with the help of Sultan Masood Mayar, the grandson of a former provincial governor, and someone whose leadership helped transform the village for the better, an international organization called Afghans4Tomorrow was able to build a school in the valley for the girls of many villages. It was built by an American engineer from Colorado, George Nez, who came and lived in the valley for about five or six months. But later some unknown people set it on fire, perhaps hoping to intimidate people not to send their girls to school.

We still don't know who burned it. We think it is people connected to the Taliban, but no one knows for sure. If you asked at the school, they didn't know. It could have been someone in the village who was unhappy with the property. There could be multiple reasons why it was burned. But it's always easy to put the blame on the Taliban: "Oh, they did it." But I think we must be very clear that there are small village grievances that also play into this type of act.

Things in Afghanistan are very complicated. There are local grievances, local tribal wars, local village disputes that the Taliban has nothing to do with. Everything bad that happens is not simply because of the Taliban. But unfortunately we lost that school. Many of the girls are still in school, they just study like they used to, inside people's homes.

Even now, though, I don't want to talk too much about how the girls are studying. I don't want to put anyone at risk.

But I can proudly say, that after eight years of efforts, we were able to reopen the girls' school with funding from the Zakat Foundation of America through Afghans4Tomorrow. The school even opened a computer lab and I have seen pictures of girls studying computers. For me to see girls in our valley sitting in front of computers is equal to women walking on Mars. Maybe that is what one of these girls will do at some point. I carry that hope in my heart, mind, and soul.

A lot of the opposition to girls' education, it's a tribal thing. As an Afghan man, I want to be honest about this and to say that in order to fix this, we need to admit that we have a problem and the problem is much more tribal first. Only second is it religious. The tribal view is that women just need to be at home. That's it. Period. From the tribal perspective, there is nothing more to talk about. Women should be at home, and women in school just doesn't make sense. Women in school is not seen as acceptable and they won't allow it.

But for women, it's more than school. It's not just that women are treated as second-class citizens—in some cases women are not even treated as any class at all. They are expected just to serve like farm animals and bring children into the world and things like that.

FOR ME TO SEE GIRLS IN OUR VALLEY SITTING IN FRONT OF COMPUTERS IS EQUAL TO WOMEN WALKING ON MARS.

There are some horror stories that I've seen personally. That's why I'm standing for girls' education. We need to get those girls out of slavery. Some of the things I've seen, it's unbelievable. One of the cultural practices is that if a brother kills someone from another family, in exchange that brother's sister has to be married off to someone in the dead person's family. The sister did not commit any crime; she has nothing to do with it. But she will be forced to marry someone in the victim's family, she will be under their control, and for all of her life she will be enslaved. Enslaved in the sense that she will have to do whatever they tell her and live under any conditions that they force upon her. If they will not let her wear shoes, she cannot have shoes. In a village near us, there was a woman who that happened to who did not wear shoes for decades. Things like this may have happened back in the fifth century. But it shouldn't be happening today.

I am not saying this to blame tribal people or culture; I am saying that no one has come forward with a better set of ideas to transform tribal culture into a more positive and decent culture. This is something that we need to work on, and I believe people will ultimately welcome it. A determined struggle always has the chance of victory.

There are many more examples of tribal issues that we Afghans are not talking about. When people marry, one of the main criteria is whether she can cook very good breads or not. And whether she can serve and care for animals, like a cow. In many houses, the woman is responsible for the cow; she has to do all the milking and clean up after the cow. Those are the criteria, not whether she is educated or not. But if we as Afghans want to be a progressive society and solve our problems, then we have to take care of our sisters. Even in my own family, when my sister graduated from sixth grade, my dad was not entirely supportive of her being considered to go on to the next grade. We had to convince him to allow her to get more education, and there were some difficult days and arguments with our own dad, although in my heart I believe that he really does like education.

Part of the problem is that for many men, in a sense, a daughter is goods and money. There is money to be made from marrying off their daughters. In my own village, a girl was married off when she was only two or three months old. The guy was about five, six, or seven years old. She was taken to live at their house when she was around eighteen months old. But when she grew up, the girl was not happy with this situation. She was afraid, and she went to her parents' house and said I don't want to be married to this guy. And what happened? The whole village went to her parents' house and brought her back to her husband's house. She had no choice; she had to stay. She has a child now.

Women are treated in a way that we have to change. We have to say that it is wrong to marry off a three-month-old girl. If we want to have a country that is prosperous, where people are treated as equals, we have to change this. If we want to be a good country, a responsible country, a responsible society, we need to change our bad traditions. Take the good things and leave the bad things to the past and to history.

We need women doctors. In the whole district I think we have three or four women doctors. That's it. And women, our own mothers and sisters, are dying. We need to fix this. But to fix this, each man needs to be courageous enough to support his daughter or his sister to become a doctor so she can save lives, the lives of other mothers and sisters. Not allowing your daughters to go to school, it's the same thing as letting your mothers and your sisters suffer. Because this same traditional mind-set says that you cannot allow a woman to be seen by a male doctor. So if there are no women doctors, that means the women should just suffer and die. I am not only talking about this, but I am doing this. My older sister is in her first year of college and would like to become a doctor. I am supporting her as best I can.

In fact, when we were trying to convince my dad to let my own sister go on to school, the first thing we talked about is that we need women doctors. People in rural areas don't want to hear about gender equality, forget about it and shut your mouth. But they can understand about the need for women doctors.

And we don't just have to convince fathers. We have to convince mothers as well. When I was visiting Washington, D.C., I came across an Afghan-American family and the daughter wanted to go to Columbia to do her medical studies, but her mom would not allow her to go. I was sitting there and I was like, "You're kidding me. This is like Washington, D.C. How are you going to ignore your own daughter and not allow her to go to medical school in this country?" I used very strong language. This is the United States. For the sake of God, how you can do that? Her dad was willing to allow her to go, but her mom would not. Her mom was mostly concerned about her daughter being outside and whether she might date other men and things like that. But her daughter had a dream to go to Columbia and become a doctor.

I told the daughter, and the mom was sitting right there, but this is what I said, "I received the United Nations Youth Courage Award. If your mom continues to refuse to let you go, I will go public about this. I will send my Youth Courage Award to you, and I will try to do anything that I can to help you go." Because I don't accept this. That mother is educated, but part of that mom grew up back in Afghanistan. She has the traditional mind-set.

One of the best ways we can change minds in Afghanistan is through storytelling. In rural areas, people are uneducated and storytelling is the most powerful part of the local culture. I'd like to take stories of some of the successful girls from across the country and present these stories on the radio in an appealing manner. I think this would do a lot to change the minds of parents in a community to stand behind their daughters' education. It won't be quick. You cannot change the village overnight. It took about fifteen, sixteen years for my family and dad to change. And it will take even longer for more families in rural areas to change. I grew up there. If you take a hard approach, if you pressure the society to send their girls to school, that is not going to work. But I think the power of storytelling can.

There are millions of girls out of school in rural areas. And these issues are tribal; they are religious; and they are economic as well. Girls are helping support their families; they are caring for cows, working in the fields. Poverty plays a role in that. The real responsibility in this case is for the younger generation—we have to ask what type of country do we want? What type of future do we need to have? Some of our culture is good for strengthening family and family values. But for me, culture should not be something that suppresses us; culture should be something that empowers us. And an empowered country is one that empowers our sisters too.

Even among Afghan youth, we are a very young country, but we are a complex country. A huge portion of our younger people are still subject to radicalization. People like me, we don't necessarily have momentum. I'm going to give you an example. A week ago there was a guy who posted online a picture of a girl in Kabul who was riding a bicycle. And an engineer, a guy who graduated from Polytechnic University and who is working, he replied under that post, "We're going to hell because girls are riding bicycles here. This society is becoming a completely Western society. And that means we're becoming a bad society."

When I saw this I was like, wait a minute. In the United States there is a thirteen-year-old girl who has a dream to go to Mars, to be the first human to walk on Mars. The BBC had a short video about her. So I took this video and I took some of the passages from the video and translated them into the Pashto language and I asked the engineer, "Do we want to become a strong society?" And then I said, "In that case, if you don't allow women to ride a bike how are you going to allow an Afghan woman to sit in a machine and go to Mars? The answer is, you wouldn't allow that at all." And the engineer wrote back and said, "Well, now that you've been in the United States, you have been brainwashed by the Americans, and now you're trying to change this country to something different, to Western society. Look at the West, look at how they treat their women, how they allow nudity and all those things."

So inside Afghanistan, it's a very difficult discussion to take on, and not just in the rural areas. That's why I think narrative and storytelling can be powerful, can be a good way to change minds and hearts. But we also have to realize that even a big chunk of the more mainstream younger generation still believes in the tribal stuff. As they grew up, they were exposed to the radicalization process: East versus West and West versus East. We need to talk about that. We need to stop thinking whether the West is good or the East is good. What we need is to make a good place for our sisters so they can live and they can survive and they can become productive human beings.

There are three reasons why I became so committed to education, and especially girls' education. The first one is my mom. Even though she was uneducated, even though she had suffered a lot during the Soviet invasion and the mujahideen civil war, she wanted us to learn. Every morning when we were leaving for school, she knew in her heart that we may not return back. But she still let us go, she was determined to give us education, and she accepted that risk. She raised chickens and sold eggs and did handicrafts to support our education. She did not spare any effort. So how can I give back to my mom? I can't teach her; she's somewhat old now to learn. The best way is for me now to give back to my sisters. If my mom can stand up for our education, why cannot we as brothers stand up for our sisters' education and support that?

The second reason is that when I used to teach in the village, the girls there were so talented. They were very smart. The sound of teaching in that kitchen is still echoing in my ears. I would give them some homework, and say, okay you just need to read the next chapter. The next afternoon, they would come back and they had not just read that chapter, but the next chapter as well. They were asking more questions than I would be able to answer. They would do all their homework, and they would also do all the women's work and housework, like take the cows out to feed them or bring water. And they would still read a chapter ahead.

The third reason is my dad. My dad would always say no guns. He fought back against the Soviets, but with us, he would always say you don't need to take up guns at any time. Never any guns, never. He had seen how bad it is.

I've traveled around the world and I've traveled in the United States. I have lived in San Francisco and gone to school, and it is like a tiny paradise. I never imagined anything like it. But as soon as I go back to Afghanistan, I will think, why are you still living in muddy houses? We have got the potential. We can be a wealthy country; we have a lot of natural resources. But we have to choose: are we going to become Saudi Arabia or become South Korea? If we don't educate our women and we don't ask them for help in using our future wealth and turning it into dollars, we will be something like Saudi Arabia. We will not be an equal society;

we'll be a closed society, a society of a few men ruling the rest. But if we educate our women, if we educate our sisters, we will be a country like South Korea, which is a prosperous country. And it's a very competitive country too.

> WE HAVE TO CHOOSE: ARE WE GOING TO BECOME SAUDI ARABIA OR BECOME SOUTH KOREA?

So now for Afghanistan and for the younger generation we first need to recognize and to admit that we have problems. And then we need to address those problems. And I think in my sense all this begins with educating our sisters. If we educate our sisters, they will educate our future children. If we educate our sisters, we can better and equally use our natural resources. We are a rich country in terms of resources—how can we not use 50 percent of our talent to become a wealthy country? But if we don't educate our sisters, we'll be in deep trouble. If all our people are educated, there will not be any need for other countries to invade us. There will be no need for Russia to invade us or for the United States to invade us or maybe China in the future. But if we don't educate our women, they will have an excuse. They can say, "Well, you're not a good society."

We're a tiny country, less than thirty-two million in population, and we're surrounded by nuclear powers: Russia, China, Pakistan, and India and Iran, which is almost a nuclear power. We're their playground, and the best thing for us to get out of this situation is to be educated and strong. If we are uneducated, our potential will be used for radicalization and wars that are not ours. If we are educated, we can transform the region into a new area of growth, into a new Europe, and Afghanistan will be the new Switzerland, peaceful and powerful.

So for the good of the society we need to educate our sisters as well.

*   *   *

Anyone who wants to be a reformer needs to have an extensive understanding of every local culture. At this stage, I think pretty much what most foreigners have tried to do is to take a Western narrative and apply it here. For instance, in the United States, if you want to change something or do something in an Amish community, you need to understand the Amish. You need to know how they think. You need to know how they have adapted. And based on that, you can bring a form of education or whatever to the Amish community. The same goes for tribal communities in Afghanistan. You need to understand the society, to what extent they will adapt, to what extent they will accept. And then you proceed slowly, step by step. But if you try to go all out right away, there will be an all-out reaction in opposition to it.

Look what the insurgents did in the past decade and a half. Western aid came in and said, we support girls' education; we are building schools for girls. And they went all out. Often, they applied the same example to the whole country. In some schools, people distributed jeans for girls. I see that and I think, "Come on, you want to help people educate their girls and you bring jeans from the U.S. or Europe and start distributing them in rural Afghanistan? Girls don't have pens and pencils and notebooks, and you're distributing jeans? That is a negative thing to do according to local people." And the one reaction was that the schools were burned, some of them by the Taliban, and maybe some of them with the assistance of local people.

My message for Western society is if you don't know the local culture please don't start just by yourself. I come across people who say, "Oh, we wasted a lot of blood and treasure in Afghanistan and it's not worth it." And I wanted to say, but you wasted your treasure the way you wanted to waste it. You never listened to us about what we wanted. We don't need your blood or your treasure. What we need most is just your moral support and the moral support of the Western communities to give us training, to give us education, to stand behind us. But if we're opening a school, don't send us jeans.

I use the example of the Amish because the Amish have their own setting, their own culture. And step by step, the Amish are being educated and they are accommodated or integrated in the society as well. So the same applies here; there are tribal societies with rules. If we understand those rules, step by step, we will be able to solve the problems. In the southeast, in one province, back in late 2001, there was not even one girl going to school there. But then one organization held a lot of discussions with local and tribal elders about girls' education. And they reached a kind of understanding with those tribal leaders; they came to support girls' education. Today there are about 115,000 girls going to school, according to government statistics. Last year, they had the first girls graduate from high school, and this year they built a separate dormitory for girls so they could study at the university. It took a long time, but it happened, and it happened with the consensus of the communities. One hundred and fifteen thousand girls in one province is a good number. It's a good change. I'm not saying that we need to give authority to the tribal elders. What I'm saying is that the best way is to work with the communities, step by step, to over time change the communities.

There is personal risk for me, because the country is experiencing a lot of culture wars and I am very outspoken about this issue. Assassination may be one thing. I'm not scared exactly, but I know that it may happen at some point, or it may not. Because the extremists and the opposition want to target people who are bridging the relationship between the two countries or bringing in new, shared ideas and things like that. And since I'm coming from the countryside—I'm one of the rare Fulbright scholars coming from the countryside—I know the local narratives. When I speak I know how to speak with the local accent.

But my life has been a continuous struggle. My parents tried hard to educate me and now I'm educated. I'm sure my parents never imagined their kid going to study in the United States on a Fulbright scholarship. I think it's very fulfilling for my mom. I think: it's not time to give up; it's time to give back to the country. Even if a practice has been around for a thousand or five thousand years, I think in history there has to be someone to stand and say, "Well, these things are wrong and we need to change them and this is how to change it." Not for the sake of Western society, not for the sake of any other country, but for the sake of the girls themselves.

English was a subject that was offered in my high school, just for a couple of years. They had beginner one and beginner two. The grammar is very hard for us, but we had little lessons, sentences like "Adela is washing the dishes. Pablo is washing the dishes." And they would have little pictures alongside, so we could figure out the sentences from the pictures, and we would ask our teacher, is Adela a girl or a man? And he would say, Adela is a girl. So we would ask, but is Pablo a man? Why is a man washing the dishes?

We also learned to write letters and we exchanged letters with two American students. I think they were high school students. They wrote to us about their summer trip to the Grand Canyon. The letters were very difficult to read for a beginning English student. So when I would be in the mountains getting wood or taking care of livestock, I would sometimes take these letters with me and read them over and over. I would read and think, if the Grand Canyon is such an incredible place, I hope to visit it someday.

So when I came to the United States, the first thing I did was to visit the Grand Canyon, after eleven or twelve years of holding that dream.

Lina Shafaq grew up with an absentee father who fought as a muja-hideen against the Soviets and a mother who was working two jobs, sewing clothes and cleaning offices, and struggled to pay rent. She went on to graduate from university, become a veterinary doctor, and along the way, learned English. Her work took her into local villages, where she saw women die before her eyes as they tried to give birth. She saw families that would not let their women access the most basic healthcare. Today, at forty-four years old, she sits in her house, the fading light coming through the window as the day winds down. The walls are blue, the curtains thick and full. At some point she will have to light a lamp and draw heavier curtains for privacy. She lives in Herat City in Herat province, one of the most conservative parts of Afghanistan. She says that among the biggest problems for today's Afghan women is their own fear of expressing themselves, of saying what they think and what they want, of mak-ing their own decisions. As she speaks, her passion grows. Her words come with their own emphasis; she speaks in exclamation points.

. . . .

I was born in the Faryab region, to a rich, land-owning, and open-minded family, but I came to Kabul when I was seven years old.

My father was mujahid, so he was rarely home. He was traveling back and forth to Pakistan, to Iran; he was resisting the Soviets. My mother was living alone, and we had a lot of problems. My mother struggled just to pay the rent on our house and to pay all the family expenses for my sisters and myself. She worked two jobs, as a tailor and also cleaning government offices, but that wasn't enough. When I was thirteen years old, I decided that I needed to start working, so

I began to sew dresses for my neighbors and my classmates, and they paid me a little money. I was happy that I had my own income and that I was helping my mother. Just earning a little income encouraged me to work harder and to work more. My mother didn't like it. She wanted me to continue full-time with my education and study, but I am also a human, it was my responsibility to fight for myself.

During the conflict period, much of my family was forced to leave Afghanistan. Our lands were seized and like many people, my family migrated to Iran. My father's jihad against the Russians made us suffer many difficulties.

I did go to university, where I studied veterinary medicine, and I paid my own school fees. I married a man who was training as a doctor, a surgeon, from Herat province. I first saw my husband when he was in medical school and I was in veterinary university.

Then the war of Kabul started, and the mujahideen came.

My husband and I fled to Herat, but I was not prepared for my new life. The mujahideen already controlled Herat, and there were a great many restrictions there. It was so difficult for me to start covering myself, wearing the big headscarves and also the burqa. I had never worn anything like this growing up in Kabul. In Herat, it was the first time I had ever seen the burqa up close. For the other local women, it was easier for them, because they had already worn the chadri, the big scarf, from childhood. Some of them had even worn the burqa.

My husband's family were poor people, poorer than us. And during those first years when the mujahideen were in Herat, it was very difficult for people to find jobs and earn an income. Things had been very different for us in Kabul.

It was so hard for me especially seeing the women's problems. I saw it all around me, even with my mother-in-law, my sisters-in-law, all the women in my husband's family. We lived together in one house and when I sat with them, they cried. They had nothing and they felt like they could do nothing. I decided then that if I had money, it would be good for me to help other poor women.

In 1994, after one year, I found a job working as a veterinary doctor with the German Afghan Foundation. It was so good for me to finally be able to help my husband and our whole family, my mother-in-law and my four sisters-in-law.

As a veterinarian, I traveled to many local villages. I was paired with a female health worker. I would take care of animals and teach animal husbandry, while my colleague helped women take care of their children and themselves. But I didn't just treat animals. I spent a lot of time with the local women in these villages, talking to them, listening to their problems. I encouraged women to start small farms and to have their own animal and to take care of their animal. After one year, I began working for another NGO, International Assistance Mission, as a social worker. This was also the Taliban time, because the Taliban came to Herat one year before they reached Kabul. By this time, schools had closed in the cities and there were more restrictions. It was a very black time in Afghanistan, and especially in Herat.

But I did not worry about the Taliban. I had already survived the mujahideen. Instead, I wanted to do something where I could help more women in these villages. They faced so many issues, especially health problems.

In the villages, there was no access to doctors, to clinics, to any kind of healthcare. In one year, I saw two or three women die in front of my eyes. They were pregnant and when it was time for them to deliver, there were no doctors, no clinics, nothing to help. It was so painful for me to watch these women, suffering and dying. And the children too, because so many children were faced with diseases.

The hardest part of my memories from these years was seeing how many villages didn't have any educated women, didn't have any educated people at all. The families would not give permission for the girls to go to school and study, even before the Taliban. But it wasn't just being able to read and write and traditional education. These women and girls didn't have the most basic knowledge of how to take care of themselves, their families, and their societies. Everywhere it was so dirty, their life was so dirty. No one had taught them even basic hygiene. There was a lot of disease, and it was so hard to watch all those poor people die, often just from lack of knowledge.

I have so many bad memories from this mujahideen and Taliban time. Most of the young people in the villages understood what we were trying to teach. They wanted to learn these new things, but the old women didn't believe any of our ideas. They didn't want to change their ways or do anything new.

I worked in the same villages for three years, going back year after year.

The first year it was so hard for any of them to understand what we were trying to do. Then, in the second year, some families began to change how they did things, trying to make a better life for themselves. After a few families began to make changes, slowly, others followed them. They understood that what we were teaching them was actually working.

During the Taliban time, I started a course. I told the Taliban it was a Koran course, but it was really a literacy course for smart girls. In 2014, almost twenty years later, I went back to some of these villages. I saw a lot of changes. The situation was so different, and I got so happy. Now some villages had schools and girls were in school. The girls I remembered as the smartest children in the village had grown up and now they were teaching at the girls' school. We taught for them, and now they are the teachers at the local schools.

Some of them have even come to Herat City to go to university. It gives me hope if we teach young people and children. After so many years, we will see changes, and they will change their lives.

Another thing we were able to do in the later years of the Taliban time was to make women's *shuras* and men's *shuras*, which are a way for people to have meetings and consultations. These *shuras* have grown up to be important organizations. They have started clinics. Ten villages share one clinic—they even have small clinics for their animals. Now the villagers know about medicine and vaccinations and use vaccinations for their children. Now they give permission for women who are in labor to go to the clinic and see a doctor. Twenty years before, men would not give permission for women to go to school or to go to a clinic.

It was difficult for me to understand why women needed permission to go to a clinic or see a doctor to have a baby. But many Afghan men think women are like a toy or like something they buy. Even today, there is a little change, but it is still not enough.

In some families, when a woman gets married, they still think the woman is like a thing they bought. If they feel like it, they give permission for a woman to go somewhere. But if they are angry, they say, "No, you don't have permission to go anywhere." Twenty-five years ago, most families in this region thought like this. Today things are a little bit better. Some families now realize that women are also human, that they need to take care of their health, they need to see a doctor, and they also need to take care of their children's health.

Many things have helped, NGOs and organizations going into the villages, and radio and TV, communications; all of these things have helped people to learn new things and to change their minds. The government has also sent doctors and teachers into the villages and helped open clinics and schools. But it wasn't easy in the beginning.

When the Taliban fell I was in Pakistan. In 2000, the Taliban wanted to kill me and my husband and my family. They closed down our office. We had to leave. Day and night, we would follow the situation in Afghanistan, watching TV, listening to the radio. When the Taliban was removed, I came back to Herat and I started my work again. Then in 2010, with some of my friends and my family, I started a smaller association to work with women and to teach women. I thought, I have knowledge, I have experience, and I have a little money to start the association. I could make a difference.

When we teach women, especially young women and girls, it is easier to change the family's lives for the next generation. I named my organization the Life Skills Development Center because I see this as one of the biggest problems that we have in Afghanistan. We don't have the skills of life; we don't have good communication with our neighbors, with our family, with our own people.

Women in particular don't have the skills for making decisions. They haven't learned how to share their ideas with men or with their families or how to make decisions with their families. I didn't recognize this problem at first. I had seen how illiteracy was a big problem for women. But then, even when women went to literacy courses, they were still ashamed to speak and to express their ideas. I took notes on what I saw. Day by day, after eight years, I thought the biggest problem for many women is that they are ashamed to do such basic things as speak up for themselves or go outside the house. It is even difficult for some women to go to the bazaar and buy what they need. They don't have self-confidence and self-esteem.

For this reason, I thought I needed to work with both illiterate women and also literate women who are still living inside their houses. In Herat City, I saw a lot of our neighbors, where there was a school near their house, the family had given permission for the girls or young women to go, but the young women themselves said, no, it is not good for me to go outside my house. These women and girls thought it would be too difficult for them to go outside of their houses and talk with other people.

This problem also became clearer to me once I had traveled more outside of Afghanistan, particularly when I went to India. On my visit, I saw that the Indian people have a lot of problems. They are poorer than Afghan people. I got to travel to some Indian villages, saw the life of the villagers, and they have more problems than Afghan village people. But still they had their own ideas, and the Indian women wanted to share their ideas with the Indian men. They wanted to work outside of their houses or even work inside their house and earn an income. In Afghanistan, we don't have these things. Our women don't believe in their own selves and their skills. They don't believe they have skills that they can use to make life better for themselves and their families. They don't have self-confidence.

> WE DON'T HAVE THE SKILLS OF LIFE; WE DON'T HAVE GOOD COMMUNICATION WITH OUR NEIGHBORS, WITH OUR FAMILY, WITH OUR OWN PEOPLE. WOMEN IN PARTICULAR DON'T HAVE THE SKILLS FOR MAKING DECISIONS.

Even when I went to Pakistan during the Taliban time, Pakistani women were better off than Afghan women had been. When I saw the Pakistani women, they were proud when they worked outside of the house, but in Afghanistan, our women are ashamed. It made me so sad to see such differences between women who are neighbors. Why was it only Afghan people who did not give permission for their women to see doctors, to become educated, to hold a job? I went to Kyrgyzstan and I saw the same thing. I thought it is time for me to start this organization and give women a turn to come and learn something and improve their self-confidence, to learn how to talk in a group. In this way, we can encourage them to go home and to share their ideas with their families and their husband and father or brothers.

We started with a group of volunteers going house to house. My daughter, my sister-in-law, my niece, my cousins, and some of my students from my NGO days also wanted to help. We wrote a questionnaire. We asked each woman, what do you need: a literacy course, a Koran course, an embroidery course, a self-confidence course? We asked a lot of questions. Most women wanted to participate in literacy courses. Some wanted to participate in skills courses like sewing and embroidery. We had one question where we asked can you talk with your family and can you share your ideas with your family? Most said, no, we can't. And when we talked with them about self-confidence, they didn't know what it was.

The Center has different programs, long-term courses and short-term seminars and workshops. We teach basic skills courses like sewing, embroidery, candle making, weaving, and knitting. We also offer literacy courses, and we have English courses for young girls, and Koran courses for old and for young women. Step by step, month by month, year by year, the women learn about our organization, then they get permission to participate in our courses and seminars, and then they get new ideas.

We have the women start in very small groups where they can get comfortable with sharing their ideas. We teach them basic steps for solving problems. We present them with a problem and then we ask one of them to speak in front of the class and share their ideas with the group. Every month we also have a big meeting. Often, we have a ceremony or a party, for example on Mother's Day, and I will ask some of the young girls to speak before everyone there.

After a few months to a year, many of the women who attend our center change a lot. Most of the changes they make come from having worked together. In Afghanistan and in Herat City, women often have a lot of problems in their homes. When they sit together in literacy courses and sewing courses, for the first time, they find a lot of new friends. Gradually, they start to share the problems in their houses with their friends. And they ask for help and advice on ways to solve these problems. Sometimes they see that some of the other women have more problems than they do. They can even share an idea to help these women. Slowly, they learn that they do have knowledge and skills and that they can believe in what they are doing. When I see these women, when I see how happy they are to learn something and to work together in a group, when I see them smiling, it gives me hope for our future.

I hope, after they finish with our courses, many of the young women and girls whose families did not allow them to go to school will go on to school. I hope that many others will be able to go to the bazaar and find a market for their products, like sewing, embroidery, and candle making. Right now, some Afghan women know how to work, but they can't access the bazaar and the market, and they don't have money to start their business. We started offering a seminar on how to write a business plan to help them, but they also need things like micro- and small business loans and machinery and good-quality materials to be a success.

Encouraging women to be a part of Afghan society, to continue their education, to participate in the economy, and to have their own income is very important. If a woman has her own income and money to spend in the family, the men also believe her. They can hear their wives. If women don't do this, then things will be different. Then the men will always think that women are their things, that they have bought their women.

I wish and I hope that in the future all the young girls in Afghanistan will continue their education and will have their own income for their family and for themselves. I'd like to see them have access to markets outside of Afghanistan, to sell their products, and even go to other countries to learn what they have and what they do. When they come back, I believe they will change our society. I wish for all our women to be a part of society and government, and for them to be strong women in their families and be part of the decision making and problem solving. These are my wishes for my Afghan women.

I started by myself to follow my beliefs with my own daughter. I wanted her to start out as an equal in life. I sent her to continue her education in Kyrgyzstan, where she is studying economics at the American University of Central Asia. If I believe in her skills, if I give permission for her to go outside of Afghanistan to continue her education, I can say to other people, you should do this too. But if I keep my daughter inside Afghanistan, my words and my ideas have no meaning for other people.

Now we are trying to find a scholarship for her to get a master's degree, because I believe if she comes back to Afghanistan she will have to get married. A lot of people already come to our house and ask for her to be engaged to their son. But I want my daughter to continue her education and get a master's degree, and after that she will find a good boy to marry.

I look at all the young girls and I hope they will continue to have better lives than their mother's life. I wish for my daughter that the problems I faced she won't have in the future. I wish for my daughter and all the other girls to have an easier life and a better life, a peaceful life.

For many Afghan women, there are few greater cultural taboos than playing sports. Mastoora Arezoo broke that taboo when she spent five years as a member of the Afghan Women's National Volleyball Team. At age twenty-three, she became the president of Afghanistan's Badminton Federation, making her the first woman director and the youngest sports director in the nation. In just six months, she expanded the federation from two provinces to fifteen. She also founded a radio station and a newspaper called Voice of Sports *to help promote women's sporting events. Today, at age twenty-six, she heads the country's Olympic Badminton Committee and is committed to creating new sports opportunities for all women. But her toughest battles have been off the playing field, where she has faced physical harm and repeated threats. Just driving a car, alone, as a woman, puts her at daily risk.*

When Mastoora sits down to speak, beneath a black chador, she carries herself like an athlete, eyes tightly focused, no movement wasted. Her every gesture uncorks in a single fluid motion. "I like to be in the forefront of the tension," she explains, "breaking the traditional models of what women should be."

· · · · · · · · · ·

My father never took me shopping at the bazaar, but he took my hand and took me to a sports club. He got me training at that sports club, and for the rest of my life, I will never forget that day. He was a general in the Afghan army, but sports was his greatest love. He gave that love to me. But it is not simply a love of competition. I am very competitive, but I believe also that sports has the ability to transform lives in Afghanistan, women's lives and also men's. If we want to stop battery against women, if we want women to live longer, healthier lives, we need women in sports; we need women to exercise.

Every day, we hear about women who set themselves on fire, who kill themselves to escape their family situations. We see the extremes of family aggression. I believe that sports is one way we can truly reduce family aggression. When women, and also men, play sports, they have a good outlet for their emotions and frustrations. They gain more self-confidence and an inner strength to fight and stand against life's problems. I don't have to look any farther than my own family to see how people who once might respond with bitterness and disbelief can discover kindness, smiling, and a different outlook. In the ten years that I have been playing sports, I have seen their whole attitudes change. It is my regret that my father did not live to see this change in his own family, to see all that we have accomplished.

I was born in Kandahar in 1989, one of six brothers and five sisters, but we moved to Kabul when I was a young child so that my father could work in the defense ministry. When the Taliban came, we left Kabul for Baghlan province. There, I received a religious education to become what we called a *talabeh*, which roughly translates as a religious student, literally a seeker of knowledge. To be a *talabeh* was a blessing, because with that kind of education, which is rare for a woman, I would be given work in society, no matter what the political situation.

I discovered volleyball in middle school, after the Taliban were overthrown, and although I trained in journalism and business administration in school, I always made time for volleyball. Not only did I play on the national team, but I began to take on different management responsibilities for the team.

My toughest opponents were almost always off the court. My family is very traditional, my uncles were very religiously strict and they were not okay with girls being involved in sports. What started to change their minds was when they saw that my part of the family didn't get sick the way their wives and daughters did. My sisters and I did not have to take medicine; we did not get diseases. The one difference between us and our cousins was that in my branch of the family, the young girls all played sports. When my mother developed back pain, she started doing exercises and the pain went away. Slowly, watching this, my uncles started encouraging their daughters to get involved in sports. Today, we are a sports family. We play volleyball, basketball, and do Tae Kwan Do.

But to create this change, we need thousands of families like mine in Afghanistan. And even to get to where we are now, it has been quite a fight.

Too many Afghan people still think that sports are evil, are an evil influence, and are a particularly evil influence for women. For years, when I have traveled around the country and worked to get women involved in sports, I received all kinds of threats. Local mullahs have told me that if I didn't leave their town by a certain hour, I "wouldn't see the face of the next day." All because I wanted to give girls the opportunity to play badminton. Early on, I decided that I could either give in to these people and their threats, or I could pretend that they did not exist. I could ignore their threats and live my life. That is how I have survived.

There have been times when I am afraid, when I have wondered if I should give up. I drive a car, which is also something that many men in Afghanistan do not agree with. When I first started driving, only my mother and my brothers knew. My extended family had banned it for women. My mother and brothers allowed me to take the car to school, but when I came home, I had to stop and park the car three bus stops away from our house. Then one of my brothers would have to meet me and drive me and the car back home and park it in the garage. In that way, no one in our area, most of all my extended family, would know that I was driving.

I drive almost every day. I drive to work; I drive home. I have even driven in Baghlan province, where it is basically forbidden for women to drive. I had my family in the car to keep me safe. But even in Kabul, men have broken my mirrors and smashed my rear windshield to prevent me from driving. I live with the worry that someday, some men will stop my car, force themselves inside, and chop off my hand so that I cannot drive. One time, I was picking up some people at the airport and along the road a group of guys surrounded me in my car. They started to call me filthy names and got very aggressive. Fortunately, I saw an Afghan police car and flagged it down. The officers got the men to disperse, but if I hadn't seen them, I don't know what would have happened. I considered stopping driving after that, but I did not want to give up. I want to be a woman who can prove that women are not always dependent on men. I chose as my motto "Impossible is nothing."

In Afghanistan, independent women are seen as very dark. But for years it has been my dream to bring about changes in Afghanistan. I want to see a decrease in the death rates of mothers. We have one of the highest death rates for women in the world. I want us to have one of the lowest. Right now, men usually have three or four women, three or four wives, in part because they think that if the first woman gets sick, he needs the next ones to take care of him. But if women can live longer, healthier lives with less disease, a man would not need to make that decision.

I want women and men to play sports also because sports have good values; sports are benevolent in society. Women especially have been victims of war and political events. I want to see an end to women being victims, and I think one place where we can start to change that is through sports.

I CHOSE AS MY MOTTO "IMPOSSIBLE IS NOTHING."

I try to spread my message in several ways. Some of it is personal experience, literally going house to

132

house and street to street. But also when I get warnings from religious figures, I have tried to answer that by going to the media. Radio, television, the print press are all ways to reach women in our country. I have studied journalism and I started two sports newspapers and a youth radio station. In this way, I can talk to more people.

My biggest personal obstacles are being young and being a woman. When I started as the head of the badminton federation, everyone doubted me. They only had questions, would I be capable? Would it just be a symbolic role? The man who had the job before me was angry that I had taken away his job. But I was not a figurehead. I played an active role in the federation. In April 2015, I was picked to be director of sports programs in badminton in forty-one Asian cities. Next, I hope to work internationally, not just in Asia but around the world. Now, because of my work, men who had big problems with me have more respect for me. Life is just like sports, you have to get up each day and improve and prove yourself.

I have many goals for the future. I would like to see Afghan women winning medals at the Olympics. I would like to have the Afghan flag respected in sports competitions around the world.

Personally, sometimes I wish I were married like most other girls my age. If I were married, maybe I would be a better cook. But I also know that if I had gotten married, I would not have been able to progress the way I have. I would not be able to travel, to have worked in journalism, to work for sports federations. Right now, I'm married to sports.

Working

Weaving

Woodcarving

Surgery

Photography

Sewing

Clothing design

From rug weaving to medicine, women are transforming Afghanistan through their work. Today, more than three thousand businesses are owned entirely by women.

WORKING

· · · ·

In the 1970s, 40 percent of doctors and 60 percent of teachers in Afghanistan were women. Today, most women must have permission from a male guardian to work, and many may only work if they do not leave their homes. When women enter male-dominated business fields, the reaction is often swift and violent. Death threats, attacks, and kidnapping are what await them, simply for growing a business and employing others. Many have been told again and again that they will fail. Their response? To go and search for opportunity, because, as one entrepreneur says, "Opportunity will never come and knock on your door."

Today more than three thousand Afghan women own and run their own businesses. They are building networks and associations to support other women. They want to be the pioneers leading the way for a new generation. They want to change minds. And many of these women have discovered something else about work: when women work, they suffer less domestic violence. They suddenly have a role and a voice in their family and in their society. Work does far more than improve their economic situation, it improves every facet of their lives.

As Mina Sherzoy, founder of the Afghan Women's Business Federation (AWBF), explains, "We taught them business skills; we introduced them to microfinance. And after that I would let them go and fly. Believe me, they did fly."

*Mina Sherzoy could be sitting in a room with a view of San Fran-
cisco. Instead she is in Kabul, with a hard, blank wall behind her
and an ugly lamp throwing out harsh light. It is always night when
we speak, always the end of a long day. Mina was one of the first
members of the U.S.-Afghan Women's Council. She is the founder
of multiple nonprofits. The daughter of a diplomat, for years she
collected traditional Afghan clothing, richly colored and richly
embroidered. When she had almost nothing else left of her culture,
she kept those clothes with her, moving them from place to place
and home to home, bringing them out to show her daughters, never
knowing if she might be able to take them back to the country from
which they had come.*

. . . .

I left San Francisco for Kabul on March 14, 2002. I came back after
twenty-three years.

I was with my friend Sandra Meyrose. We used to do fundraising
for an NGO that had collected a lot of blankets, clothing, all kinds of
things, and Sandra and I were transporting them. It took us almost
three days to get from San Francisco to Kabul.

When the pilot announced that we were entering Afghan air-
space, all of a sudden I started shaking. The tears came down my
face. And finally, I realized why I was crying. Because I had cried
for these people, for this country, for this moment all of my adult life.
I told myself to stop crying, that I should be happy and I should be
strong. And if I feel weak, if I shed tears, that means I cannot help
this country. I have to stand strong and be confident so they can learn
from me and in the end be even better than me.

*   *   *

I was born in Kabul and I was raised here until the seventh grade. My father was a career diplomat for the Afghan government. After the seventh grade we traveled to the places where he was posted: India, Pakistan, and Czechoslovakia. When my father became the ambassador to Czechoslovakia, I was about seventeen, and there were no American schools in Prague, no English school, nothing. So I had to come back to Kabul and study very hard to take my final exams and get my high school degree. I spent four months going to school and working with two tutors so that I could take my exams. That's how I graduated from high school. I was very happy.

When the Soviets took over, I had just arrived in London.

I was very lucky, we were all lucky that we were out of the country. I was living with my cousin so that I could attend the university there. My brother, my mom, and my dad were still in Prague. One day I came home from my class at four o'clock in the afternoon. My uncle was sitting there and he said, "Afghanistan is gone for good." I asked, "What are you talking about, Uncle?" And he said that Afghanistan's president Daoud and his family had been assassinated and that a few members of our family had been jailed or killed by the Russians. I was eighteen at that time. At first, I couldn't understand because I did not grow up during a war. My cousin and I didn't know politics at that age. It's not like the kids here in Kabul today. They know exactly what's happening. They hear the suicide bombings or some attack and they will say, "Oh, the explosion came from the left side, I think, from a fifty-five-degree angle." And I'll say to myself, how does this little kid know? But they've become experts on war and attacks. They hear it. They see it. So we were very naive compared to the children today. It took me a few days to really understand what had taken place.

My parents and my brother came to London, and then we decided that we should go to the United States because my father had a cousin in North Carolina. But even my father couldn't really believe what was happening. When he went to the American Embassy for our visas, he kept telling the ambassador to give him a temporary visa. The ambassador offered to give him everything, citizenship track, green card, social security, right there in his office. And my father said no, he wasn't going to take it, he just wanted a three-year visa. In three years, he said, everything will be fine. He ended up staying in the United States for twenty-four years.

When we arrived in North Carolina, I couldn't go to school and my father couldn't get a job because we didn't have any social security numbers. The late U.S. Senator Jesse Helms, bless his soul, helped my father get green cards and social security numbers. Then we started to build a new life in the United States of America.

After North Carolina, we moved to northern Virginia and then to Orange County in California, because by that time most of our family had escaped to California. I only lived there for a few months before I got married and moved to the San Francisco Bay Area. I had two daughters who are now thirty-one and thirty-two. Both are married and one of them has a child. After I emigrated to the United States, I did not forget Afghanistan because that is where my roots were—no matter where I was living that was home. My father was also very involved in the Afghan community as a senior leader. I tried to help as well. We were always trying to raise money for the people in the refugee camps. Since I was a kid, I have collected traditional Afghan clothes. A group of us started doing exhibitions of Afghan culture—the food, the poetry, the calligraphy, the clothing—to keep the Afghan culture alive and going and to show it to our children. We would also raise money at these events, $5,000, $10,000, whatever we could, and then we would send it to the refugee camps along the Pakistani border. Whenever we had an event, the elderly Afghans would attend.

We also used to watch underground videos from inside Afghanistan that had been smuggled into Pakistan or Iran and eventually made it to Afghan stores in the United States. Everybody would watch them. It was horrific. First we had Russian atrocities, then we had mujahideen atrocities among the Afghans themselves. When the Taliban came it was like the last nail in the coffin. At first, when the Taliban arrived, a lot of people in the U.S., including in the American government, thought that all the unrest would settle down and Afghanistan would have discipline. Instead, it was another nightmare. It was like Afghanistan was invaded all over again. And so many of these Talibs were Pakistanis and Arabs, they weren't even Afghans.

Around 1999, I lost hope. So much devastation had taken place, but no one in the international community did anything. They just watched and let it happen. I stopped listening to the news. I stopped going to Afghan community events. Then it was September 11. I'll never forget that day, watching the Towers, watching all that tragic death. For the first week after September 11 we stayed home. I didn't let my kids go to school or anybody go out. We felt scared, with everyone saying, "Afghanistan, Afghans did it." But then the media, and I truly appreciated the media of the United States for this, started educating people about who is an Afghan? Who is a Talib? Who is a terrorist? Who is a Sikh or a Christian . . . ?

Before September 11, people would ask me, where are you from? I would say, "Guess." They would go all over the map—that I'm Indian, Italian, Mexican, you name it. Iranian, everything. Nobody in the United States ever told me "You are an Afghan." And every time I said, "No, I'm from Afghanistan," they would say, "African?" or "Is that in Africa?" I would explain that it's not in Africa; it's in the heart of Asia. It's in between Pakistan and Iran and Kazakhstan, and most of them had no idea what I was talking about. Now, if you ask an American ten-year-old, most would say, "Oh, yes, I know." It's amazing.

*　　　*　　　*

After September 11, my body was in the United States but my mind was in Afghanistan. I wanted to do something. I wanted to come and make a difference. I felt good and I felt bad. I cherished my life in the United States. The U.S. gave me security, the U.S. gave me everything, but I wanted to share what I have with my Afghan people, with the women, with the men. Because if I had been there when the Russians invaded or when the mujahideen fought or when the Taliban came, I could be dead; I could be illiterate; I could have been tortured. Anything could have happened. I still have this feeling, fifteen years later. It hasn't changed a bit.

When I landed in 2002, I was supposed to be here for three weeks. I was picked up at the airport and we went to the U.S. Embassy to register for security reasons. While I was registering, I looked around and I saw this little boy, maybe ten years old. He was barefoot, and he was kneeling on the ground, polishing somebody's shoes for one dollar. March is cold here. He had no shoes, but he was polishing someone else's. It was so heartbreaking for me. That scene changed my whole life. I thought of my own kids—how they were and how they were raised when they were ten years old. I thought of my nieces; I thought of my cousins; I thought of my friends' children. I thought of myself when I was that age.

I called my daughters, one of them had just started university, and I said, "I have traveled around, and I see girls that are twenty years old who can't even write their names on a board." I told them that the girls and the women here need me, and I asked them, do you need me to come back? My daughters were so nice. They said, "Mom, we're working, we're studying. We know how to read. We know how to write. We have a car. We know how to drive." You know, typical American girls. They said, "You go help those women. Help those girls that don't know how to write their names." That's how every-thing started. Instead of three weeks it has been thirteen years.

It's a roller coaster. One day you move ahead and the next day you go backward. Much of that has to do with the war culture. The country still lives in a war culture. For example, we have a lot of good laws, but there is no enforcement of the law. The result is that each person has to make his or her own system in order to achieve their goals. You've got to work with all sides, whether it's the mafia or the government, or people from the international community, or your friends or family or your colleagues. I always think I've learned how to deal with this situation. But then something new happens to me the next day, and I realize that I'm still learning. And I'm only one person, I can only do so much.

The challenges are very difficult. There is a lot of poverty, a lot of illiteracy. But my attitude from day one has been to do whatever it takes. I'm here to work; I'm here to help.

When I first came back to Kabul, I could not believe how drastic the changes had been. In the city, most of the roofs were gone. I would be out crossing a street, and I would look up, and I would see all these houses without roofs. And the other thing I could not believe were all the bullets in the walls. Every building had at least a thousand bullet holes. If you've ever seen those polka dot fabrics, that's what it looked like—every house, every building. I used to wonder how many mil-lions or billions of bullets have been used in this country over the past two and a half decades—now it's almost four decades.

And now we have suicide bombers. We don't need bullets. They blow themselves up instead of firing.

My first years here, when I'd go out walking, I'd have to watch every step because there were always holes in the ground from the bombs and the rockets. And in some ways, it has gotten worse. It's not like in the United States, when you grow up in a city, in a community, and you can see that people are building and making it better. Better roads, better buildings, better this, better that. Here, in some places, it has gotten worse. I still drive around and I say to myself, I remember that hotel. I remember that restaurant. I remember this boutique. I remember this

> EVERY BUILDING HAD AT LEAST A THOUSAND BULLET HOLES. IF YOU'VE EVER SEEN THOSE POLKA DOT FABRICS, THAT'S WHAT IT LOOKED LIKE—EVERY HOUSE, EVERY BUILDING. I USED TO WONDER HOW MANY MILLIONS OR BILLIONS OF BULLETS HAVE BEEN USED IN THIS COUNTRY.

hospital, this clinic. Even my high school. When I first went back, my high school seemed so much smaller, but what I realized was that there were no blackboards, no windows, even the garden was gone. It had all been ruined.

It's going to take probably three generations to get it back to where it was thirty years ago. It's not just the buildings and the atmosphere and the roads. It's the quality of life, the culture, the mentality. People have been brainwashed. They have been brainwashed during the communist time. They have been brainwashed during the mujahideen time. They have been brainwashed during the Taliban time. Forty years ago, people had one way of living, one way of understanding their religion, one way of understanding their culture. Now, however, everything has changed.

Historically, Afghans have not interfered with other nations. We have minded our own business. We have lived a comfortable life. Yes, we were a poor country. We have always been a poor country, but we have not interfered with or attacked anybody. But everybody is always attacking this country. If you look at the history, everybody's proxy war was here. Today, the natural resources in Afghanistan—the minerals, precious metals, and natural gas—make us worth attacking. The resources we have underground are our own enemy. We are a landlocked country in the heart of Asia. We have so many enemies. And everybody exports their garbage here. Products that in China or Pakistan or Iran they would throw into the garbage, they sell to Afghanistan. Our handicrafts used to be beautiful; we had some of the best cotton in the world, our rugs, our agricultural products. But the war has destroyed everything.

When I remember what it was like growing up compared to when I came back, it was devastating. I tried not to cry but sometimes the scenes of poverty, the unfortunate people, what they have gone through, their stories, as a human being, I can't control myself.

One of the first things I did was to start an organization that I called WOMAN, World Organization for Mutual Afghan Networks, all for widows. I thought if we could start these women working on embroidery, at least that would be something. Eventually, I registered ten thousand widows. But at first, I couldn't find anyone to participate. I kept looking for women. The Taliban had just fallen, and I couldn't find anybody—even under the burqa. Then a man suggested that I go see a local mullah, that he could help me find women. The mullah told me to come on Friday and he asked how many women I needed to see. I said maybe twenty—not more than that. At the time, I was staying with my dad, who had also come back to Kabul. I told my dad that I had an appointment. I didn't tell him where I was going. I put on a traditional Afghan outfit, a big skirt and the big pants and a big scarf on my head. And I left. When I went into the mosque, there were more than four hundred women in burqas sitting there, waiting for me. I said to myself, "You've got to be kidding me. How am I going to talk to four hundred women?"

*　　*　　*

I believe everything happens for a reason. God provides you with an opportunity and then He has the answers for you too. I started talking to these women, and I kept telling them that I am here to help. I need to know their skills. I need to know what I can do, what assistance they need, how I can help them. And how I'm happy to be back. Starting with those four hundred, I got my ten thousand women. The majority, probably 98 percent, were illiterate and all they knew how to do was carpet weaving or embroidery, and some were involved in agricultural work.

I started tailoring and embroidery projects, as well as English classes and literacy classes. One hundred and fifty women were being trained every day in that NGO. Once I found what their talent was, the next step was to introduce them to business. One thing I don't believe in is charity. I didn't want to make them into charity cases. I also had a system, I trained them and then I followed up with them. Next, I started the Afghan Women's Business Association to teach them the basic business skills. We taught business skills to women who were literate and illiterate. We taught them marketing, pricing, and budgeting, so if someone was willing to lend them $100, they would know what to do with it. Then we introduced them to microfinancing institutions. And after that I would let them go and fly. Believe me, they did fly.

All this was at the start of 2003, and during that time, I kept going to the U.S. Embassy and to the United States Agency for International Development [USAID] to ask them to help fund women entrepreneurs. And they kept saying, no, you're going to get everybody killed; you can't do it. But I kept going back. Finally I said to them, "Women working is a religious thing, because our Holy Prophet Muhammad's wife was a businesswoman; she was a trader. So why can't you fund women entrepreneurs for development projects?" And they looked at me and said, "We'll get back to you."

After a few days, I started working on American-funded projects and they housed me at the Ministry of Commerce. I was doing that and I was doing my NGO, I was running everything at the same time because I had to connect everything. I couldn't lose the momentum.

Then I started a young businesswomen's association. Ten women had come to be trained, and they were all literate. From ten women it ended up being twenty women, then thirty women, then seventy women. We couldn't fit them all in the ministry, so eventually in October 2005, I put everyone together in the Afghan Women's Business Federation. After that came programs like the Artemis Project at the Thunderbird School of Global Management at Arizona State University, PEACE THROUGH BUSINESS, and Goldman Sachs's *10,000 Women*. Everybody started doing women's empowerment.

Here the work is difficult, but the rewards are great. The minute I see success, I forget about everything that I've gone through. We had an illiterate woman, a widow, who came to our NGO for six months. Six months she spent learning how to read and write and how to do tailoring, sewing. When she graduated from that, she went through more training, business training, finance, and we connected her with microfinance lenders, where you can get a loan of $100 or something like that. Two years later, I ran into her. I didn't recognize her at first because she looked so different. She looked beautiful, and her dress was so modern. She was hugging me and kissing me and saying, "I've missed you, Mina." I kept thinking: wait, I know her from somewhere. And then I realized, she was one of my students. I asked her about her life. She told me that she started out sewing. Through microfinance, she borrowed $100. She bought a sewing machine for $25 and then she spent the rest on material. She sewed three traditional Afghan dresses and then she took them to the market, sold them for a profit, paid off her loan, and borrowed $150.

With that money she bought more fabric to make more dresses, but she also started another business. She bought a tandoor, a round oven where you bake flatbread. You have to stop for a moment and look at how clever this woman is. She bought that tandoor and put it in her house. But it's not a house, it's a small, muddy, mud-brick home because she is a very poor, illiterate woman. After she bought her oven, she told the women in her neighborhood, "Okay, ladies, come and bake your bread in my tandoor. Don't buy from the bakery. Bring the dough to me. I'll only charge you two AFs while you have to pay to the baker ten AFs for one bread." Afghans eat bread at every meal, at breakfast, lunch, and dinner. So you can imagine this woman and the market that she made. She says she has a line in front of her house every morning, every afternoon, and every night. Her daughters and son have been able to go to school, and when they are not going to school, they are helping their mom. So now you tell me, how smart and how strong are these women?

If you really want to help these women, they have to feel that they can trust you. Only if they feel that they can trust me will they talk to me, will they let me into their lives. Trust begins with something as basic as how you look. Sometimes even in Kabul I dress three different ways in one day because three different places can have three different perceptions. When I go to Kandahar, I wear a burqa. If I go out to the marketplace with the women, I wear a burqa. Same if I go to Herat, I wear the big scarf that they wear. I dress like them, I travel in their cars, I don't want anyone to say, "Oh, Mina, she's different from the rest of us." In Kabul, our general assembly is called the Loya Jirga. I've worked there a couple of times, but the funny part is when the people see me there they don't recognize me because I am wearing a hijab. When the Jirga meets, almost three thousand people show up, and many are elderly from the villages or tribal leaders, people from the whole country. I can't go dressed in a scarf, jacket, and pants like I would in the rest of Kabul. In Afghanistan, it doesn't matter if you're a professor or a doctor or what you do, people look you up and down, see what you look like, how you're dressed. Then, based on that impression, they will talk to you and respect you.

It wasn't always this way. My mother, when she traveled, all she wore was a little scarf over her hair. Back then, wherever you were, women walked. They went shopping. Nobody wore the burqa or was afraid of not being accompanied by a man, and they were respected as women. A woman was respected no matter how she dressed. If she wore pants, slacks, a skirt, or the burqa or whatever or the big scarf, it wasn't a big deal. Now it is a problem.

Afghanistan now is also in many ways the opposite of the United States. In Afghanistan, the minute you raise your profile, everybody is going to ask questions. They are going to wonder who this person is and if they are important. Even the people with private security guards, they don't want to have guards standing outside, you want the guards inside and at most you want just one or two. In California, if you have a nice car, nice house, nice clothes, it speaks of your success. But here, it's the other way around. If you show your success, people start saying, okay, where did she get that money? What did she steal? Is she into drugs? Is she part of the mafia? I drive a 1995 blue Corolla, and I love it. All I need is a car that has four wheels and takes me around. No one looks at me. It's funny because when I go to places like big Western-style hotels, where there's a lot of security, in my little car, sometimes the men out front don't want to let me in. They see me in that car and they are not thinking of me as anything.

When I first came here, there was no electricity, no telephone, no Internet, no television for almost three months. There was a disconnect with the outside world. It was good for the first couple of weeks. After that it was tough. But for me, I couldn't believe I was in Afghanistan again. I thought I would never come back. I was so happy to be back. My family would say, "How could you do this? How can you leave San Francisco, go to Afghanistan—we thought you were going for two or three weeks—are you crazy?" I kept telling them, "I don't know what it is, but I feel centered there. I felt an inner peace that I have for myself that this is where I am supposed to be." When I come here I miss my family, the Bay Area, my friends, everything there. But when I'm over there, after a week or two, I think, "Oh my God, I have to go back to Kabul. I need to do this, I need to do that." I am lucky to have the best of both worlds.

Afghanistan is not the same Afghanistan it was fourteen years ago. In some ways, people have come a long way. Kids that started going to school fourteen years ago are in universities today. And these kids were not brought up like their mother or father, who were brought up during war. These kids are into technology, the Internet, games. They are in another world. I see a very good future for some in this generation.

But there is still a great divide, particularly between the urban areas, especially Kabul, and the provinces. Let me give you an example for women. Women are about 50 percent of the population, but about three-quarters of them are illiterate. What do you think this three-quarters does? They weave carpets, they embroider, and they do menial agricultural work. And women do most of the difficult work, the picking, the harvesting. But who takes the harvest to the bazaar to sell it? The man. He takes the profit; he takes the money. And this woman doesn't even know what she is worth. Most of them don't even get paid. They think that's a part of life, that they have to work for their husband. So we have one generation, working in the offices, using technology, mobile phones, texts, Facebook, everything. But when you go to a village, they don't know what we're talking about. How do you connect the people living in villages with the people in the cities?

In Afghanistan, some provinces are connected to Kabul, but in other provinces, nobody knows what on earth is going on. You have to build roads; you have to build the infrastructure in order for people to connect; you need technology, telephones, communications. People in villages are literally disconnected. We also have to work with people based on what their skills are. In Kabul, everybody's talking about doctors, engineers, and computers. Okay, but how do I get a woman empowered in her village? The way to do it is to make these women better at the skills they have.

For example, for the woman who is doing embroidery, teach her how to design, how to mix colors, how to cut a garment to become a better tailor, and teach her quality control, so she can have a bigger and better market and sell her product. And if an embroidery or sewing machine comes into the area, teach her how to use the machine. Because a lot of the handicrafts are being done on machines and the people doing machine work are all men. If a woman is around forty years old today, she is not going to go to a master's program and graduate. But if she can earn a better living with her current skills, she can send her kids to school. So the next generation doesn't become like her.

We also have the problem that donors, NGOs, people don't come here and ask, what are your needs so that I can really help you become sustainable? Instead it's all what they think is right for these people. Too much of it is looked at from a Western point of view; it's not from a cultural, religious, social point of view that tries to understand Afghanistan. Too many people come here and say, "Okay, let's have computers, Internet," while in these villages, people don't even know how to read and write.

I'm not against computers. I can't live without computers myself. But you have to know who you are helping. When I first came, most of the women I worked with didn't even know what a phone looked like. One day, I was talking to a Dutch donor that I knew. He said, "Mina, what are you doing?" I said I had done my survey and then was going to offer tailoring classes so these women could do a better job and make more money with the skills they already have. And he asked me, "Who will teach them computers?" I said, "I'm offering literacy classes; they have never learned basic letters or numbers. You think they're going to learn computers right now?" And he said, "Well, I have all these computers." And I said, "You're in the wrong place. You have to wait. They don't even have phones. They don't know what to do with a computer." People come in with their own ideas, without doing their homework.

> I'M NOT AGAINST COMPUTERS. BUT YOU HAVE TO KNOW WHO YOU ARE HELPING. WHEN I FIRST CAME, MOST OF THE WOMEN I WORKED WITH DIDN'T EVEN KNOW WHAT A PHONE LOOKED LIKE.

When the high schools were fixed, that's when I started bringing in computers. I had high school girls come in to learn English and to learn how to operate computers. You have to plan things so people can benefit. We have people who come in to do human rights training. But if you have a widow with six children who has lost her husband and is illiterate and we put her in a room with thirty other women in a similar situation, and someone starts teaching her human rights, does that work? I don't think so. She's hungry. All she's thinking of is her hungry children. She can't absorb any lessons. I've seen so many times when these training sessions are offered and the women are promised lunch and travel money. The women come just for the lunch and the money. I have seen mothers taking their plates and filling them, but not eating. Instead, they carry these little plastic bags to put the food in and take it home. So I would rather teach them something so they can earn money and learn their rights through labor. And when women have more income, there's both a decline in domestic violence and they get decision-making rights within their own families. The correlation is huge.

The international community, their funding and their assistance, has played a major role in this country. There is no doubt in my mind that women wouldn't be where there are today if it weren't for the international community. But there are flaws in what's been done, and those flaws need to be fixed. If you really want your investment to pay off, you want to make sure that person is going to benefit. You don't just bring in thirty people to a seminar, take a picture, and write a report to say, "I did it."

We also need more schools in the villages. Most of the kids have to walk for hours to get to school. There is no school bus. There is no transportation. We have to bring awareness to the villagers but first we need to reconsider our whole approach to education.

Politically all the numbers sound very nice. We have this many millions of girls in school, this number of women in Parliament. But you know what? It's only quantity that they're talking about; it's not quality. Yes, we are getting close to having ten million kids going to school. That's fine. But what's the impact? Three hours a day for a student. I would rather have five million kids go to school and study six hours than to have ten million going to school. We need good education here.

Along with that we need to talk honestly and openly about our mental health and addiction problems. I'll give you an example. Afghanistan is known for its carpets, and about 95 percent of the carpets are woven by women. But when a woman has children and has to weave carpets, who is looking after the children? Too many women give their children opium poppies to make them fall asleep, so they can weave and make money. We need to fix this situation for the women so they don't have to give their kids drugs in order to be able to work. We need daycare. We need women's centers. We need rehabilitation centers for drugs—we have about one million people here with drug problems. And we need psychiatrists.

So many people are depressed, especially people who have gone through the war. They have seen it all. I give them so much credit; I don't know how they do it. They're still walking. They're still living. They're still working. But they need help, emotional help, psychiatric help, which we have very little of here. There was a report done a few years ago that found that more than 60 percent of Afghans are depressed or have some kind of psychological issues because of the war. Our president, Dr. Ghani, said that we are an entire nation with PTS [post-traumatic stress]. But what have we done about this? Why did we do the survey? Just to put it in a file?

We have to do more. We should have done more. If we want to move forward, we must fix the lingering trauma. Most of all, we have to give people quality of life.

Yes, Afghan men are protective of their women. They have always been. And we all respect that. But during the war years, they became overprotective, because enemies were taking away their daughters, raping them, all kinds of things. Even before the Taliban, they sometimes couldn't send their kids to school—their sisters, or their daughters. When the Soviets came, those Russians were more open-minded about women, but they didn't believe in Islam at all, or any religions, so people stood up against them. And during their years and then the war with the mujahideen and then the Taliban, the women vanished. They had to vanish to be safe. If you think of a kid from those days, now he's thirty-five or forty or forty-five, for his entire life his mentality has been: protect your woman, don't let her go out, cover her up, don't show her to anybody. We have a culture of possession and protection that is embedded into men's brains. Today, even in Kabul, beautiful girls are often still hidden out of fear that some mafia guy is going to see her and take her. Beauty is admired in the West, but beauty really works against you here.

I see this desire to protect even in my own family. I love my father very much, and I'm proud of him and he's proud of me. He has taught me so much, but I remember when I first came here and I was starting all my programs, he was always worried about me. One night we were talking, having a discussion—and my father always taught me that I should keep learning and learning. There is no stopping point for education at any age, anytime, anywhere. And he taught me to always be able to defend my ideas. So this concept has been in my head since the day I was born. But a few years ago here in Kabul, the two of us—he's a politician and a diplomat and I'm pretty much a humanitarian activist focused on the developing world, so we come at issues from totally different angles—were discussing an issue, and I started reasoning with him, and I was very serious. He looked at me and said, "How dare you talk to me like this? I am your father." I just sat there and said, "Dad, you told me to defend myself and I'm defending myself. You taught me; you brought me up this way, so what do you want me to do?" I had him there. He started laughing. He said that I was right, that this is the way to be. But not everyone has a man like my father, who is capable of really listening.

TODAY, EVEN IN KABUL, BEAUTIFUL GIRLS ARE OFTEN STILL HIDDEN OUT OF FEAR. BEAUTY IS ADMIRED IN THE WEST, BUT BEAUTY REALLY WORKS AGAINST YOU HERE.

I know girls who have graduated from university and have even gotten their master's degree. Then they marry a guy who has his master's or a doctorate. This guy wants the best, so he goes and gets an educated girl, and as soon as they get married, he makes her sit at home. No, you can't work, he says. You have to stay home and raise children. Where does that mentality come from? It comes from the way they've been raised, it comes from the culture of war; by now they don't know why they are keeping these women at home. They just say it's our culture. But as a society, as people, we have invested just as much in this girl. She worked just as hard as he has in school. Men have to learn to realize why they are asking their educated wives to stay at home and not work at all.

This mentality is going to take generations to change. It's like peeling an onion. So every generation is one step at a time. It's going to have to be parents, especially the mothers, who train their boys, telling them to respect their sisters, their mothers, their female cousins, and eventually their own daughters.

We also can't just go ahead and teach human rights and then not do anything else. I'm a big believer in human rights. I'm working for women's rights. But when you're working for women's rights you have to deliver the foundation for them so they can use their rights. If you don't put the foundation together, then what's the use of teaching human rights? And when women are in the workforce they learn their rights more than at any other time. Their human rights are economic rights too.

From here, we can get women involved in all levels of the economy. They can become bankers; they can become financial analysts. Once they get into these areas, I think things will change. They will start something as basic as counting women's labor as part of the GDP. Right now, when most women work, it doesn't count in the government's statistics. According to the government's figures and definitions, women are useless economically. And women need to be involved to play a role in the rest of Afghan life. If you want to get into politics, to be a successful minister or even if you want to become the president of this country, you need to be economically aware and sufficient in order to do that.

We do need to get women into the important decision-making councils, however. Right now, almost all the policies for women are made by men. We are going to have to push men to include women, to say that women need to participate whether you like it or not. Because men are not going to do it voluntarily.

But the most important thing, for men and for women, is economic empowerment. My passion from day one has been economic empowerment. When people are economically empowered they can live a normal life. For example, if they get sick, they can pay for a doctor. They can pay for a hospital. If they need somebody to defend their rights, they can hire an attorney. They can send their children to the best schools. I would rather economically empower a woman than move her into politics. A poor woman in politics is going to be bought by a man and is going to be told what to do and what to vote for.

What breaks my heart here every day is the violence. You never get used to these things. Every time I hear about an incident, it shakes me. And I don't know how people could do this to other people if you are a true Muslim. If you are a true Muslim, you don't blow yourself up. That's against Islam. Suicide is against Islam. And it's very painful to watch the people suffer because it's shown all over national TV. Most of the time I look at them, and I say, I could be one of them. You don't know your destiny—where you'll end up and what destiny brings for you. With my heart, truly, I hope that one day I see this country really peaceful. Yet every morning when I leave, I say goodbye to everybody and we say, "Inshallah, see you tonight." "Inshallah" means with God's will, we will see you tonight. Everybody lives like that here. You have to watch where and what time you are going; you have to watch who you're dealing with—everything. Every day, every single move you make you have to analyze first.

One thing I've learned during the past fifteen or so years being here is that there is nothing wrong among people, the local people, the Western people, even with Pakistanis, with Iranians, because individual people get along very well. People appreciate each other. They want to learn from each other. They respect each other. Most of the bigger problems have to do with the politicians and the games and the region. It's like a chessboard. Who is moving forward, who is moving sideways, who is killing who, who is taking over what, who is taking credit?

All this war has really split us as a people. I know there is a big divide between the Afghans who stayed here during the war and the ones who were overseas. But I still speak the same language. I was born here, I was raised here. My feeling is that the diaspora has to come here and put their hands together with the people who have lived here during the war. They have to join hands and build this country. And you just can't do that from the comfort of your new home—no way.

Sometimes people come here—they think it should be like Paris or London. There should be electricity twenty-four hours, there shouldn't be dust, there shouldn't be dirt. I'm not kidding you. And I sit here and I think, "Oh my God." If you want to work here and really help here, you have to accept the society the way it is. You have to respect the people of Afghanistan for who they are and what they have been through. There is so much negative news here. You get up in the morning and the first news is that there has been a suicide bomber. You have to be very strong to face these things, you have to have an inner strength to live here, because if you are not internally strong, mentally strong, you will not last.

But every new day here, I believe that we are planting the seeds for the future.

> YOU HAVE TO HAVE AN INNER STRENGTH TO LIVE HERE, BECAUSE IF YOU ARE NOT INTERNALLY STRONG, MENTALLY STRONG, YOU WILL NOT LAST.

Like many Afghans, Zahra goes by a single name. She grew up dirt poor, the child of subsistence farmers who worked on other people's land. She has survived the Soviet invasion, being married off at age sixteen, the mujahideen civil war, and fleeing the Taliban. She found her profession of rug weaving as a refugee in Pakistan during the Taliban time and today weaves rugs for the nonprofit ARZU, a Dari word meaning hope. For many years of her life, until she began working, she had never seen an Afghan banknote and did not know what money looked like.

. . . .

My name is Zahra. I am forty-three years old and was born in the Dehe-Surkhak village of Yakawlang district. I grew up in this village. I had two sisters and three brothers. My parents were farmers, but they did not have their own farm. They used to work on others' land.

During the Soviet war, we lived in the same village. I was five years old then and I would hear the war stories from my father and the elders in the village. They said that foreign forces had invaded the country, and that these foreign forces would throw in jail or even kill anyone who opposed them.

One day when I went outside, I saw that a large number of villagers had gathered. Some had shovels and axes in their hands and two of them had guns. They said they were going to fight the Soviets. After a few minutes my father came home and told us, "I am going to fight the Soviets, bye." We did not dare to ask why, we just said bye. Then I found my mother and asked her where my father went.

My mother said that the Soviet convoy is passing near the village and the villagers are going to attack them as they pass. What

I heard later is that the sheikh at our mosque issued a jihad against the Soviets to drive them out of our homeland. After a few hours, we could hear the sound of gunfire and tanks coming nearer. We were scared and we all went home. When my father came home at night, we asked him about the war. He said that a large number of villagers were killed and wounded.

The war against the Soviets lasted too long and a large number of families left their homes and migrated to Pakistan and Iran at that time. But we could not afford to go to a safer place and so we had to stay in the village.

After the Soviet forces left the country and the situation was a little calmer, my father asked me to marry someone from our village who was much older than me. I was sixteen years old.

Shortly after I got married, the civil war began. One day, a number of mujahideen came to our village and took some of the men. When they came back another day, I hid my husband in a cattle barn. I kept him hidden in the barn for about three months, so that they could not force my husband to go with them.

The mujahideen did a lot of violence and treated people very badly. They would kill our sheep and kill our goats and force us to cook the meat for them. They would take our eggs and kill our chickens. I have too many bad memories from that time. I was just married and I expected to have some good days in my new life. But instead I lived in fear.

By the time the Taliban attacked Bamiyan, my province, I had three small children. Every day we would hear the sounds of the Taliban's violence. The Taliban did not have mercy and killed even newborn kids and old men. We were very scared and we escaped to a nearby mountain. For two weeks, we stayed on that mountain living in a tent.

When we came down from the mountain and returned to our

home, there was nothing left. The Taliban had burned all of our belongings. They had killed some of our relatives who had stayed behind. The Taliban had changed our green village into a hell. After seeing those scenes and all the destruction, we could not continue living there. We left the village and went to Kabul.

On the way to Kabul, a man got up on our bus, he looked at me with anger and said to me, "Why you did not wear a burqa? If Taliban see you they will beat you." I was very scared and hid my face with my scarf.

We stayed in Kabul one week and we never went out for fear of the Taliban. After one week, we left and made our way to Pakistan. In Pakistan, we lived in a refugee camp. There, I learned carpet weaving and this was the first time that I got money for my work. I was very happy. I bought some new clothes for my kids with that money. I never thought that one day I could work and earn money. Since then, I decided always to continue this work and to help my family.

We stayed for four years in Pakistan, and when the situation got better in Afghanistan we returned to Bamiyan. But we did not go back to our home village. We heard that the new provincial governor was giving land in Shash Pul to refugees, so we went there and got a piece of land, which is our home now.

I kept weaving rugs in Shash Pul. When I work and earn money from rug weaving, when I spend the money for my needs, I remember the time that I was not a rug weaver. For a long time I did not know Afghani banknotes. My husband bought us new clothes once a year. Now I buy things when I need them with my rug-weaving money. When I get the money for the rug I have made, I feel proud of myself and feel that I am not weak. I am useful for my family and this makes me happy.

Today, I have seven children—three sons and four daughters. My elder son and my daughter are studying at universities and the other children are at school. It is a big happiness for me that my children are educated.

I had a miserable life in the past and I hope my children never have such an experience. I help them to continue their education and make a good future for themselves.

Freshta Hazeq has endured death threats, threats to kidnap her children, fires, and property destruction at her office. Bribes have been paid to try to drive her out of business. The Afghan police have told her to hire personal guards. And all of this because she decided to start her own company in a traditionally male field: printing. Born into a liberally minded Kabul family, she would otherwise be like any other busy, working mother of small children. Except that she has chosen, as a woman, to build a business and reach out on behalf of other women. She began this effort from the time she was in college, and she has even sought to train Islamic mullahs to rethink the rights and roles of women.

. . . .

I was born in Kabul and I grew up there until the Taliban time. When the Taliban came, we went to Pakistan and from there we went to Iran, and then we went back to Pakistan. We had an easier time than some families because my father was an electrical engineer. But from a young age, my brother and I were going to school and working in Pakistan so our family could survive. We came back to Kabul in 2002, and I studied social science at Kabul University. I liked social science because after the years in Iran and Pakistan, I felt like I didn't know anything about Afghanistan. Even when we lived in Kabul, it was too dangerous to travel to the provinces. I only knew Kabul.

Along with going to school, I kept working. I had studied English, and I was hired to be a translator for an international nonprofit. For the first time, I traveled to all the different provinces in Afghanistan, and because I was translating for a gynecologist, I saw up close many of the issues facing women. When I traveled to the Central Highlands, I saw that nearly all the women didn't have shoes, they were walking in their bare feet. And they didn't have soap. They washed their hands with ash, which damaged their skin. If these women were lucky enough to live in a small house, all their farm animals lived inside with them. But many of the women didn't even have houses—they lived in caves. And most were hungry—they didn't have anything to eat.

When I went to villages in the province of Badakhshan, which is on the border with China, I saw the people living in the mountains. They had spent their whole life in the mountains and at that time nobody traveled to their province. They didn't know that other people were living in places beyond their own district. They thought they were the only people. The only grain they had was barley, they had never seen or heard of wheat bread. All they cooked was barley. And they also ate a plant that they fed to their animals. The plant was poisonous and would completely explode their stomachs, but they had no choice because they were hungry and there wasn't anything else to eat.

As I traveled around, I thought of my own life. I was such a demanding child. I wanted my parents to get me this new dress or that new jacket. I'd say, I'm tired of this outfit; let's change it. But when I went to these provinces, I saw their life and I said oh my God, it was too much. All of these experiences made me want to do something for the women of Afghanistan. I spent six years working as a gender specialist for Oxfam International, which works to end poverty.

Although I was young, I was assigned to do gender training in the provinces, and one of the groups I was conducting gender training for was the local mullahs, the religious figures in the community trained in religious teachings. They are often the ones who preach and who oversee the practice of Islamic law; they are the local learned

Islamic men. I would arrive and the mullahs would really make fun of me, saying, "This young girl has come here, she is like a child, and she is teaching us gender." They kept teasing me. But I didn't give up. I would use Islamic sources of the Holy Koran to teach them and to try to convince them that women matter, that women have rights, and women have value. By the end of the training days, some of these same mullahs even started to call me a teacher and they told me that they had learned so many things that they didn't know.

In Afghanistan, particularly to Afghan men, gender means "women." So we have to change that whole understanding. First, I would try to explain that when we talk about gender, we are not encouraging women to become the enemies of men. What gender means is that we are talking about the equality of men and women. And when we talk about gender, we are talking about respecting women and providing them space to grow up, a space to practice their rights. Gender is about freedom of life, to give each person enough empowerment to think about themselves, to make decisions, and to be involved in the decision making. And for everyone, men and women, to understand that a woman is a human being. They have certain rights, and they also can enjoy those rights like men in our society. I explained that the society we have now is not something that has been given to us by God. Instead, we have made this society ourselves, and when we rule over a category of society that is called women, we have done that as human beings, it has not been decided by God.

Of course, at the beginning it was very difficult to make the men and particularly the mullahs understand that. I explained that we are not bringing a new concept to them, but that this concept already exists in our Holy Koran and has been explained to us by our God, that our Prophet has explained this. Unfortunately, I would tell them, this concept has not been explained to us by our scholars and our religious leaders. We are not asking them to follow some new manual or new book, we are asking them to follow the original and most important book, the Koran.

In the provinces, they think of course women are human beings, but that they don't have any rights. They are not there to make decisions. They are just there to deliver babies and to cook at home and that's all. And when it comes to working, the men also say that the women do nothing. Most men don't see women working in the household as doing work. So, I would ask these men, if they had to hire a servant to look after their kids, or a servant to do their cooking, or hire a servant to do their household chores, how much money would they have to pay someone to perform all of these activities? And many women work for their husbands growing crops and doing other farm activities, so if they didn't do those things, the man would have to hire someone for those jobs as well. Then I would say, so if you count all this money, how much money are you saving simply by having a wife who is willing to do all these things? I would try to give men many reasons to value women differently. And to convince them that women deserve a greater role in the society and should go hand in hand with the men in society.

When I was doing this gender training, most of the men tried to show that they were really accepting of the training; they tried to show some changes in their behavior. Doing this training also made me realize that it is very important to involve men, because there were many organizations that came into Afghanistan that only focused on women. But you have to involve men, to make them understand the conflicts in Afghanistan, because at the end of the day, the men are ruling the women. I saw that even if we are empowering women, they are still consulting with their men; they have to get permission from their men. So we can't just focus on changing the mentality of the women, we also have to change the mentality of the men. We have to do the same work with them that we are doing with the women.

But I saw something else from my work. I saw that we need more women in business—and not just traditional businesses. I saw so many organizations that were just reinforcing women's traditional roles, putting them into business making jams, cooking, sewing and tailoring, or handicrafts. So I decided that I wanted to enter business myself, and not just any business, but a male-dominated business. Men always say that women cannot do heavy work, I wanted to be a woman who would change their minds.

I set out to try to establish a printing company. My company was the first and only printing company that was owned by a woman and run by a woman. When I established this company, I entered into a completely different society. The men in this industry never thought that a woman could do this sort of heavy work, dealing with heavy machinery, inventory, timing, working late, and other stuff. If you can imagine, when I opened my own office the men from the other printing companies would come in and start laughing at me. They would say, "There was no other business that you could do, so you just had to open this business? This is not a woman's job. It's not a woman's business. How are you going to do this? I'm sure you are going to fail."

Everything they said to me was negative. But fortunately my husband is a really great man and he's a completely different type of Afghan man. He's very generous, and he was always there to give me positive energy and to tell me, "Don't ever think that you cannot do this job. You can do it. You just carry on and go on. I'm here. Don't worry about anything." So I have carried on, and

WE CAN'T JUST FOCUS ON CHANGING THE MENTALITY OF THE WOMEN, WE ALSO HAVE TO CHANGE THE MENTALITY OF THE MEN.

the business is running. I have faced lots of challenges, really lots of challenges, and I am still facing them, but I have never stopped.

Even some of the other men that at the beginning were really negative; when they saw that I could run the company and that I had achieved lots of goals and progressed, they started coming to me and saying, "Oh my God. We didn't think you were that much of a hard worker and that a woman can do it. Now I can see that a woman can do it." So my work also gave me the satisfaction of knowing that at least I have changed a few men's minds, that they now think, yes, a woman can do it.

The first challenge for me in starting the business was that I didn't know anything about printing. I didn't know how to quote a price. I didn't know how the printing process really worked. For the first six months, I had to educate myself all about printing work, about the machines, how everything worked, how to give a price, how to reach clients, how to get orders. All these were challenges for me. And of course, on top of all that, I had the negative comments and the actions of the men who were coming in and telling me that I had to stop. They would tell me to quit because printing doesn't have any income. But when I started to achieve results in my business, then the men became very negative competitors. Whenever I would go someplace and bid for a project, they would also go there and try to bribe people.

I'm a person who has never tried to bribe anyone. I've never given money or taken money, but I couldn't stop the men from doing that. I faced a lot of difficulty in getting contracts or winning contracts because of all the corruption. I wanted to compete on my business skills. So I would prove to the clients that the quality of my product is better than the quality of my competitors'. One company that agreed with me gave me a long-term contract. They switched to my business from another contractor. When he found out, he called me to threaten me and to say that he had paid money to have me killed.

So now, he told me, you have to be ready for that. But if he thought I would back down, he was wrong. I told him, okay, come on, kill me. Because I'm sure those men who are coming to kill me aren't going to be calling on the phone first.

After that call, though, I was really shocked and upset, and I told my husband. He said, don't worry, nobody's going to do anything. But what happened was that this competitor burned my paper stock and he bribed my staff to break my machinery. He put a spy in my company, and then he even dropped off a letter threatening to kidnap my kids.

One time, I was going to a meeting and a man called me on my cell phone and said, "We saw you, we know where you are right now," and he gave my location. "And at this moment we can kill you." I said, "Okay, come on, kill me." And I said, "Oh my God, how much time do you have to spend calling me? Just go on and shoot me. You are spending lots of your money, just come on, kill me."

That's what I have faced—it has been very bad.

Of course, we did contact the police. We gave them the phone number that the threatening calls were coming from. The police tried to do what they could, but in the end they said, "Unfortunately we cannot do much because the people calling you, they are very clever and we cannot track them." They also told me, "You have to hire a security guard for yourself because we have a shortage of inspectors in your district, and we cannot hire someone to watch your area or your house. It is better to hire private security guards for yourself, and you have to build a fence around your wall. You have to cut your trees so nobody can climb over your walls or walk on your walls." They said they were sorry that they could not protect us more. They ended by saying that sometimes people in this position "just leave the country."

I have never been afraid for myself, but I was frightened for my kids. I didn't want them to be kidnapped. I hired a guard to take them to school and bring them back. I also found an explosive device in my office. It had been thrown in the trash near my generator. My security guard at the company saw it, and we called the police. They said it was an explosive that hadn't detonated. They investigated it, but they never came back with any reports.

When the threats didn't work, the men who were my competitors kept trying other ways to drive me out of business and to make it very difficult for my company to survive. Again, they attempted to break my machinery and to make me late with my deliveries. But I overcame that. Then they finally found a way to bribe the service manager of the company where I had a big, long-term contract. It was good income, and I had already had the contract for a year and a half. Making me lose the contract was really important to them.

One day, the service manager at the company called. He said, "I want you to come and talk to me about the contract." Then he openly told me, "You have to pay me 300,000 AFs each month, and then I will keep this contract with you." I said, "Of course I will not pay you." He called me again that night, and again, I refused. Then he said, "Okay, I'm telling you for the last time, if you're happy with this amount, I'm going to give you the contract. If not, I'm going to take the contract away from you." I didn't take him completely seriously because he was the service manager, not the owner. But the next day, public bidding was announced for my contract. I asked why, because the contract was not finished, and I was told that there had been some management changes. I met with the company president, but even though I had proof about the bribes and records of the phone calls, at a certain point, I just said, "Okay, I'm walking away. I don't want this anymore."

*   *   *

The aim of these men and these competitors was to make me shut my company, and my aim was to never give up. If I stopped my business or closed down my business, I was accepting that I had failed. And they would have succeeded in ousting me. Truly, the company that I started is like a baby to me. And how difficult is it to accept that you have lost your baby? So I'm trying to fight all the time, trying to rescue it, to keep it going, and never giving up.

What I've learned from all these experiences is that women themselves should have confidence to stand up. Then they should commit themselves to never quitting. Of course, as an individual we cannot change the whole, big society, but to a small extent, we, each of us, can be a change maker. Previously in Afghanistan, even before the Taliban time, only a very few women had businesses. But today, fifteen years after the Taliban, there are more than three thousand companies that are woman-owned. It's a huge change. But if we truly want to succeed, we have to have that desire and that commitment within ourselves first. No one else can do it for us or give it to us. Opportunity will never come and knock on our door. We have to go in search of it. We have to take advantage of any opportunities we can find.

I'm very hopeful about the future and what will happen next. In addition to my printing company, I have established an import-export company to export leather and dried foods. I'm also one of the founders of an advocacy platform called LEAD, Leading Entrepreneurs for Afghanistan Development. We are a group of women business owners that came together and established this platform to advocate for the women who are coming up behind us. We want to be the women who pave the way for those younger women who wish to be businesswomen.

At home, I teach my children that they should be a good friend because I remember what we faced during wartime. I've also tried to provide them with lots of opportunities. But they have to learn to make use of those opportunities and try to be different, especially my daughter. I want her to be different from the typical Afghan girl. She should learn to stand on her own feet. She should learn to protect herself in our society. She should be independent. And the same for my boys also—they should learn to protect themselves in our society. They have to focus on their education as much as they can. And they should explore both inside and outside our country. I try to take them away at least once a year so they can see the outside world. I want them to see the differences between other societies and our society. And, of course, they have so much more technology compared to us; for them, the Internet and computers also make the world smaller. They can reach for whatever they want.

Life does not wait for bad things to stop; life is running all the time. We have to go ahead with our lives, whatever the obstacles. We have to find new ways to be change makers and to bring change to our society. If we don't have the courage to start, nobody will push us. If we are always going to say, no, it's not time yet, it will never be the right time. The time is never going to be safe, so we just have to start now. And then one day, our society will change.

So I'm hopeful for the future.

Najiba Faiz was a top high school graduate in Helmand province with a scholarship to study abroad the year that the Russians invaded Afghanistan. Instead of completing her education, she was married off to a distant relation, who did not trust her to leave the house. He would lock the door when he left for work in the morning and open it only upon his return. It took her more than ten years of fighting to gain her freedom to go outside when she wished. Today, Najiba has worked successfully for major nonprofit organizations and even a construction company. Here she speaks about her deferred dreams and about finding her place as a devout Muslim woman in the Afghan work world.

. . . .

I was born in 1964 in Lashkar Gah, a city in Helmand province in southeastern Afghanistan that was built by Americans. The city was home to different soldiers for many years, but in the 1950s, it became the headquarters of the U.S. Army Corps of Engineers, which came to build a major dam project in Helmand province. Lashkar Gah was built in an American style, with wide streets and many trees. The city worked better than the dam, which the local people called the crooked dam. Lashkar Gah was also a very free city. There were no problems before the revolution.

My father was a trader who sold women's goods—perfume, makeup, and clothing. He was very open-minded and encouraged education among all his girls. Like many typical Afghan men, he had three wives and a total of twenty-one children.

I did very well in school. I graduated twelfth grade with honors and earned the highest score on the exit exams, the Kankor. For years, the student with the highest grade in the province would receive a scholarship to study abroad. And because at that time Afghanistan was allied with the Soviet Union, I was given a scholarship to study law or political science in East Germany or Russia.

Though my father was very open-minded, when the Russians came and the wars began, he feared that I would get involved with the mujahideen or that they would get involved with our family. Many of the mujahideen in our area were allied with the socialists, rather than the communist Russians. Mujahideen supporters also lingered around big educational facilities—many of the open-minded, educated people became mujahideen at that time.

Once the Russians came, my father refused to send me away. I was so upset that I went on a weeklong hunger strike and was ready to kill myself. So my father made a concession and said I could retake the Kankor exam the next year and go to Kabul University. But by the next year, the situation had gotten even worse.

For a while, my father said that he would give me the option of going to Iran or Pakistan for my education, but soon he got too worried to send me anywhere. The political situation completely changed him and his outlook on life. Instead of continuing my education, he decided I should get married. I did not want to get married, and I did not want to marry the man my father had selected, a distant relation of his who lived in Herat. But my father insisted and my mother was okay with it, so I went ahead and got married. Four years after I had graduated with the highest exam score, I was married off to a man I barely knew and I had moved to Herat province and started a new life with him and his family.

My husband was a manager in the electricity department of Herat province. Initially he was very ugly, very mean, and very suspicious, almost all because of the political and economic situation in Afghanistan. The coming of the Russians and the mujahideen and later the

Taliban changed Afghanistan. There was so much fear and insecurity. No one trusted anyone anymore.

My husband was one of those men who didn't trust me, who didn't want anyone coming to visit me or for me to leave the house at any point when he was not around. He objected to me talking to people and seeing people during the day. I could not go to the bazaar. I had no freedom of movement. In the morning when he left for work, my husband would lock the doors to the house and then open the doors only when he got home. At first, I tried to reason with him, then I would cry, then I would object. It took me a good ten to twelve years and a long and arduous fight until he finally agreed to give me my freedom.

I have convinced my husband that I am trustworthy to the point that now he lets me travel around Afghanistan with no worries. Today, I can earn good money. And also he says that I am old—I am over fifty now—so he does not have many worries about me being out by myself anymore. In part, he let me out because I am old.

One of my first steps toward my freedom was that I was able to teach at the local lycée. I had a teaching background and did additional study, but with the coming of the Taliban, all the schools closed. My two oldest children were in the fourth and fifth grade, but all they could do was stay at home and do religious studies. They did manage to graduate from high school later, and they now work in business and trade, but they did not go to college. It was too long. My youngest son is getting his master's degree, and my daughter is married. We chose my sister's son for her, and she was okay with that. We needed to go the traditional route in marriage. In the culture, it is not acceptable to do something else.

By 1997, the money situation in our house was very bad because my husband was out of work, so I managed to get a job with an NGO. I've worked for a British NGO, Ockenden International, which focuses on helping refugees and displaced persons. In Afghanistan, it helped train women to knit and weave and also taught them the basics of household economics. I eventually became the program manager, sending people all over to train rural women. After that, I worked for USAID and then for a Spanish construction company.

I had no preconceptions about my work; I just took everything that came to me. In each job, I wanted to work really hard to prove that the Afghan women can do whatever their Western peers can, that we are not less than Western women. As far as being humane and being a decent human being, I see no difference between the Afghan and Western cultures. The big difference was in the religious components, in maintaining my faith. It was very important to me to keep my hijab and maintain my Muslim character and Muslim persona as I did my job. I wanted to maintain who I am as an Afghan woman throughout the workday. I believe that nothing can stop your progress, not religious barriers or cultural barriers. To outsiders, it might seem inconvenient to stop for daily prayers, but not for me. Observing my religion is not going to hold me back from progress.

My latest project is to start a company that empowers Afghan women and enlightens them about their rights. I think one of the best ways to do that is to start working with the local mullahs. I want to train mullahs in four provinces, because many of these religious people have no concept of a woman's value or her rights. These mullahs lack proper Islamic knowledge and if we have educated mullahs going out to teach the uneducated ones, it can make a huge difference. Then we will not have incidents like the killing of Farkhunda. Religious leaders won't manipulate uneducated women. We have already seen this make a great impact in Badghis province. After the mullahs were taught, it helped lower violence against women.

I did finally get to go abroad, first to Dakar in Senegal to study and then to Arizona for a training program called Project Artemis.

All the building and progress that I saw in America amazed me—all the progress that women had made, all the roads, offices, and homes, the large amount of technology. As I traveled there, I would think of Afghanistan and how it had regressed, or at least not progressed as much as it could have, how it is still enmeshed in war, killings, burnings, and destruction.

When I did travel outside of Afghanistan, particularly to the United States, I regretted that in my youthful years, with all the energy that I had and the sharp mind that I had, I had been held back from studying abroad and continuing my education. But as much as I regretted that, Project Artemis showed to me something else. It showed me that I was complete, that I am a complete person. I have a position in society. I am capable and accomplished.

Nasim Gul Azizi stood out as the quietest woman in her business development classes at Project Artemis, a special initiative at the Thunderbird School of Global Management at Arizona State University in Glendale, Arizona, to train Afghan women entrepreneurs. When she arrived in the United States in 2010 to learn business skills, she already had twenty employees. In 2012, when Artemis checked back to see how she was doing, Nasim Gul had over two hundred employees. Stunned, they asked her what had changed, and she said, "I grew my business through negotiations. You taught me how to negotiate with men."

She had found her voice and her self-confidence to expand her business and make her case. Instead of being outwardly shy, she became newly determined. Everything about Nasim Gul is serious, except for the brightly colored headscarf that frames her face. She has completed not one but two stints of educational and business training in the United States, opportunities for which she remains "highly appreciative and thankful." During her second trip, she traveled to Texas A&M to learn about cold storage. Back in Herat province, she built the region's largest cold storage facility. Along the way, she has adopted many of today's hot development buzzwords, such as "capacity building" and "gender mainstreaming." They roll off her tongue with more certainty than other, far more common English phrases.

· · · · · · · · ·

In Herat province, where I live, many women still do not have permission to leave their homes. They cannot go out to go to school, to shop, and especially not to work unless a man accompanies them or says that it is okay. Afghanistan is still a very masculine society. People, particularly men but also many women, believe that men should have all the decision-making rights. But I fight that with this face. I am a woman, but I am showing that I can run a business. From the beginning, I wanted to hire other women. I make the effort not only for myself, but also for other women. As women, we should not just see ourselves, we should try to increase all women's empowerment, not just our own.

Devastated Afghanistan requires professional people and expert people who can really work hard and rehabilitate this country. It is my dream to be an active member in the reconstruction of my country.

I got my idea to start my food-processing business when I went to some of the villages where my relatives live. Herat is an agricultural province located in the western region of Afghanistan, but many farmers were not able to sell their products. I saw fruits rotting on the ground and vegetables dead in the gardens, all wasted. In the villages, many families have a bad economic situation too. I knew if we could buy products from the farmers and from the family gardens and gather the women from the villages to work together, we could change many things.

When women stay in their homes, they stay illiterate and they do not have decision-making rights. In the families in rural areas, women also do not have rights because most of them do not have skills to generate income. If women work, they can earn money and that money will give them a decision-making role within their families. When women earn money, they also can decide how to spend what they earn. Almost always, they will spend their money on their house, for their children to go to school, for food, and for clothes. And some of their money can be saved. When a woman works out of the home, she empowers herself and supports her family.

*   *   *

My idea was to start a food-processing plant to make jam, juice, dried fruits, and tomato paste. I had to find $5,000 to start, and I also got a grant from a program funded by the U.S. Embassy. It was a challenge. The women we hired did not know how to make any of our products. They had never even used these products, because many Afghans don't cook with them. We trained some of our women workers to give cooking lessons to other local women so they could learn to use what we made. We also discovered that we had to teach many families about nutrition because they did not know about nutrition for their children and themselves. And we faced many problems with the villages. When we started our work, the women in our villages did not have permission to work outside of their homes or even to go to the market. But after we worked with the communities, the members of our processing centers can now go outside of their homes for working and for shopping. They have been given permission by the men in their families to leave their houses. Our biggest persuasive tool was economics. Families need income.

Now, we have 350 women working for us. Eighty of them are widows, so they are the only ones supporting their families. We have 18 processing centers in different villages and districts inside the province. But we don't do just food processing, we also do vocational training. We call ourselves an association because we train women in areas like record keeping, management, leadership, and marketing, and also in human rights, women's rights, and gender mainstreaming.

Each of our food-processing centers has a savings box for the women. We started putting in savings boxes when we first opened. The women can save small amounts of money in the boxes and if a member of the food-processing association or a person in the community has a problem, she can take a loan from the savings box and then pay the money back. They can use the money for emergencies or for important things that they need, as long as they pay it back.

The most difficult part of our business is security, which means whether people feel safe from attacks, from insurgents launching attacks and trying to get control or create unrest. If the security is good, if people are not worried each day about their own basic safety and the safety of their families, the work will be good. We need to purchase more machinery for things like packaging and quality control, but our biggest problem is security: do our employees and our customers feel safe? It is also hard to be a woman in business. Women in Afghanistan face many problems for their business such as a high tax rate, high power costs, lack of sufficient government cooperation, and little information about the running of a business. In our business, we have to pay the government money for licensing, for registration, and our tax rate is 20 percent. I think the government should consider decreasing the tax rate for new businesses, for all companies, those owned by men and those owned by women.

I believe more jobs means less violence. Women can bring more peace and improve the stability of the economic situation. And women will have more decision-making rights if they can join in the larger Afghan society. More people are already starting to believe that women are half the population and should have influence in their families.

. . . .

My own story begins in Herat, which is a very agricultural province. I was born there on December 1, 1989, not long after the Soviet Union left Afghanistan. I have two brothers and two sisters. In Afghanistan, my father worked repairing bicycles. He was illiterate and never had a chance to get an education. My mother is a literate person; she was educated at a university. But both my parents wanted their children to have an education. Although I was born in Herat, almost immediately after I was born, my family fled as refugees to Iran. The mujahideen forces that had formed to fight the Russians were now fighting each other. It was civil war, and it was too dangerous to stay. We were lucky. My aunt was already living in Iran, so we did not have to stay in a refugee camp. But it was still hard. My father worked as a day laborer, but he could not always get work. I went to primary and secondary school in Iran. When I graduated, I studied computers, first-aid skills, and some English. I even learned how to be a tailor. For a while I worked as a teacher in a school for refugee kids. After my last sibling graduated high school, in 2005, we moved back to Herat.

It had been almost four years since the Taliban fell, but even in 2005, we had a bad feeling when we came back. We were scared. We knew that the Taliban were still in many parts of the country. At first, my brothers and sisters and I did not like Afghanistan. Not long after we moved back, my father died. We were not a rich family and without my father we had to fight with the difficulties of life. My first job was at the Welfare and Development Organization for Afghanistan as a finance officer. WDOA really motivated me to want to serve my country and help people through business.

Most of the families around Herat have the idea that women should not be educated past the sixth or seventh grade. Some of that is also security. These families won't send their children to school because of the security situation. But education has always been my prime target throughout my life. My mother has always played a very important role in my education. When I needed to go to college in Herat, she told me, "Don't work at home. Study more." She did my chores around the house so that I could spend most of my time on

I LIKE THE SENTENCE THAT SAYS, "WHEN YOU EDUCATE A WOMAN, YOU EDUCATE A NATION."

school and my business. She spent her money to buy me books. When I was invited to the United States for different training programs, my relatives didn't like me traveling out of the country and told me not to go. But my mother supported me. She would say, "Don't think about what other people are saying about you, just go ahead and follow your dreams and your ambition for your country. We will support you as much as we can to be successful."

And true to her word, my mother, my brothers, my sisters have all supported me to try to make a change in Afghan society. Now I want to get a master's degree in the United States, so I will need even more support.

I like the sentence that says, "When you educate a woman, you educate a nation."

After the Taliban fell, Kobra Dastgirzada started work as a teacher, but she soon discovered that her passion was in being an entrepreneur, despite the personal risk. Her first major undertaking was to establish the Sisters Cultural and Sports Gathering (SCSG), which offers women a fitness club and vocational training. SCSG is the largest female sports center in Kabul; two thousand women have been trained here in fitness, as well as in sports like volleyball, basketball, and badminton. For three years, Kobra also operated a driving school for women, but she received too many threats. "My job is not safe," she explains, "but I want to be a good person to my country." But Kobra's desire to build a better Afghanistan has come at a personal price: danger for her daughter. It is a hard reminder of the precarious position Afghan women still face, even after they have achieved success.

· · · · · · · · · ·

I believe in new ideas and new ways to help people. I believe that every woman should be independent without being under the supervision of men and should have their own businesses and become an active member of society. I have started four very different businesses. Three have succeeded. But my family has paid a high price for my beliefs and my success. We have had some big defeats and setbacks.

When I started the first fitness center for women in Afghanistan, no one understood my idea. No one wanted to encourage me. Many people had very bad reactions because it went against Afghan culture. But I did not give up.

A fitness center was a natural choice for me because I knew about methods and techniques of fitness. I played sports when I was young; in college I played basketball. I liked it very much. I liked running, jumping, and getting to the ball. Sports are very important because they make a person young and healthy too, and it is relaxing to exercise. When I had a baby, I used fitness to get myself strong and healthy again. But my view is not shared by many people in Afghanistan. For my fitness center to succeed, I had to work very hard to gain the trust of women and their families. It is very difficult for families to allow their mothers, sisters, or daughters out of the house to go to a fitness class.

I spent a lot of time explaining the center to people in my community. When families came to see the center, they saw that my employees had good behavior. Everyone wore sensible clothes. At my center, women only do their fitness exercising according to the values of the culture. For example, we do not play loud music because then people would think that we have bad ethics, that we are holding dancing classes, which is not acceptable. People who came also saw that the atmosphere is very friendly for all.

The most popular activity is running around the gym. Only young ladies play basketball and other sports. It takes a lot of trust for men to let their mothers and sisters come to a class. The success of my center is all based on trust. I really also appreciate the mothers who brought their daughters to the fitness classes. I thanked them.

My business was not only for physical profits. I wanted to use it to help change the image of women in society, to tell the ladies that they are human beings and they should play a positive role in society. I wanted to teach women especially that they should be their own people, they should know who they are and what they are, and they should look for ways to improve society.

My message to women is not only to be a leader but to become your own leader.

Still, many women say being a leader is too difficult; they say, we cannot do it, we don't have the capability. They think they have to follow the men and can only be an employee. Few say, yes it is a great idea; it is a great job for me.

I have not always succeeded. Along with the fitness center, I opened a driving center for women. For three years, I taught ladies how to drive and also basic knowledge about the parts of a car and how a car works. But the reaction against the center was very strong. I was harassed on the street and even received some threats. All the other driving centers were owned by men and they didn't want a woman owning a center or teaching women how to drive. They used some very negative tactics to compete against me, and I had to give up the center. It made me very sad to have to give up the driving center.

I also had to learn a lot about business. When I started, there were many things that I did not know. I was very fortunate to be able to study with PEACE THROUGH BUSINESS in the United States and with Goldman Sachs's *10,000 Women*. I trained in the U.S., in Japan, in India, and in Kyrgyzstan. After that training I started two businesses, a food-processing plant that makes nine kinds of jam and five kinds of pickles and a basket weaving business. When I went to Japan, I got the idea to make baskets. Many food products need packaging, and in Afghanistan, we were using plastic baskets, which are not always good for food. In Japan, I saw traditional straw baskets being woven. When I came back to Afghanistan, I searched for these baskets, but I could not find them.

So I began to look for someone who knew the art of basket weaving. Then I created a training program to teach women how to weave all different sizes of baskets, from a five-hundred-gram size to fifteen-kilo size. I applied for a grant from USAID. Today, I have ninety women who are trained in the art of basket weaving. They can work from home and produce one or two pieces a day.

I supply the raw materials, and they deliver the finished products and earn an income. I now have a contract to supply five thousand Afghan farmers with baskets.

I've faced lots of challenges and obstacles. It was not only the new business that no one had done before, and there were bad reactions to it, and repeated efforts to make me fail. The biggest problem I have had to face came from within my own family. While I was working on my businesses, my daughter, Farah, got married. Then her husband started to beat her. Her husband and his family threatened to destroy my family's image in society and to ruin my business. They had planned to get control of all the businesses that I was running and to use Farah to force me to give them half or more of my businesses as my "partners." But I did not give in. Instead, I took my daughter back from that family.

I went to court and presented documents and evidence of my daughter being beaten. There is a law for families who face such violence. According to the law, a woman who is beaten by her husband can be divorced, and I got my daughter divorced. I had to stop those people.

In my family, we have all learned a lot from these defeats, but most of all, we have learned that by struggling and by strengthening our efforts we could succeed. Even during hard times, we found opportunities by standing up to these difficulties.

My daughter got a very positive lesson when she got out of that very bad situation in her marriage. It was a very tough lesson for her, but now she can start to use her experience to help others. Many girls and women are living in the same situation as my daughter, and their mothers cannot do anything to help them. I want to teach my daughter how to help others, especially those women who are under pressure from their families or are facing violence. She is studying law in the university so that she can work for women in society. Farah saw how difficult it was to rescue her from that situation. I hope she can help rescue other women and girls.

If I start another "business," it would be going into politics. In Afghanistan, politics is not going on the right path, there are lots of gaps. We need the government to work for the people, not be on top of the people. The people shouldn't be used as slaves for the government.

We also have too many issues with the countries surrounding us. Too many of these neighboring countries are interfering with Afghanistan's politics. Once the ancient Silk Road ran through Afghanistan on its way to China, bringing civilization and profit to the area, but today the other countries in the region are just trying to keep the Afghan economy weak so their own economies will profit. When China makes business deals, it looks to Pakistan, not to Afghanistan. Afghanistan has a bad image, and it is hurting our economy.

We will be a much stronger and better country if we have a very good government. The people shouldn't suffer so much from insecurity and low economy.

Right now, in my area, community councils are being established. I'm on our local community council. I'd like us to start a community center, where women can get more knowledge and income. If we open the center, I'm thinking about starting a women's driving school through our local council. I believe the opportunity is there—we just have to find a way.

Manizha Wafeq was sixteen years old in 2002, when Afghanistan started to reopen after the Taliban were removed from power. The second of five daughters and two sons, her parents were both doctors who worked for the military—"they are very educated but they love to have children"—and they assumed Manizha would follow in their footsteps and go into medicine. Instead, she wanted to go to work in an office and to apply the English and computer skills that she had learned as a refugee in Pakistan. As a petite, teenage girl, she endured insults and innuendos. Her experiences and her work with women in business have focused her views on why and how Afghan society needs to change.

. . . .

In 2002, all the international aid organizations were opening offices in Afghanistan, and I asked my father to allow me to go out and work. At first he denied me because he wanted me to go to university. But I convinced him that I wanted to start working. And I also knew that I needed to give him financial support, because we had grown to a big family, five daughters and two boys and both parents and only my father was earning any money. So I thought it was time for me since I knew English and computers and there was a good demand for young girls and boys who knew English and computers. We were easily recruited by international organizations as administrators and translators.

One thing I always knew, since I was twelve and living in Pakistan, was that I wanted to study economics and I wanted to become a businesswoman. I was always curious. I was fascinated by economic issues, and I loved to watch the news. I never really lived the life of a child. I was always full of ideas, thinking about different types of businesses that I wanted to start. I planned on opening a boutique and a salon and other things for women.

I remember one day when my dad came home from work and I told my parents that I had decided that I would do business. And my mom's answer was, "Umm." She said that neither she nor my dad were businesspeople, so they didn't know how I could possibly become a businesswoman. Her view was that your job had to come from your parents' profession. But my father said, "Leave her dream, whatever she wants to. I'm sure if she dreams something then she will go after it and she will do it. She will make it happen for herself."

My father's words and his attitude were what really encouraged me at that age, the trust my parents had that I would be able to do anything and that I could do anything in my life if I wanted to made me achieve a lot of things that I am proud of.

So at age sixteen I was hired as an administration and finance assistant for an international agency. I started taking care of all the cash for the office, taking care of the day-to-day expenses, slowly learning to do payroll for the staff, and taking care of other administrative issues like writing letters and handling the office communications with the Afghan ministry. Sometimes I attended meetings, wrote up the minutes, and also translated for my boss when he met with Afghan government officials. What I didn't understand was how different a work environment would be from a school environment. I wasn't able to handle that. After a week I started crying every day when I was coming back from the office. I was short, and I was also very young, sometimes I think I was behaving a little bit like a child. The whole office was men, two South Korean men and five Afghan men, and they were

MY FATHER SAID, "LEAVE HER DREAM, WHATEVER SHE WANTS TO. I'M SURE IF SHE DREAMS SOMETHING THEN SHE WILL GO AFTER IT AND SHE WILL DO IT. SHE WILL MAKE IT HAPPEN FOR HERSELF."

nice to me, but unfortunately they were not nice all the time. I was the only girl working with them. My Korean colleagues expected me to stay longer hours just like my male Afghan colleagues.

But in Afghanistan, the rules are different for girls and women. My family kept saying, "You cannot stay longer hours because of our neighbors." My parents didn't have a problem with me working late, but we lived in a community where if I came home from the office at eight p.m. and was being dropped off by a car from some international organization, all the neighbors would be watching, and they would start talking, saying, "Oh, she's a bad girl. She's working for foreigners. And her parents are bad because they are allowing her to work with foreigners." So I had pressure at home from my parents and pressure in the office. But my father gave me a book, *How to Win Friends and Influence People: The Only Book You Need to Lead You to Success*, by American author Dale Carnegie. It had been translated by an Iranian, and my father told me, this book is to teach you success.

I read that book two times. And it helped me to become the master of my life and the owner of my life, the owner of my happiness and my well-being and my success. That book taught me to love myself and to respect myself. It says that you have to respect yourself and love yourself first if you want the world to respect you and love you—that only if you take care of yourself and if you value yourself, will other people value you. And I realized as I was reading it that the way my colleagues were treating me was very devaluing. Yes, I was a girl, I was very young, I looked small because I was short, and I was inexperienced. But I started practicing the lines from that book, and I started not caring about what all these other men thought and did.

In Afghanistan, there are all sorts of situations that are difficult for women who work. There are all kinds of ways for male colleagues not to respect you. I remember one time I had to make name cards for a very high-level meeting between Afghan and South Korean officials. I had never made name cards for a table before, but they were considered very important. My other colleagues had gone ahead to the hotel to set up, and I was back at the office. The other Korean man, Mr. A, that I worked with had remained at the office too, but he was asleep. I kept waiting for him to wake up to check what I had done, since no one had ever taught me how to make name cards. He woke up late, but he said everything was fine. I was almost finished with the cards when my other colleagues called me, wanting to know where the cards were. I said that I was almost done, that I had been waiting to have them checked. Immediately, the other Korean guy, Mr. B, started yelling at me. Mr. B said that I wanted Mr. A to check my name cards because Mr. A was paying for our office expenses and our salaries, but he said it in a way that sounded like there were personal favors involved. And one of the Afghan men supported Mr. B. At first, I was stunned. I said, "What nonsense are you talking?" But then I felt angry. I did not deserve this disrespect. It would be insulting to any woman, but for an Afghan woman, accusations like that are particularly devastating.

I finished the cards, I sent them with the driver, and then I went home. The next morning, when I came in, I didn't go around to all the offices and greet everyone, as was my usual custom. I waited until I could see the overall boss, who was also Korean. I told him what Mr. B had said. And I told the boss, "From now on, I'm not going to work with him, and I'm not going to take whatever projects or assignments he gives me. If this is not acceptable to you, then I'm going to resign." And the boss said, "That's fine, Manizha. You can work with Mr. A, and I'll tell Mr. B not to give you assignments anymore."

After that experience, I knew that I really wanted to have my own business and that I wanted to help empower women. But I had also promised my father that I would go to university and get my bachelor's degree. I waited until 2008, because before that there was only Kabul University available. I wanted a private school that offered economics. By the time I enrolled, I was working full-time and going to school part-time in the evening. I got married in 2011, and graduated in 2012 with my husband and my sister.

It's a lot to do all that at the same time, but I had learned multi-tasking and fast working from my mom. When I observed her as a child, she was always very fast. She used to go to the hospital, walk back home, make us lunch, and then go back to the hospital. Wherever she went, she would walk very fast. She would also do all the household chores and take care of her children in a very efficient way.

By the time I graduated, I had some savings, and I started a company called Wonderland Women Clothing Company. Clothing has a huge market here, especially party wear and party dresses, called *Saleeqa*, which means "elegance" in the Dari language. One woman over the course of one "party evening" will sometimes wear two or three dresses. And each dress costs a minimum of $200. When I calculated the cost for producing one of those dresses, I thought this was a good profit margin. Also almost all of the clothing being sold in Afghanistan is imported from China, Pakistan, or India. I was asking, why don't we develop our own Afghan brand? My thought was let's start small and then someday we can become a very big factory that produces Afghan-made women's clothing. I wanted us to use local employment to help our economy. I also wanted Wonderland Women to run its own retail shop with women as sales representatives—sales is a position that was previously considered "for men only." I wanted to give women the confidence that they too can work in the same profession as men.

I started the business with my husband and my sister, but it was very difficult. It was the wrong time to be starting a business because in 2013 the international forces started talking about withdrawing from Afghanistan by the next year, 2014. Almost overnight, our economy and our security and political situation became unstable. Then in 2014, the whole year was taken up by the presidential election. Again the whole economy was down. We have been hoping that in 2015, everything would pick up and the business will keep expanding. But if you watch the news, you will see that almost every day we have an explosion in Kabul. Yesterday my mother-in-law barely survived an explosion. She was about fifteen meters away from the explosion. The explosion took place in the parking lot of the Ministry of Justice. And she was just standing outside to catch a taxi.

The fear that we have today we didn't have until 2012. Even in 2012, when the bombings started, most of us were like, okay, some days an explosion takes place. But back then, the suicide bombers and car bombers were only attacking military and international targets, so most of the people who lived in Kabul were just careful to try to avoid those places. We thought, out in the rest of the city, it's okay. We thought, we will survive and live a normal life. But not now. Especially in the months since the new president has taken over. Now, there are bombings everywhere. So many of us are so afraid. We all think, today when I go out I may not come home alive. I might die in an explosion. Personally, I will not change my travel routes and plans, but now that fear exists in my mind whenever I leave home. Even when I'm just talking about it, the fear exists in me. The bombings and the attacks have created a very horrible fear in almost all the population. And people and their lives are kind of on hold. They don't want to invest, they don't want to do something new, they don't want to buy a house, they don't want to do a lot of things. Many of them say, let's see what happens. Let's wait two, three months more and then, if the government doesn't improve, let's leave the country. That's what everybody around here is saying and everybody is thinking.

What keeps me going is the vision that I have for this country, for the people of Afghanistan and for me and my family. There are times when I think, okay, I have to stop now. But then I think, I'm in a very good situation, I'm working and earning money, I've created jobs for people, and I also work teaching women entrepreneurs how to start and grow their own businesses. I start thinking to myself, I should create more employment, I should help more people, I should change the situation. And I think, if I stop my work, what will happen to all the others? If I don't do this, then others won't be able to live. That feeling of responsibility makes me keep going.

A lot of things in Afghanistan have changed and improved since 2002, the number of girls in school, the number of families who have a better attitude and mind-set about girls going to schools, about girls going to university—all that has increased. The idea of women working outside the home has gained acceptance. Women's participation in politics has gained acceptance. In 2002, it was a remarkable thing just to have women seen outside on the streets. During the Taliban years women were not even seen outside. And if they did go outside, they were underneath a burqa, fully covered. There were no schools for girls. There were no women in government offices, in the workplace, no women in the public. In 2002 when all of a sudden women came out, especially in the major cities when men saw us outside without burqas, it was very shocking to them. But today, more of our men have been exposed to the outside world. Some have gone outside of Afghanistan for education or medical treatment, or just to travel; some returned here after being refugees abroad. In other countries, they saw women working; they saw women who are athletes; women who are students; women who are managers in offices and they're walking outside without covering their heads or their whole bodies and it's fine. So that exposure to the outside world has changed men's attitudes a little bit.

But while all these things have improved, we still have major challenges—primarily the fear that some men and especially our religious leaders have about losing their power. Their power is also very much connected with the money that they can have. If women get educated and women are in power, they think, oh, those women will take our positions. They'll take our jobs. They will take our place in politics.

Too often these men use religion to keep control, preaching to people that Islam does not allow women to work outside. And unfortunately our people, even the educated segments of our society, listen so much to these religious leaders and preachers. That's the biggest challenge that we have, because those ideas and those words shape everything for us—our political participation, our economic participation, our access to education and higher education. Because it is not just our religious preachers, our mullahs, but all the men they train who follow these ideas. Today, this is less of a problem in Kabul, but in the provinces it is very, very strong. And it is only going to improve very slowly.

I've been involved with advocacy for over half a decade as a board member of the Afghan Women's Network and as the country director for PEACE THROUGH BUSINESS, which offers training programs for Afghan women in business or looking to start businesses. Right now, my dream list of what I'd like to do consists of three things. First, I'd like to work with the minister of hajj and religious affairs. After the killing of Farkhunda, our Afghan Women's Network asked to meet with him because we need his help to put together a long-term plan to work with the mullahs. We need to train a whole different society—a different mind-set for the men, especially. But to do that, we need the mullahs in our mosques to change. In our mosques, on Fridays, only men go to worship. It's not like in your churches where the women go, here only the men go for prayer, and on Fridays, the minister of the hajj gives our mullahs a subject or a theme to talk about. A lot of the time, they talk about religious practices, but one of their versions of religious practice is that the man should control his woman.

So we talked to the minister of hajj and we told him that the men going to mosques are all Muslim—they already know about religious practices. They know it is their duty to pray, it's their duty to take fast, it's their duty to recite Koran. Now it's time to tell mullahs to train these men to be kind human beings, to love other human beings in their society, to stop fighting, to stop cruelty. They need to talk about all the good things in humanity. And those ideas exist in our text, in our Koran. No one is asking them to use some outside concept from international human rights laws or to use some foreign idea from the Americans. These principles can be found in our own culture and our own religion. We just need the mullahs to teach them to our own people.

Next, I'd like to work with the minister of education to make sure that these values and principles are taught to girls and boys in high school and middle school—that both girls and boys can learn these things. The third thing would be to work toward women's economic empowerment. If we can improve the environment for women to start businesses, to expand their businesses, and to create more employment, we will be improving things not only for women but also for men. Those are the three things I would like to do immediately.

I've learned a lot since I started my own business. I was very lucky to get involved with PEACE THROUGH BUSINESS. It's a very unusual model for us here in Afghanistan. Most of the international community that comes here does what I call "one-shot training." They bring in women or men for one class, maybe for a day, or for half a day or for five days. They "train" them and then give them certificates and imagine that they all have become experts. This program has a totally different approach. We have an in-country class for two months.

And during those two months we only have one class in a week. Then throughout the week, everyone has assignments and they have to put their business plans together. It's a long process—it's not that we train them very fast and we bombard them with a lot of knowledge. We give them the knowledge over time and then we have them apply that knowledge putting together a business plan. Then after being in the program for two months, in February and March, then in July, they come to the United States for the second portion of the program, Leadership Development. In the U.S. they attend some classes and they are mentored by an American woman, which is another valuable piece. Being mentored, studying, traveling to a different place, you broaden your view, you broaden how you see your business and your life, and your whole world. These women come and see a lot of different things in the United States. And they get inspired. They love it. I love it.

The third portion of this program is "pay it forward." The program taught us—which I love the most—to take responsibility to share the knowledge that you've gained from the program with other women. It says if you are privileged enough to receive training, then you should go back and give it to some other people. You can be a multiplier, sharing it with others.

We have a saying in Afghanistan that men and women are the two wings of a bird, and a bird cannot fly with only one wing. My dream for the future of women in Afghanistan is to achieve "bird-wing," to become an active wing of Afghanistan's bird. In Afghanistan, men are one wing. Women need to fly right alongside the men, to be the "other wing."

Surviving

Old and young

Supporting each other

Cooking

No longer behind closed doors

Mother and child

Determined to overcome violence and devastation, women are rebuilding their lives. After years of cruelty, they are at last being treated with compassion.

SURVIVING

. . . .

Afghanistan is often described as "the worst place in the world to be a woman." Afghan women have their survival threatened on many fronts, starting from the moment they are born. Women often have no access to prenatal care, and many women still must get permission from male family members or even their mothers-in-law in order to be treated by a doctor. And it cannot be a male doctor; it must be a female doctor, midwife, or other female healthcare worker. Those prohibitions and the limited supply of midwives help explain why even a decade after the fall of the Taliban, one out of every eleven women was still dying over the course of her childbearing years. But the dangers do not end there.

Girls and women often must survive a gauntlet of abuse. This, however, is not simply an Afghan problem, lying only within its borders. Asía Frotan, whose mother "was always black and blue," did not set foot in Afghanistan until after the Taliban fell. She grew up in West Germany and the United States. She lived in fear in both Western nations. Indeed, the very first office of Women For Afghan Women, which provides shelter, aid, and assistance for women facing abuse and violence, opened not in Kabul, but in New York City. Then there is the larger culture of societal violence and conflict that oppresses millions of Afghans inside their nation, particularly women.

For Afghan women, survival has so many meanings. Here are the stories of women who are trying to give the gift of survival to others, who want to teach their nation and the world that, in the words of Manizha Naderi, of Women For Afghan Women, "There is no honor in punishing women."

To the outside world, Asía Frotan loves vintage fashion and seems like so many other early millennials, posting her likes on Facebook, tweeting, and sounding as if she too grew up watching The Fresh Prince of Bel-Air *and* Saved by the Bell. *Like the Fresh Prince, Asía did make it to California at the start of the 1990s, but her journey was vastly different from Will Smith's sitcom existence inside a laugh-track-enhanced Hollywood studio.*

· · · · · · · · · ·

My friends always tell me that my story should be a movie or a book. But it's really my mother's story first. My mother was born in Kabul and raised there until she was nearly sixteen. They were a successful, well-regarded family. My grandfather worked for the Afghan Justice Department, one of his brothers was a provincial governor. But in December 1979, everything changed. That year, the Soviet Union invaded Afghanistan. My grandfather's brother, the governor, was kidnapped, and my grandfather wanted to get everyone out of the country. He had nine children, five daughters and four sons. They all made it across the border to Pakistan and the city of Peshawar. Refugees were everywhere in Pakistan, but still no one was safe. In the refugee camps, in the cities, Afghan girls were being kidnapped. In Afghan culture, once you have been kidnapped, once you are suspected to have been alone in the company of men, you are ruined. No one will want you, not a future husband, not even your own family. You have been shamed and have brought shame upon your family. So my grandfather did the only thing he knew that would keep his daughters safe, he started arranging marriages for them.

Someone in the Afghan community came to him and introduced

him to a man, an architectural engineer working in the city of Peshawar, a man who spoke five languages. This man was a Palestinian, living in Jordan, and the best news of all was that he was looking for a wife. My grandfather was interested. He quickly saw a match. My mother was sixteen, this man, my father, was thirty-five. He married my mother and not long after they left the mounting chaos of Pakistan for his home in Jordan. I can only imagine my mother boarding her first plane to take her to what she thought would be her home. When they arrived in Jordan, my mother saw that her new husband had a good-size house. He also already had another wife living in that house and eight daughters. He had married my mother in the hopes of having a son.

When it came to having a son, my father was determined. His first wife was pregnant at the same time as my mom. In fact, she got pregnant first. Two months before I was born, she gave birth to a son. Then, not long after I was born, she got pregnant again and had yet another son. I was born in between two boys, and after the second boy arrived, my father had no more use for my mom. He screamed at her, he hit her, he took out every frustration on her. I was still a small child when she picked me up and fled back to her family in Pakistan. But she couldn't stay in Pakistan for too long. Conditions were no better, and inside the Afghan community, it was a shameful thing to have left one's husband and one's home.

My mother's older brothers had already gone to West Germany as refugees. My grandfather paid for my mom and me to follow them. He got her papers saying that she was a widow. Or that is what she wrote on her papers and then signed them. No one said anything. Inside Afghanistan, the mujahideen fighters were battling the Soviet troops. Widows were common. And it was the 1980s. In the world of geopolitics, we were cold war refugees and West Germany was the actual dividing line between West and East. They were the place to take us in.

ASÍA FROTAN

*   *   *

What I remember from the beginning was it being so cold. We had all arrived in our thin cotton clothes; we hardly needed coats in Pakistan, but it was freezing in Germany. At first, we stayed in what was basically a warehouse for incoming refugees, but later we were put into special housing.

The houses looked to me like little vinyl boxes, all laid out one next to the other. When you walked in, a bedroom was in front, then there was a living room to the right. Off to the left was a hallway with another bedroom, a small kitchen, and a third bedroom, plus a bathroom. There were four rooms for living spaces, split between families. My mother, my aunt, and I were crowded into one bedroom. We shared the rest of the space with an Afghan husband, wife, and their two children. We were lucky. Many times, three families shared one apartment, each taking turns with one kitchen and one bathroom.

We had a place to stay, but we were never really welcome. I was old enough by then to go to school, and school for the most part was okay. There were enough other refugees in the classes that none of us felt alone, and many of the German parents were welcoming. I even made friends with some of the girls in my class. The mother of one girl, Hanna, brought hand-me-down clothes to my mom. But outside of school, Germany was a scary place, because every day we lived knowing that we were not wanted there. All around the Afghan community, there were stories of kids disappearing. Neo-Nazis waged periodic attacks against the immigrants, and there was always violence. One time, a homemade bomb was put outside our front door. Someone saw it and we ran outside. It was a small device, I don't know what kind of damage it could have done, but just the fact that it was there at our door was enough.

Even our housing told us that we weren't wanted. Our develop-

209

ment was set apart from the town, completely by itself. We had to walk to everything, often crossing a large field. I would walk home, alone, from the bus station after school across this field, and there was always a sense of threat. Everyone told us, if someone even comes close to you, run.

Many of the people living in this housing were single mothers with children. Most found it hard if not impossible to learn German, and there was also the sense that we don't have our men to protect us. All of the Afghans largely kept to each other. But even that didn't make us feel safe.

At night, in our room, I slept on top of my mom, in her arms. I believed that if or when kidnappers came, they'd have to take both of us because we were literally bound together.

In the daytime, we had to be apart. The German welfare system wouldn't allow refugees to work. If you worked, you would be cut off from German welfare. That was hard on people like my mom, people who were naturally hardworking and wanted to save. My mom went out and found work anyway, on the side. She cleaned retail stores. She worked on an assembly line in a cookie plant, for one of the cookie brands that the Germans export and you can now find in American grocery stores. And while she was working, I was running through that big field to get back to my room.

Even regular things were hard as a refugee. Because our housing was built so far away from the town, just getting groceries was difficult. The housing complex had one or two bikes for everyone to use. We had to wait until a bike was free and then ride to the grocery store and fill as many bags with whatever we might need. It would take us forever to come back because the bikes would be so slow as we tried to ride with all those heavy bags. Sometimes my friend Hanna's mother would help us go get groceries, and that really meant everything. And to a certain degree, we had it easy. By the late 1980s, more refugees were arriving in West Germany from other conflict zones. Many of these new arrivals were also Muslim, and the Germans put them alongside us, but packed into rows of temporary trailers rather than our box homes. The number of immigrants was overwhelming, and their living situation was way worse than ours.

When my mom was about twenty-six years old and I was about eight or nine, an Afghan man flew to Germany. He was living in the United States, but like my mom, he had grown up in Kabul and he had a brother living in Germany. He had seen my mom at a wedding before the Soviet invasion. She would have been about fifteen then. His brother let my mother know that he was interested in her, and my mom agreed to meet him. Because of my grandfather's position, my mother always felt like she was being watched closely within the Afghan community, that people were monitoring her behavior and talking about her. She felt very much like a single woman with a fatherless child. She was also living in limbo, unable to have a good job, struggling with German. When this Afghan man from America arrived, they met once, talked, and that was it. They decided to get married. We took what little we had and traveled across the Atlantic and across America to Fremont, California.

We stayed there until I turned seventeen. Then, over two nights, we packed everything we could into a compact car. Between us, we had about $100 in cash. But it was enough to flee, driving east to Colorado, to Boulder, where I had already been admitted to the University of Colorado on a scholarship.

At first, when we arrived in California with my new stepdad, it seemed like it would be easy. We were coming into an established Afghan community. We moved straight into my mother's new in-laws' apartment, and there were lots of people around to show us the way. And English was much easier to learn than German. My mother had even taken some English classes back in Kabul and when she lived in Pakistan. We didn't have to struggle to get somewhere or to see a doctor. The problem was not outside; the problem was inside our home.

My mother was always black and blue. My stepfather drank, he did drugs, and he hit my mom. There were so many times. Once, they had friends over, and my father threw a crystal glass at my mother's face. The force of it shattered her cheekbone and her eye socket swelled until she couldn't see anything. The emergency room doctor kept asking her what happened, and each time my mom would say, "I just fell down."

Another time when my stepdad was beating my mom, and I was crying in my room, the cops came to our door. They knocked and came in, and my mother and I both said things were okay, but they looked around and took my stepdad to jail anyway. That was in many ways the most terrifying. We were even more scared for when he would be released and what he would do then. We went and stayed at his parents' for a while, but then we had to go back and pretend everything was okay, to act as if nothing had happened. My stepdad's mother knew about the beatings and so did his aunt, but they just said things like "he'll grow out of it."

My mother was afraid all the time. She was so fearful of what her in-laws and the Afghan community would say. And she feared my stepdad. For years, he threatened to have my mom deported back to Afghanistan. He told her that because the papers she had used to leave Pakistan for Germany had said that she was a widow, her entire immigration was based on fake information, and for that she could be deported. Of course, a lot of people came into Germany as refugees under fake information, but my mother believed him. For years, she only really had contact with her in-laws. But finally, one of her own friends in the Afghan community told her that was not true, that he could not have her deported. My stepdad also wouldn't do the paperwork so that my mom and I could get our green cards and ultimately our citizenship papers. My mother only had work authorization, nothing more.

It was 9/11 that changed things for us. After 9/11, a lot of Afghan TV channels started to pop up. Some from cable, some from satellite. My stepdad's mom and my mom watched together and sometimes I joined them. I remember one commercial and it was done like a joke. The husband does something and then the wife says, "If you touch me, I'm going to call 911." I was watching and thinking, "Why couldn't we call 911? Why do we have to live like this?" That spring, I was accepted to the University of Colorado at Boulder on a scholarship. I hadn't even finished high school, but I told my mother that I couldn't live like this any longer. Now my stepfather was not only turning on my mother, he was turning on me. My mother agreed to go.

We made it to Boulder in our little car. I finished high school and enrolled in college. I worked three jobs the first year while taking eighteen hours of credits, and we were also on welfare just to survive. But it was still very hard for my mom. She found it very hard to live in Colorado without a tight-knit Afghan community. The Afghans we knew there were an interesting mix. Many had come to the United States through Canada, and there was also a Hazara community, the Shi'ite Muslim minority that lives in Afghanistan. But most people kept to themselves. They didn't mix with each other. After I had been in school for eighteen months, we packed up and moved again, this time to northern Virginia, because we knew that there was a large Afghan community there.

*　　　*　　　*

Just as each city inside Afghanistan is different, each diaspora community outside Afghanistan is different. Fremont, California, our first home in the United States, is often called "Little Kabul." It's an established community, but in the 1990s, there were only a few well-educated Afghans and only a few immigrants we knew who were interested in furthering their own education. Many of the Afghans living there stayed on welfare, and actually took steps backward from their lives in Kabul. The teenagers joined gangs, many got involved in drugs and other bad practices. Even people who wanted to help my mother and other women like her in the same situation didn't feel empowered to do much. But the Afghans who lived in parts of Southern California were different. For them, education was much more highly regarded.

In northern Virginia, things were again very different. Many of the Afghans living there had originally settled in New York, but when they found New York too overcrowded, they came south, to Virginia. For them, the trees and the natural beauty reminded them of Afghanistan. They liked that the area had four seasons, also like home. And many were very dedicated to their education and to their community. You don't hear about Afghan gangs where I live now, instead kids join Afghan student associations. And the mosques are very proactive. They offer a lot of services and help for any struggle you might be having. It's a completely different environment from the one I remember back in California in the 1990s.

Our story does have a happy ending. I got my college degree and a master's degree. My mother went to school for cosmetology. Ten years after she left my stepdad she married again. This time it was because she really wanted to, and her marriage is a happy one. I reconnected with my biological father, and despite our very difficult beginnings, today our relationship is in a great place. He has evolved and grown. I am happy to call him "Dad," and he is happy to have me as his daughter. The changes I have seen in him make me hopeful that anyone who truly wants to can change. I also got married, to an Afghan man, something that at one time I never could have imagined doing, and now I have a young son. And before all that happened, my mother and I went "home" to Afghanistan.

When the Taliban fell, my grandfather, my grandmother, and two of their children who had stayed in Pakistan moved back to Kabul. As my grandfather said, "I am going to die in my own country." Conditions were very primitive, but they went. And not long after, my mother and I went to see them.

I know a lot of Afghans who haven't gone back since the war. My own mother-in-law and father-in-law haven't gone back. They left when my husband was only one year old. But when she was raising me, my mom would always talk about the good times in Kabul. I wasn't born there, I wasn't raised there, but through my mom's love for the country, I became attached to it. And I always grew up thinking that I wanted to go to Afghanistan. At the start of 2002, my mom and I were among the first women to travel to Afghanistan without a male escort. It was on the one hand a culture shock like no other. The city was so devastated, so destroyed that it was hard to imagine the place my mother had described. But on the other hand, it was a beautiful feeling once we got there. Once we arrived in the airport, we just felt like we were home. The dirt of Afghanistan has a pull on you; it just feels so natural to be there. I tell my friends that it's like in the movies when the child comes home from college and sees his family again. It is that same warm, cozy feeling of connection for the ones you love.

My mother goes back to Kabul every year. I go when I can. I

haven't been back since I got married, but I really want my husband to experience the country.

But for me now, the United States is home. No matter what, I know that it is home. In the beginning, when it was hard, it was very hard. It was hard too after 9/11, because we became the enemy in the U.S. Just when we thought we could take a deep breath and say this country is ours, we were rejected again.

All of these experiences, the bad and the good, have taught me to believe that there will come a better time. The fact that my mom and I can share these stories and not fall to pieces, even that is a remarkable thing. I try to use my experiences as a way to empower others.

We spent so many nights sleeping in terror, in Germany with the Neo-Nazis, in the U.S. with my stepdad. At least now at night we are able to sleep peacefully. I am so grateful just for that.

Massoma Jafari sits in her office. Behind her is a large board covered with photos of women and smiling babies. Massoma works with the Afghan Midwives Association. Afghanistan has one of the world's highest rates of maternal and child mortality. In many rural areas, men will not even allow their wives or female relatives to give birth in a hospital, insisting that they remain at home. Finding ways to reduce the large number of deaths and serious complications is a passion for Massoma, as is training more women to work as midwives. And she notes that midwives play a vital role beyond women's health. In many communities inside Afghanistan a midwife is often "the only educated woman you can find." A mother of two small children herself, Massoma is always on call, day and night.

· · · · · · · · · ·

My mother lost her mother when she was born—my grandmother died giving birth to my mom. My mom faced lots of hardships due to her mother's death. Then, my grandfather gave her away in marriage when she was just twelve years old. At age thirteen, my mother was pregnant, and she faced many, many health problems and many complications. She had her next baby at fifteen, her third child at seventeen, and I was born when she was about twenty years old.

My mother's story and my grandmother's story are what inspired me to become a midwife. I wanted to change the situation so that no woman and no family should have to suffer like that.

I started to study midwifery in 2008. At that time, one of the biggest problems was that most women were illiterate, even in the city.

Also, many families still wouldn't allow their girls to go to school and get an education. They had really bad memories from Taliban years. Families would keep the daughters in their house. The situation was particularly bad in the provinces. There, girls can't make their own decisions about their health, they are almost entirely dependent on their family and have to follow whatever decision their families make. A pregnant woman couldn't go to a clinic without permission from her mother-in-law or her husband—even often from her father-in-law.

One of my first cases when I was a student was a woman in labor who came very late to the hospital. Her baby was already in serious distress by the time she arrived. I remember our whole team asked her why she had come for help so late; we had to tell her that she might lose the baby because the situation was so serious. She was crying and she said, "My mother-in-law tried to manage the delivery at home." She explained that her mother-in-law had refused to allow her to go to the hospital because she said, "In the hospital, you don't have any privacy and everybody can see your body." So she had stayed at home. We delivered the baby, but it was born not breathing and unresponsive. One of our teachers said the baby was dead, that it had meconium and debris in its lungs. I remember how one of my classmates started crying, but she went over to the newborn baby's body and tried to clean its lungs and get it breathing. She tried and tried and tried for a very long time. Finally, after many minutes had passed, we all heard the baby's cry. The baby was alive. Then the mother-in-law started crying. Because that baby was a boy, it was the first son of her son. In Afghan culture, fortunately or unfortunately, the son is very important for the family, and without the midwives, this baby boy would have died. After that day, this mother-in-law changed her mind. She became a big advocate of going to the hospital and using midwives.

*　　*　　*

But even now, it is difficult to convince families to use midwives. We do a lot of education. Sometimes we use points from the Koran. We talk about passages in the Koran that say that a woman needs to be an independent person and that a woman's health is reflective of the health of the society. If the women in a society have good health, then that society and that society's families also have good health. And sometimes we show them evidence. We show them mortality statistics, such as how many women and babies died before there was a midwife and a clinic in the area, versus after there was a midwife, or how many women and babies suffer complications from giving birth at home, versus in a clinic. And we explain these comparisons in the local language. We also try very hard to get the families to use the clinics by explaining that their women will be seen only by trained female workers, and that we have invested a lot to train good female workers. More and more, people are willing to use midwives and clinics for delivery and to treat pregnancy complications. But for other issues, like family planning and domestic and sexual violence, we need to educate more and more.

Often in the community, when there is sexual violence or domestic violence, the midwife is the first person who faces this problem, because the victim may come to the midwife's house for treatment. Seeing this firsthand makes the issue a big concern for midwives. But according to Afghan laws on gender and sexual violence, we can't do anything beyond the most basic medical care. According to our job description, we need to intervene and to help, but according to Islam and our culture, we can't do anything.

What I think midwives can do and are doing is helping to change attitudes about women across society. There are about five thousand midwives in Afghanistan. Most of them are not just working as midwives; they are also leaders in their communities. In many families and villages, the midwife is the only educated woman you can find. Midwifery is a medical profession that requires education and it is also a business, where women can earn their own income. So, in one profession, you have women who are saving the lives of mothers and babies and also achieving economic independence. That has changed the minds of many families about the idea of women working outside of the house, even in places like Kandahar, where the position of women is very insecure.

Midwives are also in a better position than some of the other professions in Afghanistan. We have a very active association—more than three thousand midwives belong. The association is a way to build a bridge among people, a way for women all over the country to have better communication. Each midwife can have access to the experience of the other expert midwives or expert businesswomen to share knowledge. Our association also inspires others to work together. When you volunteer to help other people in your profession or your community, it shows that you have commitment to society. And people come to respect you.

But this respect is not true for all women. There is still a movement in Afghanistan against women's activities and against women activists. When I talk with my friends who work on gender issues, they tell me that they face many problems and sometimes they are afraid. Even though Afghanistan has increased the number of women who work in the government, who work in the police, who work in the army, the country didn't pay enough attention to making sure it was a proper environment for women to work in. If we don't fix those problems, women may

IN MANY FAMILIES AND VILLAGES, THE MIDWIFE IS THE ONLY EDUCATED WOMAN YOU CAN FIND.

be discouraged from working in the police and the army, especially. After so many years of hardship for women, women entrepreneurs, women in male fields, like policing, need extra protections or they face many problems. We are afraid even to go to the political parties and ask for our rights.

Compared to how things have been in the past, conditions for women have improved. In the last six years, there has been a lot of positive change in Afghanistan. In the cities, families are finally encouraging their girls to have education, to go outside more and be in the society, to work out of their houses and to participate in associations. We still have many problems in the villages, but in the cities, it's much, much better. But we are still not where we should be as a society. We need to think about that and we need to work on those areas where women are still behind.

Personally, I think that education and economic independence have had the greatest influence on changing the situation for women. Having more schools for girls, having jobs where women can work out of their houses, having organizations that women can join and belong to, all of that has increased opportunities for women and changed women's lives in the cities.

As a country, though, we need to improve our political situation, we need an end to war and at least to feel that we have "life security." And we have to stop the brain drain of our educated people so that we can be stronger and have a better economy.

Regarding the situation for women, though, nobody can help us except us. We need to work together, all the women of Afghanistan, and encourage each other to work hard and to be committed to each other. We need to build the capital of our own people. I think human capital—the knowledge, talents, skills, health, creativity, and experiences of our people—along with human resources and diversity are the most important things we have to help us change the current situation.

I have to believe in the future. I have one daughter who is five years old and then I also have one son who is nine months. Fortunately I have a husband who believes in me and supports me. I also try to support working women like myself, particularly with full-time programs in my private kindergarten to help care for their children and provide a good environment for them.

We say to the mothers, "Don't worry about your children, they're safe. Just think about society and your work." In that way, we can create change by starting with each other.

Afghan women experience the highest rates of abuse and violence in the world. Founded in 2001, Women For Afghan Women is dedicated to curbing the epidemic of violence, particularly domestic violence, and abuse against women. WAW runs domestic violence shelters and provides legal aid, mediation services, and help for women and girls who are victims of violence and abuse. In fifteen years, Women For Afghan Women has directly helped over 15,000 women and children. Eighty percent of the women seeking help in shelters inside Afghanistan stay in WAW's shelters. It has opened locations in 13 provinces and has more than 650 local Afghan staff. One of its major initiatives is to work with religious leaders to change the cultural dynamic inside Afghan society. But even that is not enough. Manizha Naderi is the organization's director. As she explains, "At least 15 percent of the women who come to our shelters cannot return home, ever." She describes the situation for women inside Afghanistan.

. . . .

My family came as refugees to the United States after the Soviet invasion. I went back to Afghanistan in 2003. One of the first places I visited was a women's prison in Kandahar. I could not believe the conditions. Most of the women who were jailed had been accused of "moral crimes," and had been put there because they ran away from home, because they were escaping forced marriages, beatings, or they had been raped. They were the rape victims and they were jailed. Women who run away from violent situations are often accused of *zina*, sexual relations outside of marriage, and are punished for that. Under the Taliban especially, if a woman ran away or was even simply seen on the streets alone, she was put in prison. Many of these women also had their children living with them, in the prison.

I decided right then that I had to go back to Afghanistan. I wanted to open up shelters to keep them safe, to keep them out of prison.

Many of the women who come to us are so broken. They have been tortured by their families, they have been sold, they have been burned with flames or acid. We had a girl who was not yet eighteen whose father was pressuring her to marry a forty-five-year-old man. When she refused, her father and brother beat her, stabbed her, and then her father slit her throat. She described it to us, saying, "He began to slaughter me like a sheep." Her father and brother left her for dead. When she awoke, she told us, "I pushed my intestines back into my body" and managed to get help. After she was treated in the hospital, she came to one of our shelters. She had lost the ability to speak. We worked with her to help her recover and to learn to talk again. Another one of our clients had acid poured on her face by a man she refused to marry. And then there is Gul Meena, whose brother struck her with an axe fifteen times when she ran away with another man to escape her abusive sixty-five-year-old husband. She had been married off to him when she was about twelve years old and he started having sex with her then. She fled when she was seventeen. Her brother tried to kill her for "honor." He said he was maintaining the family's honor.

There is no honor in punishing women.

What warms my heart is when I go to one of our shelters and see women who have been there for three or four months, women who when they first arrived didn't want anything, didn't even want to talk. Now they are taking literacy classes. After never being educated, they are learning for the first time how to tell time, how to count money, how to write their name.

Shelters alone are not the long-term answer. We have to change the entire view of the culture, men and women. Most Afghan women want to stay with

THERE IS NO HONOR IN PUNISHING WOMEN.

their families. Once they come to a shelter, it is very hard to leave.

Along with offering them a safe place to stay, we offer family mediation. We don't just meet with the family, we also send our caseworkers on unannounced visits to the homes. About 70 percent of our cases are solved through mediation, but if mediation is unsuccessful or too dangerous, we will go to court.

Every mediation case is different. Sometimes it is a girl who has run away because she is being forced by her father to marry someone. Or it is a girl who wants to marry someone else, someone she chose, not a man of her family's choosing. We start by having a caseworker talk to the girl, then, if it's safe, we call the father. We know most of the time that he wants to save the honor of the family, he wants it to stay a secret that his daughter has run away. We do have fathers who in the beginning are very aggressive, saying, "I can take her away." Our caseworkers are trained to talk to the father, to get his side. The caseworkers also try to make him understand that in Islam, it's illegal to force your daughter to get married. We will also bring in religious community leaders to talk to him, even law enforcement. We explain that there is no gray area in forced marriage. The daughter has to be old enough and she has to agree to the marriage on her own.

In the cases where the husband is beating the wife, it is more difficult. We won't send his wife home until he agrees to certain conditions. We also do a lot of counseling over a couple of months to watch the situation so that we can feel she will be safe at home. Before she leaves, we have the family sign a paper allowing our caseworkers to come into the house at any time.

We do meet with resistance. We have people who argue that we are spreading Christianity by trying to change these practices, so we often use Islamic Sharia law experts who can explain what is written in the Koran. We have one man who works with us who has debated with the Taliban on Islamic law and practices and has won. He also receives death threats from Taliban supporters, but he keeps working with us.

Our first family guidance center opened in 2007. Now we have expanded our work to 13 provinces. Often community leaders are the ones asking us to expand to their province. We now have a staff of 650 people, and we include a human rights and domestic violence training program. We also have four children's support centers to help the hundreds of children who are imprisoned simply because their mothers have been sent to jail. We take them out of the prisons, get them education, get them counseling. These kids are so hungry for learning. Many of our kids do better in school than those who have both their parents and a home to live in.

We also take in girls who have been victims of sexual violence. We had one girl, Husnia, who came to us when she was five years old. She was raped; her father had driven her hundreds of miles from her village to Kabul for medical help. But once she was released from the hospital, she could not go back to her village. She would be seen as having brought dishonor on her family and her village, and she might be killed. Her father left her at one of our centers. Eight years later, she was still living at our center and attending school. And finally, in a rare occurrence, her village said they would accept her back. This time, it was her father who said no, he wanted her to live in Kabul and only return to visit. He made that choice because Husnia, his daughter, was the only girl from her village who had learned to read. Her father wanted her to keep studying. On her trips home to visit, she has started teaching reading and writing to other girls.

In addition to our shelters and our centers, we operate two other types of housing, long-term transition houses and separate halfway houses for women coming out of prison or women who have been living in our shelters and cannot return home. In both of these situations, women have a very difficult time. They often cannot return to their communities; their families don't accept them. Women leaving prison are especially vulnerable. Most end up on the street, begging or working as prostitutes.

In addition to our shelter work, we also provide literacy and life skills training to women across the country. If women know their rights and their worth, they can also learn that they don't have to accept violence, forced marriages, and other practices. And we have a comprehensive training and outreach program called Women's Rights ARE Human Rights. We work with mullahs, community leaders, teachers, health-care workers, law enforcement, and government officials to explain women's rights under Islam and civil law. We've reached over 250,000 people just through training. And I think we've definitely changed the culture of a great many of the individual families we have worked with.

Afghanistan has always been a patriarchal country. Today, having a conservative religion, war, and poverty all together is a really bad recipe. On the one hand, I'm surprised at how well many people are doing actually, after living for almost forty years, a whole lifetime, in war.

We also have to understand that cultural change takes a long time. Think of how things were in the United States sixty or seventy years ago. Compared to today, there were almost no civil rights and not many women's rights as we know them now. I believe that in Afghanistan, if education prevails, if security prevails, then change will come.

In Afghanistan, I believe that the men have also suffered. Nobody has ever told them that the things they are doing are against Islam. For years, no one has offered them a new way to live.

When her father announced that she was to be married, Laila Hayat was turning fifteen and was a student in the eighth grade. Her fiancé was thirty-three years old, eighteen years her senior. That was more than twenty years ago. Laila considers herself fortunate—she has a strong marriage, her husband allowed her to continue her education, gave her permission to travel to see her family, and she has never suffered spousal battery, unlike so many other Afghan women—but she also sees herself as a victim because she had no say at what age she wanted to get married, or to whom.

After the Taliban fell, she heard about a UN safe house for abused women. She went to the organization and told them that she was interested in helping other women. Her youngest child was just a baby. She is now a caseworker at a women's shelter run by Women For Afghan Women and has come dangerously close to sacrificing her own life for her job. Although she has never been outside of Afghanistan, Laila speaks with the same brisk authority as many American and immigrant women who have grown up in one of New York City's five boroughs. There is steel along with compassion.

. . . .

There is a sense of shame in coming to the shelter. We have to be very patient. We want the woman to know that she is there to get help, not to be judged. We take her into a calm room; we ask her if she is hungry and offer her something to eat, we ask about her children. We have to build trust.

Women come to us with many problems. Sometimes it is family violence. Sometimes it is forced marriages, such as a seventy-year-old man who takes a young girl for his wife. Or a father may give away his own daughters to a family in a trade in order to take another wife from that same family. In Baghlan province in the northeast, a father gave away his eleven- and twelve-year-old daughters so he could buy himself a new bride. Sometimes it is economic problems, such as not being allowed to have a job or to have any money of their own. Men get remarried, so there might be other wives. Women have to take care of the other wives' children or they might be forced to take care of a relative's children, like a husband's brother, in addition to taking care of their own kids. Girls in a family might not be allowed to go to school. Many times, when a brother commits a crime, it is the sister that is taken away and thrown in jail instead. Even if the brother is convicted, he remains free. The sister serves his jail sentence.

All of these are abuses. They are caused by many problems, lack of security, lack of education, more than thirty years of war. Also, many traditions that have been going on for a long time in society are not good traditions.

In Afghanistan, what the woman wants is not important. Women do have rights because in 1948 the Afghan government signed the United Nations Universal Declaration of Human Rights, but many people do not recognize those rights or do not realize that women have them. As a society, too many Afghan people are not aware of who has what rights or what rights other people may have.

WOMEN DO HAVE RIGHTS BECAUSE IN 1948 THE AFGHAN GOVERNMENT SIGNED THE UNITED NATIONS UNIVERSAL DECLARATION OF HUMAN RIGHTS, BUT MANY PEOPLE DO NOT RECOGNIZE THOSE RIGHTS OR DO NOT REALIZE THAT WOMEN HAVE THEM.

Each situation is different and each requires a different solution. Often, after we have spoken with the woman, we try to find an elder in the family whose words will carry weight in the family. We work on that elder, we have counseling with him, meetings with him. We try to convince this person that there is wrongdoing inside the family and then ask for his help to fix it. We also have psychologists who can meet with the family and do family counseling. We discuss everything from the Islamic point of view and the human rights point of view. We also always make the woman who is there aware of her rights. With people who live in the cities, talking to them about their rights is more effective because they have more education. Outside of the cities, it is more effective to come at things from a religious point of view. That way they can research their religion and prove it.

You never know how a case is going to turn out. About five years ago, a girl from Kandahar came to one of our shelters. Her husband was a member of the Taliban and he would beat her. He did not allow her to visit her family on a regular basis. She was not happy, but she did not believe in divorce because the stigma is too great. She moved back in with her mother and brother. We checked on her for over a year, and everything seemed fine. Then four years after she had left her husband, the police came to our offices. They asked us for the reason why she had been staying in our shelter. We told them, but we were suspicious about why they were there. Finally they explained. After four years, her husband had come for her and killed her.

A few months ago, a twenty-two-year-old girl came to our door. She had studied pediatrics and was working as a pediatrician. Her father was a military man in the Afghan army. She had fallen in love with a boy that she wanted to marry, but her father was against it. He had his own prospect picked out for her. When women and girls come to us, we have them stay for as long as they need because often it is not safe for them to go back to their families. We asked her mother to come to us and thought maybe she could speak to her husband, but the mother said, "I'm not going to tell my husband what to do." It was clear that she was scared of him too. We asked the mother who the elder in the family would be, she thought it was his sister. We spoke to her, and the girl's family said, let us think about it.

In the meantime, we checked out the boy to make sure that he didn't have any problems. Then I suggested a meeting at our offices between the boy and his parents and the girl and her parents. Many times, I had heard the girl's father threaten me, threaten that he was going to kill me. He said that I was trying to destroy his reputation and his values by not letting his daughter marry the man he had chosen. But I have heard that from other fathers before.

On the day of the meeting, the girl's father saw the boy on the street outside. I watched the girl's father pull out a gun, a revolver. Without thinking, I jumped in front of the boy. The father fired three shots. I remember two of them, one right by the side of my leg, one by the side of my body. The bullets whistled by me, but each missed me. I don't know why I did it, but in that minute after those three shots, I ran at him. We struggled, and I grabbed the gun out of his hand. We stayed like that until the police came. They took away his gun because it was a government gun and he had not used it for a military purpose. And they took him away too. For three days, he was held by the police and kept in a Kabul holding cell. After they released him, he came back to the shelter with his wife to see me and to apologize. He said that he took out the gun thinking that "you would get scared, but instead you came after me and that was very brave." He asked me why I did it, and I told him that I had invited that boy and his family here. If something had happened to him, it would have been my fault.

I did not tell this father that after the police left and I went back inside the main office, I broke down and started crying and crying. Everyone in our office hugged me as I cried, and asked, Why did you put your own life in danger? I said because a young boy could have been shot, but all the time I was crying. I kept thinking about my own children, my son who is twenty and has a computer science degree, and my two daughters, fifteen and thirteen, who are still in school. I am responsible for them, what would they have done if something had happened to me?

After the father came back to apologize, we got a signed letter from him stating that he wasn't going to harm his daughter and we taped a CD where he promised that he would marry the girl to the boy of her choice. Only then did we let the daughter go home. I am visiting the family on a regular basis to make sure that everything is okay. The girl is not engaged, but she is spending time with the boy's family now.

For my own children, most of all I want to make sure that they are educated. I've reared my daughters to be independent. I don't go around like traditional Afghan mothers washing and cleaning up after them; I want them to be able to do things for themselves. As they grow up, my husband and I have given our daughters as many rights as we can at the appropriate ages.

Laila's cell phone rings. It is her father calling, worried because it will soon be dusk and she has not come home. She assures him that she is leaving soon. She explains that her father happens to be at her house tonight—it is the eve of an Afghan national holiday. If he were not there, her husband would be the one calling, wanting to know where she is. The streets of Kabul are not very safe once it gets toward nighttime, particularly for women.

Najia Nasim is the country director for Women For Afghan Women. She grew up in Afghanistan and spent time as a refugee in Pakistan. In 2013 she graduated from Bucknell University in Pennsylvania with a 4.0 GPA, an education made possible by a scholarship from the Initiative To Educate Afghan Women—a program she had heard about by accident when she was taking an English test.

Her first school in the United States was Brenau University in Gainesville, Georgia. "I taught English in Pakistan for five years, but when I arrived in the U.S., I did not know what they were talking about. The accent in the South is really different from the northern part," she recalls. She even had a hard time understanding her professors and following the discussion. "I told one of my professors and she told me that listening is also participating. I always remember that. Even when you listen, you are participating." After transferring to Bucknell, she pursued a double major in accounting and economics and worked as a teaching assistant in the economics and business departments. Her students selected her as the TA of the year. When she returned to Afghanistan, she initially worked for the Afghan government, but wanted a more hands-on experience. From her home in Kabul, Najia talks about her work with domestic violence victims and the state of Afghanistan today.

. . . .

Before I took this job [country director for Women For Afghan Women] I didn't know that there was so much violence against women going on in Afghanistan. I was raised in Kabul, I didn't have it in my own family. And in many other families, normally, most people look the other way. Only when it's some kind of shocking case, especially cases of violence involving children, do people pay attention. If it's on TV, the majority of people know, but if it's not, often only the people who are involved in our organization are aware of the case.

A lot of this problem is cultural. In Afghanistan, culture is more powerful than right or wrong. Social norms and cultural norms have their own power, particularly in the provinces and the smaller cities. These places are often very small. When something happens in a house all the villagers know about it. If someone in your village says bad things about you, that's going to damage the honor of your family. And if you live in a village, you have no option to move. So that's why people try to keep family violence and abuse as secret as possible.

If we provide services to a woman at one of our women's protection centers, they do not want their own relatives, let alone other families, to know. Especially in the provinces, most cases are dealt with by the elders. People don't want to go to the police because it causes more exposure. The majority of the time, they don't want to go through the justice system. Even just coming to our shelters has a stigma. Many people believe that the women who come here are not good people.

We also have to worry about the staff who work at these centers. Afghanistan is a country that we know is violent. We have fighting with DAESH, which is what we call ISIS in Afghanistan, with the Taliban, with all the antigovernment forces. These are people at war, and they are also against women who work outside of the home. They are very much against the type of services that we provide at women's protection centers. So, if we are visible, that could bring harm to the staff and make our clients even more worried about coming here. It takes time to change all these things, especially because we are a war-torn country.

I really do believe that if we had better security and everything was okay, it would be much easier for our organization and others to work in remote areas and reach the people who lived there, so they can see that the idea of a women's protection center is not bad, and they can see what we do.

The turmoil in society is even more challenging for us because it definitely makes the situation at home worse for women and children. The extreme types of cases that we deal with sometimes are truly shocking. They make you sick. We had a case that got a lot of attention in our media; it was the story of a two-year-old girl who was raped. But it's one thing when you see the story on TV or read about it. It's very different when, like us, you actually see that child sitting there in front of you. You can see everything that has been done to that child. Or other cases, like a woman who had acid thrown on her head and her face at an engagement party. Or a girl about twelve or thirteen years old married off to an older man, and her in-laws tried to force her into prostitution. When she refused, they locked her in a basement for six months and they tortured her, even pulling out her nails, taking the flesh off her fingers.

When you are an outsider and you read about these cases, you can stop reading or put it aside. But when you are seeing the client, it is a very different experience. I find myself asking how can it be that we are living in a Muslim country? I ask what is Islam's faith and why are people not following it? Why are they forcing these child marriages or raping children? Some days, there is an overwhelming frustration about why this is happening.

I think it's hard for people in other countries to understand or to feel what the people inside Afghanistan are feeling. It's different to be the ones that are actually experiencing the conflict. People in other parts of the world who have always lived in peace take it for granted. But for someone like me, my whole life, my country has been at war.

All I remember from my childhood is war in Afghanistan. After we were invaded in 1979, we never experienced peace inside Afghanistan. Now, it's like people are getting used to war. It's easy to say as an explanation, but it's really very hard to live in that situation. When you live like this, all you can think about is security. There is no space to think about other things. Even the mind cannot be peaceful. Only when our security is okay will we have time to think about other things.

If you live in the United States or in other countries, you learn that there are certain areas where people don't go at night. When I lived in the state of Georgia in the U.S., our host families said that there were some places where it is not safe for a woman to drive through at night. But that's something that people know, and normally those people who care about their lives don't drive there alone at night. But in Afghanistan, things can happen anywhere, at any time, day or night. When I go to the office just to do my job, I have to worry about suicide attacks. I'm not worried about my job; I'm worried about what is going to happen on the way to my job or on my way home. When people go out in the morning they have no idea whether they will come back alive because they might be caught in a suicide attack. It's completely unpredictable. So that's the kind of mind-set that people already have every day. And we can't escape that.

If you ask people what their top priority is, almost everyone would say "security." For the Afghan people, security means that there is no fighting, no guns. You can safely go from one place to another, whether from home to school, or home to the bazaar. You can safely go from one province or district to another. And nobody harms you. That is the security that the people of Afghanistan want.

ONLY WHEN OUR SECURITY IS OKAY WILL WE HAVE TIME TO THINK ABOUT OTHER THINGS.

238

Right now, people are very afraid to travel by road. Because if they travel by road, they don't know whether fighters or bandits will stop the car and kill the passengers or just kidnap them for a ransom. There is also fighting near many of the roads. A couple of weeks ago, I was out in the provinces and I wanted to travel between two towns.

IF YOU ASK PEOPLE WHAT THEIR TOP PRIORITY IS, ALMOST EVERYONE WOULD SAY "SECURITY." FOR THE AFGHAN PEOPLE, SECURITY MEANS THAT THERE IS NO FIGHTING, NO GUNS.

They are only a half-hour drive apart, but I couldn't make the trip because there was fighting and the road was blocked.

When security gets bad in parts of the country, most organizations just close their offices. But with our offices, I can't just close them down. I'm responsible not only for our staff but also for our clients and the children we have at our centers. We have a center in Kunduz that had sixty children in it. When the fighting got bad around Kunduz, we had to evacuate those sixty children on the spot. We had to put them in cars and take them away. It would have been easier to keep the children there, but we couldn't take the risk.

This lack of security affects us as a country in all kinds of other ways. Now we have more resources to send girls to school, and we are changing people's minds to believe that sending girls to school is good. But even when people want to send their daughters to school, they are afraid to because of the lack of security. So girls don't go to school, and they can't go to work. More women in a number of the provinces would like to work—their families even want them to work—but the security situation is not good enough. And when the security is bad, then there are also often not enough jobs.

From all of this, we are losing some of our best and brightest people. When I went to apply for a visa to go to India for a week, there were so many people at the office applying for an Indian visa or a visa to go to Pakistan. Some were there because of medical conditions, because we don't have very good medical treatment in Afghanistan. And when you start to look at all these issues—lack of security, no or poor education, high unemployment, little healthcare—many of us feel a lot of frustration. We see people who were good students, who have good degrees and are scholars, and they are leaving Afghanistan. They are leaving for other countries because they don't have enough opportunities here.

Afghanistan is not such a big country—it's not like the United States. It's more like a large U.S. state. But there is so much war going on and so many people are just fighting, for what? What do they want? Much of the time they are targeting civilians. It's the regular people who are getting killed. Now we have more people traveling to other countries and they can see the changes in other places, they can see the peace and security that exists in these other places, the strong implementation of law, and everything else. But then when you compare these places to Afghanistan, it makes you upset. It makes you wonder, why is it like that?

I think a big part of the problem is how many of these people that are fighting are trained. It's kind of injected into them that if you go and kill these groups or those groups of people, then you will be rewarded. You will be rewarded in paradise. And after they hear this enough, they just want to go and kill themselves and kill all the other people.

Just like the cultural norms are more powerful in our society than right or wrong, sometimes religious issues are more powerful. The people who want war also sometimes misuse religious issues. They take advantage of people who are illiterate, who are not educated enough to know what exactly the religion they believe in says.

*　　*　　*

It's not easy to change people's minds from ideas that they have believed for a long time. It's hard work. In many ways, our country is struggling with some of the same issues that we are at our protection centers. The people who do violence against their wives and their daughters have to have their minds changed, but changing those people's minds takes time. So we know that we also have to work very hard to try to change the mind-set of our clients, the women and girls who have been victims. We try to help them be strong, to see that this violence happens but that does not mean it is the end of their lives. There are solutions. We give them possible solutions and say what they need to do is pick one. But getting our clients to a place where they can be strong enough and bold enough to be more hopeful about life takes time. And we have to be patient, because sometimes the client expects to be there sooner or for things to be better sooner. It takes time, it takes patience and courage and skills to work with these types of clients, to get them to a different type of life.

The good thing about my work here in this field is that I can see the results. It is practical, it is visible; you can see what we do for a client from beginning to end. It's not like policy writing, where you can't see the results that much. It's like a doctor who is treating the patient, so they can see the improvement in the patient, or a teacher who helps a student. When I was a teacher, and I saw the improvements that my students made over the semester and in their exams, it gave me a good feeling. What I had taught my students, they got it. So if we can change even one person's life now, it gives all of us in the office satisfaction.

One of the biggest successes that we have had is with the children of Afghan women in prison. If these children stay in prison with their mothers and are raised in prison, there is a high probability that

IN AFGHANISTAN, HOPE IS A
VERY COMPLICATED SUBJECT.

they will become criminals because of what they see there. We take the children out of the prisons, and we provide them with education, shelter, food, clothing, everything. To see those kids smiling and happy and learning, it makes me proud. One of these children just turned eighteen, and he was admitted to university. If we did not support him, what would have happened to him? So that's the way we can see successes, even if they are small.

In Afghanistan, hope is a very complicated subject. We cannot just say, yes, we are hopeful. It's hard to predict what is going to happen in Afghanistan. There are many reasons, like the security situation, why people are losing hope.

But it's an altogether different kind of thing to say that we *have* to be hopeful. Everyone who is committed to Afghanistan, everyone here who is trying to do something to make the country better is putting their own life at risk. There are people who are risking their lives to work for women's rights and children's rights. Those people and their work tells all of us that there are still people who want to fight for us, for our people, for our country, for our human rights. The energy of those people, the commitment that they have, gives us hope.

Now it is our responsibility to build up a feeling of hope for our fellow Afghans. If we don't give them hope, if we don't give them support, we are not going to bring about change.

We have to make all of them hopeful to life.

Challenging

Laura Bush with Onaba Payab, 2014 valedictorian of AUAF

Farkhunda's casket at her funeral

Speaking out

Voting

"A tree doesn't move unless there is wind" (traditional Afghan proverb). Working together, often against overwhelming odds, Afghan women are leading their nation in a new direction and toward a better future.

CHALLENGING

. . . .

In 1931, the suffragette and philanthropist Alva Belmont expressed her wish that American women would serve as a beacon of light, telling not only the story of what they had accomplished, but also showing "our determination" that women around the world shall be "free citizens, recognized as the equals of men." Today, no nation needs the glow of that beacon of light more than Afghanistan. The gains for Afghan women and girls, while encouraging and even in many ways remarkable, are also fragile. And they are uneven.

A great divide still exists between women in urban areas and the millions of women who live a rural life. Conditions are particularly difficult for widows, who make up roughly 5 percent of the population and are often shunned and forced into begging or prostitution to support themselves and their children. In Afghanistan, the average age of a widow is thirty-five.

Even now, while women have political rights and the right to vote, frequently their voices are not heard. When Afghanistan's president nominated Anisa Rasooli to serve on the Afghan Supreme Court, the first such nomination of a woman in the nation's history, she failed to win confirmation in Parliament by nine votes on a secret ballot. Afghanistan has sixty-nine female members of Parliament. But twenty-three were absent on the day of the historic vote. Now Afghanistan's women must wait for another "next time."

There are, however, many reasons to be hopeful. Inside Afghanistan, there are brave women who are not afraid to challenge current beliefs and conditions. They are not afraid to speak their minds and to stand up and be counted. As they press forward to create a better nation for all Afghan citizens, perhaps around the world many more women and men will join together to help light their way.

Naheed Esar was destined to be an activist—her grandmother was a mujahideen commander. But her personal road has taken many turns. She spent years working with Afghan widows, perhaps the most marginalized group in Afghanistan, many of whom are forced to turn to begging or prostitution just to survive. Today, she works as an analyst with Afghanistan Analysts Network, where among other things she has analyzed the state of society and the events surrounding the brutal murder of the female religious scholar Farkhunda in Kabul in March 2015.

. . . .

My grandmother, my father's mother, was a commander in the mujahideen during the Russian times. She was a freedom fighter, fighting against the Russians who had invaded, but also fighting in the community to try to educate girls. My grandmother was illiterate herself, but she helped to establish two or three schools in our village. When she died, about two thousand villagers came to her funeral. She was one of the strongest elders in our village.

And not only did she have so much power in public, but even in private she was a very powerful woman. From the time that I was very young, I used to sit with her until very late at night and she would tell me stories about Afghan women, about their struggles and her struggles. One time during the winter, when she was seven months pregnant, one of our relatives beat her and threw her out of the house. He beat her so badly that she bled the whole night. And the weather in that village is really, really cold in winters, so she could barely survive until the morning. Then in the morning her children took her to the hospital.

She was a second wife, and her mother had been a widow. I've heard that her mother was a very strong woman too.

When you talked to my grandmother, you wouldn't think that she was illiterate. She was very smart. Once, I remember I told her about Hitler. I was sitting with her and someone on the radio mentioned Hitler and she asked me who Hitler was. So I gave her the whole history of World War II and of Hitler, how he killed millions of Jews and all that. And then the next day I saw her talking to a group of women in the village and basically telling them everything I told her. I wondered how she could remember all that. But she would basically take all the stories from all the people around her and then tell all the women of the village. She was a bridge. I think my desire to be a bridge came from her.

She was also a very devout Muslim woman and a very nationalistic woman who had raised twelve sons—I have eleven uncles. When the Russians invaded and took power she couldn't bear having them around. She gave all kinds of support to the mujahideen. She smuggled goods to them, she housed them, and because she was a woman, the police didn't suspect her. I don't think you can call her a spy; she was more like the mother of the mujahideen. And she was a voice for the female mujahideen. She also had the trust of the people. She had lived her whole life in the village. People knew her very well. They knew her family.

When I sat beside her and listened to her stories, she used to teach me to always raise my voice. In Afghanistan, for years, most of the women did not actually speak for their rights. My grandmother told me to risk everything to speak for my rights. And all the stories that my grandmother told me showed me from a very early age that there is so much that needs to be done in this country for women.

Let me tell you this story from my grandmother. She always used to say "A person has two hands, left and right. In many societies the right is the man and the left hand is the woman. In Afghan society, both right and left hand is the man." She said this because there are literally no limitations—no social limitations—on Afghan men. So because there is no limitation on men, women have to carry almost all of the limitations, to accept all the social barriers on themselves.

My mother also became an activist. So from the very beginning, these two women made me want to do something when I see bad things happening or when I see women who are in danger.

I was sixteen years old when I started the very first project in my village on women's teenage sexuality, which is a very sensitive subject to discuss in Afghanistan. Everyone told me, "Don't do something like this because it will turn out to be a disaster because no one will actually tell you about their feelings, considering that this subject is very taboo in Afghanistan." But in fact the opposite happened to me. Every single woman wanted to talk about it. And I realized how much we need to actually understand our own society, rather than just accepting what everyone else tells us about our society.

The women I talked to told me about their love affairs, and they told me about their internal feelings and how either their families or the society had forced them into marriages, sometimes forcing them to marry their own relatives. Both Afghan women and also foreigners have this idea that Afghan women are so vulnerable that they actually give up, that they don't fight back, and that's why they're forced into arranged marriages. But I saw that a number of women fought against these marriages right up to the very end.

After that I got very interested in studying our culture. I saw a very big need for research, especially deep qualitative research. I entered Kabul University in 2005. But even though I grew up around so many brave women, going to university, I was also afraid of ruining my reputation. Both my mother and my grandmother had told me that "You, as a girl, are like a piece of white fabric. If you do even something very small, it will put a stain on the fabric for all to see. Your brother is like a piece of black cloth, he can do anything and it will not be seen." So I did not talk to any boys in the school; I did not talk to any of my professors, because they were all men.

But even staying silent is no guarantee of safety. As in other areas of Afghan life, girls studying at the university were subjected to harassment, to older men who told them that they wanted to make these girls their "special friend." Many girls and women are afraid to speak out about sexual harassment and intimidation because to do so brings dishonor upon themselves and their families. Women who do speak out risk being killed by their own relatives simply because they are seen to have "brought shame" upon the family. But seeing women around me who were trying so hard to get an education and had to face these unwanted advances, I decided that I could not stay quiet. I decided that even if nothing changed, at least I wouldn't be guilty of having said nothing.

I went to many classrooms on campus and spoke about sexual harassment. I got other students to sign up to join my cause. We had some meetings. We held some protests. We went to the minister of education, because it is not just the women who are victims, it is the men as well. Men who harass women are victims of our culture and of decades of silence. But then a dean told me to stop speaking about these things in public; he has even told me that he can take my diploma back. There are a lot of things that people can do in Afghanistan, especially to women, because we don't have good legal protections.

My story has a good ending because no one ever did take away my diploma and eventually I got a Fulbright scholarship to study in the United States. It is one of the most prestigious scholarships you can get, and I give thanks to the U.S. government and the American people who pay for the scholarships with their taxes. I studied for three years in the U.S. Now I am back working as a researcher and an analyst.

I didn't apply for my scholarship right away. After I left the university I worked with widows for five years.

I have some friends who are widows in the United States. It's very different to be a widow in Afghanistan. In the U.S. every person is considered an individual from the beginning of his or her life. In Afghanistan, all women are dependent. Even in the educated community, a woman is often defined as being a wife, a mother, a sister, a daughter; she is defined by the identity of the men in her family. A woman is not defined by herself as a woman but by her relationship to a man.

In Afghanistan, the widow has no one. She is no one. She has no one in her own family to help her because she's been married, and once you're married you're out of the house and you're your husband's wife. She's no longer a daughter; now she's a wife. Most of the widows in Afghanistan are about thirty-five years of age, due to all the wars and conflicts. Many of these women don't have older sons, so they can't even be identified by their son's name. I think the lack of identity is what makes them socially very vulnerable. Many of the widows I talked to were harassed even by their neighbors. They were afraid because people knew that they didn't have a male to support them. Often, they are asked to have affairs with the men outside of the family because they are considered to be even less without a man, and everyone can take advantage of them. That makes them very vulnerable.

EVEN IN THE EDUCATED COMMUNITY, A WOMAN IS OFTEN DEFINED AS BEING A WIFE, A MOTHER, A SISTER, A DAUGHTER; SHE IS DEFINED BY THE IDENTITY OF THE MEN IN HER FAMILY.

Even the widows who try to get jobs, if they tell the men at work "I'm a widow," the men will ask them for affairs. In Afghanistan a girl must be a virgin until she's married. And once she's married, she has a husband. Widows are not girls, which means they aren't virgins, nor are they wives any longer. So they were the biggest targets.

I did many things with the widows. I even helped build a community of five hundred homes for widows and I did research in different communities of widows, many of whom become prostitutes or use drugs, like heroin.

When I was working with these women, after a while they would just tell their very, very dark deep stories that they did not tell anyone. At first, I was like anyone else; they didn't want to say anything. But because I kept going to their houses, because I kept talking to them, they started to trust me. I didn't even cover my face with a scarf or anything, to gain their trust I would rather not hide my face.

After I had spent so many years listening to these women, I started to feel a pain in my shoulder. I went to a doctor in Pakistan, at an Islamabad hospital. He told me that I had stress hearing all these stories, that I needed to take a break. I was wondering what I should do, when some of my friends advised me to go for my master's. They said maybe it can help to be away from the country for a few years.

One of the stories of the widows still brings tears to my eyes. I would go to each house many times. Most of them had a *toshak*, which is like a mattress or a pillow and is basically an Afghan couch. I would sit there and talk to them. In order to not distract them I would not take any notebook or anything. They would just talk and I would keep all the things that they said in my memory and write it down later. This one woman was a prostitute and she was using drugs. She was a widow, she had a second husband, who also used drugs, and she had four very cute girls. The oldest one was twelve and the youngest one was something like three and a half. And the minute I entered the house I saw the look in the eyes of the three-and-a-half-year-old girl and I knew everything was wrong. She literally started crying seeing me. So I talked to the daughters and I talked to the woman. After a really long time they told me that even the three-and-a-half-year-old girl was a prostitute.

The pain in the bodies of all these girls, even the three-and-a-half-year-old, was obvious. I took them to a hospital and in the hospital, the oldest ones were not okay, of course, and they all had inhaled the smoke from the drugs, but the three-and-a-half-year-old also had bleeding. The doctor kept telling me not to let her be forced into prostitution. But what was I to do? I, myself, am a poor girl. I can't financially support these families. Even if I financially supported this family, the husband could just take all the money and go and buy drugs, and force the girls into prostitution all over again. But I kept going to their house. Eventually the group I was working with was able to take the mother with the children to one of the drug clinics in Kabul. But that story has really haunted me.

When you go to the houses of these widows, the houses are mostly mud. They're rarely painted. Mostly they have their kitchen in the hallway—they don't even have a separate kitchen. The bathrooms are in very bad condition because poor families don't have commodes and toilets to sit on. So you can see the fluids and everything. But particularly in the cases when the widow is using drugs, the first thing you can see in the house, that you can feel in the house environment, is the depression. You rarely see smiling faces. When you talk to them, you can feel that they can't really concentrate on talking to you unless it is when they go to their deep, dark stories and they tell you how badly they live. That's when they really concentrate and talk to you. But then sometimes they just cry and can't say anything.

In Afghanistan, a woman is considered a pot without a lid, but a widow is a pot that has lost her lid. Many widows suffer from depression and trauma. They often cannot support their families and most of them are illiterate. If a woman's husband dies suddenly, all the burden and responsibility is on her; she has to take care of the whole family. It was also the tradition in some areas that once a woman's husband dies, the widow is supposed to marry the brother-in-law or someone else within the husband's family. These are the types of situations that lead these women to turn to prostitution and then to drugs to try to get rid of the depression. Sometimes, because of their occupation, because of becoming prostitutes, they started doing drugs. The more drugs they did, the deeper they got into prostitution. In some cases it was the drugs that got them into prostitution, but in other cases it was prostitution that got them into drugs.

Prostitution is not accepted at all in Afghan society. In some provinces, they actually kill prostitutes. Most of the women in prison in Afghanistan, in Kabul and other places, are women who either committed adultery, or were raped, or were somehow involved in sexual activities. That's one of the reasons why these women took a long time to tell me they were prostitutes. They are very afraid. They are afraid of their landlord asking them to leave their house, the house they were renting, because very often the minute the landlord finds that they use drugs and they are prostitutes, they are thrown out of the house. And even those who have their own houses, their neighbors will ask them to leave the house.

The widows who were using drugs, sometimes it seemed like they didn't even care. They had already been cut off from everything.

I definitely had some difficulties when I started working with the widows and interviewing and researching their lives. I had to communicate differently. It took me a while to be able to eat their food. One time I went to a widow's house and what she cooked you couldn't really eat because the amount of oil in that food was like a river. For these women, it's how they try to be super-hospitable to a guest because oil is expensive and they can't afford it. So if they cook with a lot of oil, they are showing you respect. But in my house, we eat very little oil. I think when I went home that day, I threw up because I ate way too much oil. And this widow also gave me goat's milk, which is even more expensive. But I don't like goat's milk. I got sick many times, especially from their vegetables because they barely cook them, they barely clean them. Sometimes not even with water, they might just brush them off. I got big pimples and irritations on my skin and had to go to a doctor. I even got a parasite. But in order to have their trust and to actually start a relationship I had to be part of their way of life. And over time, as I kept coming to see them, I would see a smile on their faces, at least sometimes if not always. When I would go there, even if they had never had any education, some would ask if their children could study English with me.

One thing I've noticed in Afghan society unfortunately nowadays, particularly in the last eight, nine years, is the gap among women. On the one hand, you have the elite community women who are educated, who work. But then you have a much larger group of women, women who are weak economically, educationally, socially, who live very differently from the elite; the widows and the beggars or just the normal Afghan women who are poor and who stay in the house most of the time. Today, there is barely a connection between the elites and these other women; there is very rarely a bridge between these two. It was basically for that reason that I tried my whole time to be among the widows, the regular women, the grass roots. One of the first things they would tell me was "You are different from other elite women [and here they meant educated women] because you talk to us in our language, you come to our houses, you do kiss us. Most of the elite community women don't kiss us because they think we're dirty. You also wear clothes like us, you eat like us."

So I think all of these divisions have created a long distance between the women of these two categories.

And it's not just how these two groups of women talk or eat or kiss or not kiss. Of course, when the women are educated they use English words—especially when they are educated abroad—and the vocabulary they use of course is different, the style of talking is different. With educated women, you sit in a very formal way and everything is very refined. With the widows, you sit on the floor and the voices are usually louder. Everything is different with these two groups of women.

But the biggest gap I saw, after going into these widows' houses, into their communities, is basically the lack of knowledge these elite, educated women have of how much these other women suffer.

When I went to one widow's house, she invited me to go with her to her sister's engagement. So I got a pink sari—a sari is a kind of Indian dress—as a gift to her sister. I think I bought it for about ten dollars, so you can imagine that it wasn't a very fancy one. We both went to the engagement party, and I gave her sister the gift. When the bride and the groom came out, the girl was wearing the sari that I had given her. And then the widow told me that her sister didn't have any beautiful clothes, any clothes as beautiful as the one I had given her. And I thought, here is a woman at her engagement and she can't even afford to buy clothes that are a little bit fancy.

So I see that gap, I see the lack of understanding. And it goes both ways. Some of the widows used to ask me, "Do you earn $10,000 minimum? You must earn $10,000." But my whole salary was $200.

So they think that these educated women are almost from a different planet. They think that money means nothing to them, that they should be throwing all their excess money at others. They didn't know we weren't that rich either.

One of the most difficult things for all the widows—both those who were just widows and those who were doing drugs and were prostitutes—was worrying about what would happen to their children. For all the widows, it is far more difficult for their children to go to school. And if their kids went to school, they would see the economic gap between their families and the other kids in the school. The children of widows often weren't accepted by their classmates.

But almost always, what gave most of these widows hope was their children. I would hear that very often from the widows, any category of widow, those who were just widows, those who had community support, those who didn't, those who were prostitutes, those who weren't using drugs, those who were using drugs—any kind of widows. The most common quote was about "my children." They would say, "I'm no one, but I'm living for my children." And, "I'm looking forward to them being someone in the future."

Born in Herat City, Laila Samani spent much of her growing up as an exile in Iran. Her family fled when she was only a toddler because her father had served in Parliament and after the Soviet invasion, he became a target. She returned to Herat during the Taliban rule, and it was only after their fall that she was able to have "the golden chance to follow my education." She is a founder of the Movement of Afghan Sisters in Herat. Her latest project for Afghan women is called Birth of New Ideas Organization. She is serious, passionate, and emphatic when she speaks. Even in the privacy of her workspace, she is fully covered in a heavy, black hijab.

. . . .

My name is Laila Samani and I was born in Herat City, Herat, Afghanistan. I am a women's rights and civil rights activist. I didn't plan on becoming an activist. My first job was as a professor of education, teaching people who were studying to become teachers. But I soon realized that no matter what job I did, or what job any other Afghan woman did, the situation and the conditions here were always the same: women are always under duress. Whatever your profession, if you are a civil activist or if you are a teacher, many people will be against you simply because you are a woman.

When I taught in the education department, some people complained that because I was a woman, I should not be teaching men. It did not matter what my own education was or what my skills were. They said I should not teach just because I am a woman. I decided that I needed to get other women to join together to change this situation. And that one of the best ways to do this was by becoming a civil activist.

I have seen terrible things happen to women in our society. I have seen girls forced into marriages with old men. I have seen women whose own families have cut off their noses because they think the woman has somehow violated the family's honor. I have seen women who have had hot oil poured on their heads, burning their hair, burning their skin. They have been tortured. I see women who work in the fields for no payment, forced to labor and being treated like slaves. I have seen girls killed simply because they fell in love with a boy and the family thought that was a form of dishonor, or the men were angry because the girl had rejected whatever boy they had selected for her to marry. I see many women and girls who are not allowed out of the house, who are confined inside their homes every day. I have seen where women are killed simply because they did not ask permission of their husband before they ate food. I suffer a lot watching what women in my community, particularly in the more remote areas and villages, must endure. But we also saw with the killing of Farkhunda that dark minds are supporting superstitions and working against women in many parts of Afghanistan. I believe that women must come together to change these conditions.

> I HAVE SEEN TERRIBLE THINGS HAPPEN TO WOMEN IN OUR SOCIETY. I HAVE SEEN GIRLS FORCED INTO MARRIAGES WITH OLD MEN. I HAVE SEEN WOMEN WHOSE OWN FAMILIES HAVE CUT OFF THEIR NOSES BECAUSE THEY THINK THE WOMAN HAS SOMEHOW VIOLATED THE FAMILY'S HONOR. I HAVE SEEN WOMEN WHO HAVE HAD HOT OIL POURED ON THEIR HEADS, BURNING THEIR HAIR, BURNING THEIR SKIN.

During the Taliban times, I was a totally different person. When I think back to how I was able to tolerate that period, inside I feel like dying. But today, I am stronger than that time and I am more experienced than that time.

Right now, I feel that the Taliban are coming back to Afghanistan. If they are not stopped, I am prepared to go and fight against them. I will take a weapon and fight rather than staying here and living under them again. Now many women say that we are prepared to fight against the Taliban and also ISIS, also called DAESH, which is the Islamic State in Afghanistan. If we let them control Afghanistan, we will be forced back into our homes and have to tolerate another dark era. Instead, we are preparing to fight and even to die or be killed.

But it is also very important to understand that ideology is not why people are attracted to the Taliban and ISIS. It is the economic conditions that attract people to these groups. These groups are paying money to people to join them. Unemployed men, with families that need to be fed, are being offered a huge amount of money. They accept, but they are not supporting these groups and their ideas because of ideology. They are supporting their ideas because of payment. When some of these men are captured and put in prison, they say they did it for income for their families.

I am not surprised by this. One of the most important things that we have found through years of working in the local communities is the need to find ways for women to earn income. After much research across the country, we have found that when women earn an income, they can get out from family and domestic violence. They will no longer be under the total control of their husbands and their immediate families. If they earn an income, it is also easier to convince them to send their daughters to school. These changes, income and education, will have positive consequences in the future for Afghanistan, not necessarily in the short term, but definitely in the long term.

But how we make these changes and educate people about these changes is also very important. We will not be successful if we do not also respect the customs of these communities and respect their cultures. When I go into communities as a civil activist, I keep my hijab on tight, I keep my hair and ears covered, I do not wear makeup, because the men and also women in the communities might be offended and I want to avoid further complications in the society. If people in these communities think we are trying to push Western culture on them, that we are not showing respect for their culture, they will reject what we have to say.

One time I went to a human rights training session in a rural village. I made sure I wore full hijab, I started by reciting verses from the Koran, then I talked about human rights and women's rights. Because I started out in that way, the people were very receptive of what I had to say. I had a colleague from the West who would come to do these trainings uncovered. She was giving the same message as me, but the people resisted what she had to say and complained. They looked at her and felt that she did not understand their culture. When you do not have a sensitive approach, people in the villages start to believe that the international organizations are there to promote Christianity or Western cultures against Islamic values.

In 2010, I was working with a U.S. democracy program on a project, and we invited some mullahs to participate in human rights and democracy education. But even though I had written a report on these issues, I did not want to be in the same room as the mullahs. I did not want them to see me. Instead, I stayed in a small room nearby because I was afraid the mullahs would be unwilling to express their ideas about women in my presence. We wanted to hear about their ideas on women who work with NGOs, but they would not share them in front of a woman.

If we really want to have lasting change, we need for women to be more active in their communities. They need to run businesses. They need to get involved in politics. Only then can women become stronger and help to solve their own problems.

This is a hard thing to ask of many women. Women who get involved in politics in Afghanistan face special obstacles. Many times, women in public life are accused of being immoral. They can also have their reputations ruined on purpose. I know well one woman in political life in one of the more distant provinces. A wealthy man tried to force her to have a sexual relationship with him. She refused. To get revenge against her for rejecting him, he decided to ruin her honor by paying her father a large sum of money to marry her. Then, after only one night as husband and wife, he divorced her. In Afghan society, that creates dishonor for the rest of a woman's life.

Even voting is a challenge. My first presidential election, I got up very early in the morning to go and vote. I also worked as an election observer. When I saw many women standing in long lines at the polls, I got very excited. But there are areas where the polling places are very far from where many women live. These women are unable to walk the long distances to the polls and have no means of getting there, so they cannot participate. Some families also prevent their women from participating in the elections, saying that women cannot vote. And there were also times when men stole the voting. They put pressure on the women in their family to vote for a particular person; the women could not choose the candidate they wanted. I saw one person bring forty to fifty women to a polling place and then submit their ballot cards for them. Each card was marked for the same candidate. And when I asked one of the women her family name, it was different from what had been written on her ballot.

It is also difficult for women to vote because there are no pictures on the ballot cards. Many women cannot read, and they need pictures to know which candidate they are voting for. Voting is progress, but we still have very far to go. One of our biggest problems today, outside of extremism, is government corruption. Widespread corruption in the government also leads some Afghans to support extremist groups.

*　　*　　*

I knew being an activist would be hard. There is tremendous pressure on women simply to stay home and not to get engaged in political affairs. But I also believe strongly that we need powerful women in our political system, and we need these women to support other women in particular.

After fifteen years, you can definitely see changes in every aspect of Afghan women's lives. Women now have the right to access education. Women can now advocate for their rights and can freely express their opinions through the media. Women now also have the right of access to the government and to participate in government, but they are still not treated equally as men. Yet these changes are only confined to the cities and surrounding districts. The remote districts and provinces are still suffering from violence against women and restrictions with respect to women's rights. Around the world, women's rights have been violated for centuries, particularly in Afghanistan. In the social and governmental system, women have not been able to stand shoulder to shoulder with the men.

I think women can govern differently in some aspects from men, and that this would be useful for our country. Women, due to their nature, are not as easily corrupted in government and can govern with more integrity. And we have a new generation of educated women and men who can hopefully overcome many of the challenges we face.

I hope that in ten years, Afghanistan will have political stability and much less political corruption—right now, it is in the top tier of corrupt countries. I hope that it will be a powerful state without the forces of ISIS and the Taliban and without intervention by any neighboring countries to cause problems.

But I worry that maybe all this is somehow a dream.

After decades of conflict, one of the greatest losses inside Afghanistan has been the country's rich artistic traditions and culture. Skills that were once passed down from generation to generation are being lost. In 2006, with the support of Great Britain's Prince Charles and the Afghan president, and assisted by a generous grant from USAID (United States Agency for International Development,) a program called Turquoise Mountain was established to help rescue Afghanistan's centuries' old artistic culture. Turquoise Mountain is working to train a new generation of craft artists in calligraphy and miniature painting, woodwork, jewelry, and ceramics, as well as architecture, including overseeing an ambitious project to restore part of the heavily damaged old city center of Kabul. Samira Kitman is a calligrapher who trained with Turquoise Mountain. She is seeking to preserve the past, but also to make a new place for Afghan women in the future. In 2014, she was honored as the "Best Woman Entrepreneur" at an International Women's Day event sponsored by the International Women's Center of the American University of Afghanistan. Here, she speaks about culture, the future, and peace.

· · · · · · · · · ·

I was born on November 26, 1990, in Kabul City. My family went to Pakistan as refugees when I was eight, after the Taliban had come to Kabul. We came back in 2003, and in 2010, I graduated from Turquoise Mountain.

I became interested in calligraphy and miniature paintings when I was a child. My uncle used to be a calligrapher, and we had many pieces of his work hanging in our home. There are very few women who practice this art. I am one of the first now to pursue it. Afghan calligraphy is very unique because each letter is deeply personal. How you write the letter shows the character of the artist. The person picking up the pen, the person making a drawing of a font [the letter style] is what makes it special. I also like that art doesn't have an end. It will take an artist a lifetime to become a master, and even then, you will never be able to learn everything about your art.

As a country, in Afghanistan, we have a very large, old history of art. It is the duty and the responsibility of the artists to make sure that our culture, our art, our heritage is kept alive for the next generation. But we also have to make sure that artists can make a living and have an income for their families. That is where programs like Turquoise Mountain and my own business come in.

I am the first person to pursue a business in my family. My mother does not even know how to read and write. Business is also not something that is always accepted for women. My father was reluctant to let me travel to India for a handicraft conference. I had to convince him that the world has changed. By age nineteen in Afghanistan, most girls are expected to be married and most will never get to choose their husbands. I have not married yet, and I am very lucky because my parents and my two brothers say that who I marry will be my decision, not theirs.

I have studied and built my business, but that is highly unusual. I hope to change this, so that more and more young women will decide to finish school and start a career first, then get married. The priority should be to have a better quality of life later for your family, and education is very important to that. Right now, my company and my foundation are training young women to become artists and to make a living. More than ninety girls have learned calligraphy and miniature painting.

*   *   *

It is hard sometimes for us as Afghans to think about the future. I am frustrated that the media only highlights the war side of Afghanistan. People outside of our country think that this war culture is our culture. What went on in Afghanistan in all the years before the war is not interesting to people who decide on what will be in the news. But we have as much valuable culture as other countries in the region. Afghanistan and its art have their own character, their own style. If you look at the artwork from a long time ago, it is very sophisticated and beautifully made. That is the culture that is underneath us now, that is what we must preserve.

Ten years from now, the only thing I can think about or hope for is peace. Afghanistan for me is a heaven, and I am frustrated that some people choose war instead of peace. Peace is the first thing and the last thing, and the most important thing. Without peace, there is no job security, no personal security, and we cannot know what will happen tomorrow. Even if we have nothing else, if we have peace, we will be happy.

Nasima Rahmani has fled her home twice, first from her village to Kabul during the Soviet invasion, and then back to her village when the mujahideen came. By then, she was an eager young law student. Only after nine years of upheaval did she return to the classroom and resume her studies. "Education is a gift, not everyone in the world has that gift," she says. During the Taliban time, she taught herself English by listening to BBC and Voice of America radio broadcasts. Today, she has initiated the first gender studies academic program in Afghanistan and leads the Women's Empowerment Centre of Gawharshad Institute of Higher Education, where she also teaches law. In addition, Nasima has founded an Afghan chapter of Graduate Women International.

The recipient of a joint scholarship from UNIFEM Australia and the Peace Scholarship Program, she earned a master's degree in Australia from the University of Technology Sydney (UTS), where she also received the prestigious Chancellor's Award for Excellence. The Max Planck Foundation for International Peace and the Rule of Law, through the German Ministry of Foreign Affairs, has awarded her a PhD scholarship and in 2015, the Advance Global Australian Awards recognized Nasima's women's rights work in Afghanistan. Here, she talks about her experiences, especially what it is like literally to be shut behind a door, with no access to learning or employment. "I would no longer think of myself as a human," she explains.

. . . .

I was about five years old when my family fled to Kabul, at the very beginning of the Soviet invasion and the time of conflict in Afghanistan. In our village my older brothers were in school, which meant the insurgents could force them to join their warring groups. We had to flee before that could happen.

I remember the day we left our home. To me now all these years later, that morning sits in my mind like a dream. We left everything behind, the farm, the animals, the house. I remember that we were walking on a path early in the morning. I wasn't walking; my brother was carrying me in his arms. At some point, I fell asleep, but I woke to the sound of our family dog following behind us, barking painfully. Everybody around me was trying to make the dog go back. I can still hear my father shouting at him. Later when I was older and could better understand things, my mother would tell us about that dog, how it was terribly loyal and very nice. But that morning, the dog was sent back. One of my brothers who stayed behind told us that when the Russians attacked the village, they set fire to my grandmother's house and killed the one man who had remained in the village to try to safeguard the houses. Everyone else had fled to mountains and hidden themselves in the caves to escape the bombing. Sometime that morning, the Russians also shot our dog and our cat, which was even more beloved than our dog to our family, particularly my mother. When I think about my early childhood, our cat and dog definitely come to my memories.

I stayed in Kabul with other family members for one or two years, then I was sent back to the village. My grandmother was still living there as well as one of my uncles and his family. I was sent back to be with my grandmother. When I finally returned to Kabul, I had already missed three years of school. My younger sister was in the second grade, and I was told that I would have to be enrolled below her, in first grade, which was not acceptable to me. But my brothers tutored me, and I passed the exam to be placed into fourth grade, the correct grade for my age, which I started in the spring.

What happened in that fourth-grade year helped to set me on the path to education. My first and very respected teacher, Sahila Jan, watched me take the progress exam. She told the school principal that she wanted to have me in her class. Knowing that this teacher wanted to teach me lit up a flame of enthusiasm in my heart and mind toward education and hard work. I felt proud of myself and that pride and feeling of happiness paved my way to further success. In a few years, I topped all of the school students and remained the top student until I graduated from high school.

From fourth grade until I finished school, I never went back to our village. I almost completely forgot about it. During this time, it was not possible to go back. Even my father could not return. The highways and roads were blocked; no one was allowed to travel from Kabul to there or from there to Kabul. My uncle and one of my cousins were stuck in the village. The insurgent group dominating that area had taken what remained of our house and our lands, everything. So nothing was left in the village for us to go back to anyway.

With the war and conflict, one horrible thing is the displacement from one place to another; it is really, really difficult and painful to leave everything behind and run away from your home. I felt more of the bitterness of that pain when we had to flee the intensive fighting between the mujahideen groups again in 1992 in Kabul. One morning, my father rushed into the house, calling out, "Hurry up, we have to run away before all of us die." I didn't even get a chance to take my dearest belongings, things I had treasured my whole life, not even the little money that I had saved from my pocket money during the school years and my first year of university.

> ONE MORNING, MY FATHER RUSHED INTO THE HOUSE, CALLING OUT, "HURRY UP, WE HAVE TO RUN AWAY BEFORE ALL OF US DIE." I DIDN'T EVEN GET A CHANCE TO TAKE MY DEAREST BELONGINGS, THINGS I HAD TREASURED MY WHOLE LIFE.

*   *   *

My life in Kabul when I went to school was actually a golden period. Looking back on those eight years, although there were some killings, rocket attacks, and explosions, if I compare it to what I went through after that and what's happening in the country now, it is still the most peaceful and most beautiful time in my life. Remembering those years, feelings of joy and satisfaction penetrate in my heart. This doesn't mean that Kabul was completely safe and peaceful and we did not have problems. The last two years of the Russian-backed leader, Dr. Najibullah, could be described as rather similar to the current situation in Kabul. Now, when people leave home in the morning, they have no hope to return in the evening. It was the same in those two years due to the numerous rockets that were launched into Kabul by the mujahideen on a daily basis. A common joke among my friends in university was "Oh gosh, you look very beautiful today. I am afraid you will get martyred," because we believe that if an innocent person is killed as a martyr, he or she looks particularly beautiful and has a bright face on the day of his or her martyrdom.

When I finished school and began the first year of my law studies, everything about the conflict changed, because when the opposition forces arrived in Kabul, they started fighting with each other. All of the nine groups that had been united in fighting Russians suddenly became enemies among themselves. As a result, unbelievable chaos was created in Kabul. The city was looted and ruined. May 1992 is the starting point for this very devastating period in Afghanistan's history that changed the features of Kabul City and ousted more than half of its population from the country. Among those who remained, almost half were killed or injured. That period took the best years of my life. All of my future plans and my education got delayed for almost nine to ten years.

It seems that people have forgotten what happened in those years. The eyes of the world missed much of this time because it did not matter much outside of Afghanistan, but for people like me who witnessed what happened, it was the most dreadful time in this country's history.

The Commission on Human Rights reported that sixty-six thousand people living in Kabul were killed between 1992 and 1994, but I think it is much more than that. The United States and other Western countries had filled Afghanistan with the guns and weapons they sent to the mujahideen to fight Russians, but when they left, none of these countries cared about what happened with those weapons. That failure helped turn Afghanistan into a safe nest for insurgents and paved the way for the emergence of the Taliban. Yet during that whole time, the U.S. did not pay attention to the bloodshed going on in Kabul. It did not feel responsible for Afghanistan until it was wounded itself on 9/11. Afghans assisted the U.S. in reaching its ultimate goal of demolishing the Soviet Union from the world's map, but it forgot to think of this poor nation when we needed America's assistance afterward. The U.S. should have interfered in Afghanistan in 1992, right at the beginning of the civil war, to prevent the massive destruction and killing of innocent people. In fact, the United Nations was supposed to supervise the transfer of power and the elections, but the mujahideen groups breached the agreements and defied the UN. The mujahideen flooded into the city from different corners of Kabul. They started killing and putting everything on fire, just for the sake of having more power and having control of a bigger piece of Kabul. That would have been a very good justification to interfere.

The chain of miserable war that is still going on today is a result of the United States' initial negligence. I blame all the leaders who closed their eyes to us. But I think they have also paid a huge price for these decisions with their losses in the war on terrorism.

Today, you can't even say very much about the mujahideen time because of the current overall political atmosphere in Afghanistan. Many of those killers later became national heroes and still are. They are successful leaders sitting in the Parliament and they rule the country again; they have their own followers and they are respected. The younger generation—the twenty- and twenty-five-year-olds— know very little about these killers and the crimes they committed to obtain what they have today. I have sympathy for the younger generation and their genuine feelings toward the warlords. The innocent youth just vote for them and consider them their leaders, but they don't know much about the true features hidden behind the faces they see.

It was not possible to live in Kabul in the first three to four years after the mujahideen's arrival. Those who could not manage to leave the country would escape to relatively calm provinces and remote villages. Unlike in the Soviet times, when nearly all of the fighting and destruction was happening in the provinces, now the provinces were largely quiet because the focus and attention were on Kabul. My father was always against the idea of leaving the country. He did not even allow my brothers to go abroad when they received scholarships and fellowships as he was afraid my brothers would not come back. So we did not leave Afghanistan, but we went back and forth to the village to survive the intensive fighting periods.

Every house, every family in Kabul was affected somehow. I remember one neighbor told me she counted the rockets and explosions in our area [Khair Khana] one day, and it was more than one hundred. But even so, Khair Khana was still the most secure area of

Kabul. When we were in Kabul, we would spend most of our time in basements. Those who did not have a secure basement in their house would go to a neighbor's on the street. We did not have a secure basement and it was not easy to rush to the neighbor's house several times a day. But staying at home meant thinking that every minute the house might be struck by a rocket and explode. In my mind, I can still hear the disgusting sound of rockets passing over the house. I can think of no other way to describe it.

Now, when there are explosions in Kabul, some of the casualties among children and older people are due to the dreadful noises that accompany these explosions. In particular, children's hearts may suddenly stop if they are very close to the exploded area.

During the war a rocket did hit a very big tree in front of our house, but by then we had already fled Kabul. If not, most likely some family members would have been killed. My oldest brother was left behind and we are so thankful to God that he survived the blast with only a minor injury. The incident damaged our car and some parts of the house. One of the things that was lost was my notebook. In my teenage years, I was fond of writing. I used to read lots of novels and maybe that created the passion in me. This notebook held some of my short stories that had been edited by one of my teachers. The rocket explosion tore it in pieces and that discouraged me from writing again. Just now sometimes I wonder if I should rethink that beautiful hobby, but I can't make time for it. Instead I write for work.

In one sense, fleeing from Kabul and leaving everything behind and having that kind of war and destruction in my life again was a nightmare for me because I was just in the first year of my law studies. So everything in my life was destroyed one more time. Before, I had big dreams for my future and what I would do, but in facing that horror, I forgot everything.

The first thing imposed by the new government that took power after Dr. Najibullah was overthrown was the restriction on women's freedom. Although these could not be called restrictions compared to what the Taliban did later, women still experienced a huge difference overnight and suddenly managing such a big change was not easy. For instance, women could not dress up like before and they had to wear a scarf to cover their heads, something that was optional before. But the changes were soon followed by bloodshed and fighting among the factions, and under those circumstances, survival became more important than having the freedom to do what one wanted or for a woman to dress how she wished.

We have a proverb in our language, which could be translated as, "Even bad things that happen might have something good in them." And the good thing about the civil war at that time was the possibility for me to go back to my village.

During the years of intensive conflict, 1992–94, all of our relatives who had fled ages ago returned to the village, so it was somehow also a nice time. When I look back at that time—the cooking and bread making, the fetching water, weeding in the fields, and walking with other women to collect fruits from the distant orchards—the reunion experiences were good moments. But there was also a strong sense of hopelessness and disappointment because I had lost my friends and my studies and my dreams. And I learned how tough life is for women in Afghanistan.

I experienced how the village women make the bread, a major task for women who live in the remote areas. They bake it two to three times a day in ovens that are placed inside the ground, which adds a particular difficulty to this job. In the village, I managed to do everything that the women living there would do. We would collect fruits like berries, almonds, and apricots from fields and orchards located near and far and then dry them inside the houses or on the roofs for selling. I saw how the women there managed to do the household work and look after their families and then on top of that assist men with the tasks that the men should have been doing themselves, like farming and cultivating the fruit and nut trees and collecting the fruits. I learned about all the sacrifices that Afghan women make. All of these experiences have helped me with my gender work today.

I think Afghan women are capable of a lot and they do so much, but they still are considered just second-rate humans. The moment you talk to men and you mention women's rights and equality and freedom, the response is "What are women? What do they do? They're not capable of doing anything. Women just need to sit at home and raise children." Most of them are not ready to hear that women are human beings like them.

By 1995, things were a bit better in Kabul. They even reopened the university. Some of my family members returned to Kabul, but my mother and father and I stayed in the village. My father thought that it was still not safe enough to go back to the university, especially because during the previous four years, many crimes had happened in the area where Kabul University is located. People said that women from different parts of the city were kidnapped and were taken to the basements of the medical institute and kept there as sex objects for the men who had guns. Because of the security threats, when the university was reopened in 1995, not many people allowed their daughters to restart their studies. My father was one of those. I was not allowed to jeopardize my own safety and family honor by attending the university, as there was no guarantee that things would not become bad again. So I listened to my father and did not insist that he let me go.

That time saw perhaps more kidnappings of young women than any other point in Afghanistan's history, but many of the incidents were not recorded. Instead, we heard stories and, like currency in the marketplace, they were passed around. A sixteen-year-old girl had to jump out of the window from the sixth floor in the Macrorayan apartments of Kabul to escape the gunmen that entered her family's apartment. Many other women threw themselves into their houses' wells. I remember my brother telling us, "If gunmen knock on the door, I will give you a hint and you all jump into the well yourself. And if you don't, I will not hesitate for a moment to throw you there before opening the door." And we, my two sisters and his wife, agreed with him as we knew that gunmen would enter the houses and then they would take the young women with them.

I want to share my thoughts on one more thing here. Although right now we don't have enough statistics and credible data, if research is conducted, I am sure it will be proved that polygamy reached its highest level in Afghanistan in the first half of the 1990s. Female activists who did not leave the country at that time and witnessed what was happening might agree with me. The reason I think this is that most of the insurgent commanders married for a second, third, and even a fourth time upon arriving in Kabul. They did what they wished because no one could reject their proposals. First of all, they had the power. If a family said no or did not give their girl to them, they would simply kidnap the one they wanted to marry. Second, during this time young women became a huge burden on their families' shoulders as there was continuous fear that sooner or later they would be taken away by gunmen. I know many friends and neighbors who married their daughters to very wrong men out of fear. They simply wanted to get rid of the responsibility of having these girls and the threat of dishonor that hung over them.

What women and the inhabitants of Kabul went through in those years could be called the worst ever tragedy in the history of this country, but unfortunately many of these incidents and what happened at that time were not documented. There is a report available from AIHRC [Afghanistan Independent Human Rights Commission], which was prepared after the fall of the Taliban, but I don't think it sufficiently reflects everything because just one report on all the crimes in that period cannot be comprehensive enough to capture everything. One famous case that was known to everyone in Kabul was the story of a pregnant woman who was on her way to the women's hospital to deliver her baby. Gunmen stopped the car, took the husband out of the car, and drove away with his wife. Sometime later, in another area, they stopped the car and surrounded the poor woman, telling her, "Now give birth to your baby. We want to watch how that happens." The woman died, probably right there on the ground.

Yet by 1996 things seemed to be returning to normal. I convinced my family to allow me to restart my law studies, and I completed the first semester of that year. I wish my English was perfect to find suitable words for describing the feelings of going back to university and seeing some of my old friends, who all had different appearances and pale faces that reflected the miseries we had gone through. Nothing had remained like before. At the end of the first law class that I had finished before the arrival of the mujahideen, we were almost 180 students and more than half of the class was women. When I returned, I only saw a handful of my previous classmates, boys and girls together, and that was the most painful thing to face and cope with. I think that situation could be described as being much the same way that a big flood arrives and destroys a village and its houses and takes the people with it. You are one of the survivors, thrown into another place, and then four years later, you come back and look at the ruins to see what has happened to others. You find a few people around who have survived like you, but they too have lost everything. Yet you all have to still live life, no matter how difficult and painful the absences of others.

Now as I say this, I feel the same pain in my heart again.

We heard about some of the students who had been killed; a majority of the boys and girls had left the country with their families, many others were simply missing. A big group of happy and enthusiastic young people who had every joy and hope before them had been shattered and torn to pieces. Only a few of them survived the storm to make it back to that classroom. With all of those sad feelings, I completed the first semester of my second year of law studies in 1996, but again graduation remained a dream. Because at the beginning of the second semester in September 1996, the Taliban arrived and pushed women back for five more years.

This was another period of misery and devastation in my life, which broke my heart into pieces again and killed the remaining soul and spirit in me. This time I felt I was really finished, and I gave up on every hope for the future. But there is a difference between the first four years of struggle for survival and the five years of imprisonment under the Taliban. In this period, there were no explosions and no serious fighting in Kabul. The city was to some extent calm and secure. Rather, the war was concentrated in some provinces in the north that resisted the Taliban. Last year, I read a report on war crimes against women in Afghanistan and learned what was done to women in the northern provinces like Jawzjan and Samangan. How they raped women and killed them.

But stuff like that did not happen in Kabul.

But although Kabul was not violent, there was no sense of freedom and no, I would say, humanity for myself. I would no longer think of myself as a human because as

> I WOULD NO LONGER THINK OF MYSELF AS A HUMAN BECAUSE AS WOMEN, WE WERE SHUT BEHIND THE DOORS.

women, we were shut behind the doors. Particularly in the first year, we were not allowed to go out. Women could not do anything outside of the house. Before that, many women were working at beauty parlors and as tailors; they had shops and they worked in governmental offices, schools, universities, and hospitals, but all that stopped in the first days of the Taliban's arrival. Only female doctors and nurses could go to their jobs, probably because they would not allow men doctors to examine women or operate on them. Even those women who had private businesses were denied those opportunities as they could not maintain any presence outside of the home. It was only later that some women started to open underground schools and offer English courses or teach children and girls whose parents were trying to find a way to educate their daughters. But unfortunately I could not find any of those English classes around me to benefit from.

Even so, I should tell you that at first people were very happy to receive the Taliban. Kabul inhabitants in particular were fed up with what had happened in the previous years of fighting and chaos. They welcomed the Taliban because they had heard that in the other provinces like Kandahar and Herat, they had established a very strong sense of security and they collected all the weapons. People just wanted a secure Kabul; they wanted a strong hand to be a savior. But it was also very clear to us that the Taliban would stop women from working, that they would shut them inside the houses.

Before the arrival of the Taliban, I also had a part-time job teaching in a school; I remember a heated debate I had with one of my colleagues the day before the Taliban arrived in the city. That teacher was very openly and happily saying that she was looking forward to the Taliban arriving. I quarreled with her and argued that, being a woman, how could she say something like that? Because it was clear that the moment the Taliban arrived in Kabul, we would have no more freedom. But she said she had five children, and she told me that the life of her children and their security were more important to her than her own freedom. It was more important for her to see these children grow up and be alive, rather than for her to work and to be able to go out.

Many people and even women would make comments like that. They were so weary. Nearly every family in Kabul had to have some kind of weapon, such as a bomb or gun or whatever, for their own safety and protection. In most of the houses the family members would also take turns staying up on the roofs at night to watch the house and their street for robbers and other threats. That way, other members of the family could sleep while one or two were the patrol.

I think the Taliban were also very successful in deceiving people. Through their propaganda, people believed that they would bring security and that they had a strategy to move the country forward. And there was some security. By collecting the weapons and guns, they gave some peace of mind to the ordinary people.

But in Kabul, the Taliban's arrival happened like a bad miracle. One morning we woke up and my father went out to see what was happening, since we knew that the Taliban were getting closer and closer to the city. He rushed back into the house and started screaming, "Oh, they are here, they are all over the streets." After that, we started to prepare for any unexpected incident. (Much the same thing happened in the Kunduz tragedy in 2015, when the Taliban retook that city. As one man from Kunduz told a newsreporter, "It happened all of a sudden. We woke up in the morning and the city was full of Taliban.")

During the Taliban time in Kabul, we had no TV, no radio, nothing except the broadcasts of their own news and some religious poems in the evening. The only thing I could do living inside was to make clothes. I taught myself tailoring because that way I could make some money. The biggest entertainment I had was to listen in secret to the Voice of America or the BBC. These strangers on the radio played a great role in disseminating information to the people of Afghanistan. The Voice of America and the BBC also had some programs to teach English. And that was the biggest thing I could do, to listen to them and teach myself a little bit of English. I was so disappointed that the Taliban had control over 95 percent of the land in Afghanistan. There was not much hope that things would change. There was not much hope that women would be able to do anything again.

The first year was the most difficult. Then slowly, slowly, if we were covered properly with the burqa and if we could have a male child accompany us, we could go out. We could do the shopping and I could manage to go to the bazaar and buy the fabric and stuff that I needed for my work making my clothes. But still, when you are an ambitious person and you see everything destroyed and dying in front of your eyes, you cannot have a decent life. I remember I was crying a lot. I developed a terrible crying habit during that time.

My nephews were going to school and they were attending English courses as well. If I helped them with their homework, I could read their books. I also found a little schoolboy who had lots and lots of books. He was lending books to people for a small sum of money and I would borrow novels from him. He used to charge his book clients one AF per day for borrowing a book. But if I kept a book for a month, he would still only charge me one AF. I offered him more money, but he would politely reject it, saying, "No, ma'am, you keep it. I only want one Afghani because I know women cannot come every day. I know you will only come out of your home when you have some urgent business. My mother has the same problem. I don't want to take advantage of this misery." I admired him for that level of understanding.

Inside, I sewed, I read, and occasionally I watched a movie, maybe once a month or once every two months. But just to do that, you needed to go to a basement or a small room that had no window to the street and make sure that there was no sound coming out from that room. If the movie could be heard, the Taliban would arrive to punish that family. Thank God we were so cautious and it never happened that we were captured.

WFP, the World Food Program, did a very good job during the Taliban years of saving the lives of many people in Kabul. In our neighborhood they distributed cheap bread cards to almost every household, and women who had lost their jobs and widows could collect bread from specific bakeries in the area that received free wheat and flour from the WFP. Now as an experienced humanitarian myself, I realize that apart from saving these women from the malnutrition and the poverty that hit Kabul at that time, these bread lines also helped to save women from severe depression. Collecting bread from those bakeries became great fun and provided many women with an opportunity to come together in regular spots. I myself would go to one such place mainly to meet other women and listen to their stories. I even made friends. (One of them, Suraya, was recently injured in a suicide bombing in Kabul.) Everybody was wearing a burqa and at first it was not easy to identify who was who. After a while we could recognize them from the sounds of their voices and the faces of children that accompanied these women.

EVERYBODY WAS WEARING A BURQA AND AT FIRST IT WAS NOT EASY TO IDENTIFY WHO WAS WHO. AFTER A WHILE WE COULD RECOGNIZE THEM FROM THE SOUNDS OF THEIR VOICES AND THE FACES OF CHILDREN THAT ACCOMPANIED THESE WOMEN.

In the years before war, I would find it really difficult to wear a burqa, but once the Taliban arrived, I got used to it so easily. Indeed, wearing a burqa was no longer a problem. When you experience a much, much bigger difficulty and restriction like being locked inside the house, and wearing a burqa is what can save you from that cage, so that at least for a little while you could go out and see what is happening in town, then the burqa was actually a freedom.

Even today, I still wear a burqa in some places when I go shopping. The streets in Kabul are not safe for women to walk around. If you are a working woman, and you go to your job and then you are seen on the streets, even for shopping and little things, people still have the impression that you are not a good woman, that you are going out a lot. So I wear a burqa when I go to buy the groceries and run errands. Women in Kabul would have been so happy if they were allowed to go back to their previous jobs and classes in schools and universities wearing a burqa. A typical Afghan woman would not question why she is not allowed to go out; her family and children are everything for her and she is happy to stay in and look after them. And it is much the same for the unmarried women and girls. If she has a job or other business out of the home, then she is even more eager to spend time at home. With this I want to emphasize again that it was not the freedom of appearance in public that we wanted, it was permission to work and to get an education.

What happened on September 11 in the United States obviously was the most horrible thing to happen in the history of the world and to human beings. But for the women in Afghanistan, it liberated us and it gave us the freedom to start life. Inside Afghanistan, many people at first strongly condemned the U.S. decision to bomb the Taliban. My women friends at the bakery would say that the U.S. wants to bomb us and that it has no right to do that. We were pretty upset about the bombing decision as we were not sure that we would remain safe at the end, even though it was said that civilians would not be affected.

The horror of that bombing time in my mind is worse than all of the war period I can remember. Every day when the skies were getting darker, the Taliban would cut off the electricity to make sure the bombing aircrafts could not identify their targets. And then the horrible voice of the planes overhead would stop the sound of breath in everyone's chest. There is a big military base located in our area and that made it very dangerous and terrifying for us. Going through all that destruction again was more difficult than any other time we lived with war.

But in the end, the bombing had a very beautiful result for women. When U.S. forces arrived to establish a new, interim government, things changed all of a sudden for all Afghan people and for women in particular. We could leave our homes. Immediately in that winter I could manage to go to an English course.

At first, I wasn't very sure that I should go back for my education. After the mujahideen and the Taliban, my law studies were already behind nine or ten years. I thought maybe I should simply find a job and earn a salary. I had to have more ambition to go back and to continue. And even more, I could not trust the situation. I was afraid what would happen to me if I was forced to stop my studies for a third time.

I'm grateful to one of my brothers who encouraged me to go back to school and also to my English teacher. The English course I went to was taught by a very young woman, and in the class she asked, What are your plans and what do you want to do now that the situation is different? And I said I don't think that I will go back to resume my studies as I am afraid something will happen again and stop me in the middle. She was so unhappy to hear that. She said to me, "I see that you are such a talented woman, how can you say that? If you go back to law school and finish your studies, I'm sure you will become someone. If you just go for a job, you won't achieve nearly as much." And that was my brother's argument as well. I'm still trying to find that English teacher today. Together with my brother, she made such a difference in my life with that encouragement.

I went back to the university, and I scored better than all the male students. When you are good in the class with the highest marks, then you become the first position student. Topping the class brought me all of a sudden a lot of energy and a lot of enthusiasm to finish. So the last two years of my law studies were a wonderful time. I worked hard. I also went back to my job. I was a teacher at the same time as I was going to university. I even managed to learn computers and polish my English a little. Then in 2004 I got my first job in the law sector, which eventually led me to work with the Afghan Women Judges Association. My boss also encouraged me to go for further education.

*   *   *

In 2005, UN Women Australia, formerly UNIFEM, announced a scholarship for a female lawyer in Afghanistan to complete her master's degree in Australia. I applied for it, but I was not sure if my English was good enough to win. The application asked about my life and educational experiences. I put down all of what I had gone through, and I was lucky enough that the women sitting on the board of UNIFEM liked my paper very much. Then they asked me to take an exam to see whether I could qualify for the master's studies. The requirement to pass was 5.5. I scored 4.5, simply using the English that I had managed to teach myself during the years of the Taliban. They came back to me and asked, Is there any way that you could improve your English? They told me they would wait for me to take the exam again.

Together with two friends, I went to enroll in an English course at an American NGO. They accepted me, but then one month later, the course was closed down. But my teacher, Patricia from New Zealand, knew that I needed to improve my English to receive the scholarship, and she promised to teach me in her home. Because I had a full-time job outside of Kabul and was commuting every day, she continued working with me for the next three months on the weekends, for two or three hours every time we met. I think that if Pat had not supported me, I would not have succeeded. Three months later, I retook the exam, and this time I scored high enough.

Also my thanks goes to the ladies from UNIFEM, in particular Libby Lloyd and Rosalind Strong, who decided to wait for me. They are such inspirations in my life. I think most of what I do now is from the impact of knowing them.

Coming to Australia I was also exposed to a different world—a much bigger one than my small, little world. All I had seen was my village, Kabul, and barely three or four other provinces of Afghanistan. In 2006, Kabul was still in ruins. It was still full of war memories. The destroyed buildings were pretty much the same, and they were constant reminders of all that Kabul had suffered. Also coming from a country like Afghanistan with all the restrictions and difficulties for women, and then entering a country like Australia, where you receive all of the support and attention and are given so many opportunities to grow and to improve, was such a blessing.

However, the first six months of my stay were difficult. It was hard to be exposed to the beauty of a shining city like Sydney and see how well people lived there and then have the disappointment of thinking of my own people, thinking of their miseries and of the wounded city of Kabul. But slowly I started to accept the facts and focus on the opportunities I had to do something that would be useful to serve my people and war-torn country. In my first professional job after graduation from law school, and before I went to Australia, I worked for women who had legal problems. The more I saw of women's difficulties and problems, the more it became very clear in my head that I should help women.

When I went back home, I applied for a job that was related to women's rights and gender-equality issues. After four years of tireless work there, Dr. Sima Samar, a leading Afghan women's and human rights activist, encouraged me to move into the education sector.

In 2011, I started my work with the Gawharshad Institute of Higher Education, where I led the Women's Empowerment Centre, and I started a very useful scholarship program for young women who are keen for education but face economic problems. I also started the first gender studies academic program, which had been my dream. Through this program we currently work on the development of academic materials in the Dari language, hoping that will help us to offer a diploma in gender studies. Next, I think that we need to train our children in the schools and universities to become familiar with the concept of equality and understand gender issues.

But I have not stopped my own education. I am working on my PhD, focusing on women's financial rights in the aftermath of divorce. This is something that requires our attention because divorced women in Afghanistan face serious deprivations. They have no financial rights and no legal guarantee that they will receive some kind of support through the government. A divorced woman loses custody of her children to her ex-husband, while her own family and society do not accept her back as she is considered dishonored. In a nutshell, a divorced woman is a complete loser, and I want to discuss that in my thesis from a financial perspective.

I am hoping to draw attention to this problem, but who knows how long it will take to get policy makers to accept it as a social problem that needs urgent attention. It's not easy to change minds. I worked for four years on programs and projects to benefit women in different provinces. But looking back on that and on my own life experiences, I came to the understanding that small projects will not create the major change that we need for women in Afghanistan. I think a strong political will is needed to look into women's problems more strategically, and it must start with education, as that is the most important step to take to create changes in the life of women as well as in the overall society. With education you give understanding and knowledge to women and you also pave the way for them to become employed and to have an income. And once a woman has the confidence that comes from having knowledge and from being economically empowered, then she will also become strong enough to stand against violence, to defend herself, and to make decisions for herself. Then she has a chance at a better life.

So I'm very optimistic that as we educate more women and

educate the society that things will improve for women and for all Afghans. But I'm not very optimistic about the next five years or ten years. In saying this, I consider the last fourteen years. Although we have made great progress over this period, there are certain things that are going to deteriorate more before they get better. This year, Afghanistan is going into the worst period security-wise since the fall of the Taliban. In retrospect, I don't think it was a good decision to have most of the NATO-affiliated forces leave Afghanistan starting in 2014, because that was the moment that the severe deterioration in our security situation began.

I do think that the presence of the international community in Afghanistan and people being exposed to such different kinds of information technologies has made more Afghans aware of or open to progress and development and to change. We don't want to go back to the medieval times that the Taliban want to impose. Now people recognize the importance of education and economic growth, along with the participation of women in social and economic life. I think most of the people are happy now to give women a chance to make a contribution to the family's economy and to allow them to stand shoulder to shoulder with men in building Afghanistan.

If the security gets better, I think we will rapidly move toward other improvements and other progress in Afghanistan. But for now, the ongoing war and the attacks and explosions impede many efforts and make people afraid. Unless the current situation changes, in five years, or even in ten years, or maybe even in twenty years, I don't see Afghanistan in a place where we could say, "Now it's paradise."

But, for my part, all I can do is to hope and pray for a better life and a better future. And I do just that.

In 2010, Naheed Farid was elected to Parliament from the conser-
vative province of Herat, a former Taliban stronghold. She is one
of the youngest and most educated members of Parliament, with
a master's degree from George Washington University—but she is
also very representative of a young nation, where some 60 percent
of all Afghans are under age twenty-five; they were born after the
Soviet invasion and occupation. Naheed fervently believes that the
country's younger citizens must take responsibility for their nation,
saying that "Afghan youth want to present a new identity to the
world." But she knows exactly how difficult that path will be, hav-
ing endured threats during her campaign and while in office, to the
point where opponents of her candidacy cut her face out of her cam-
paign posters in Herat City.

She can list all the accomplishments for women—28 percent
of Parliament seats, cabinet ministers, a female provincial gover-
nor, a female mayor, female attorneys and judges, women athletes,
women in the police force and the National Army, women in busi-
ness, and women teaching in universities and receiving higher edu-
cation. But that has not changed the minds of most conservative
political figures, who do not support an act to protect women from
domestic and other gender-based violence and who just last year
rejected the country's first female nominee to the Supreme Court.
Naheed says, "I really have the ambition that one day, Afghan men
and women, all together, will launch a powerful movement for
women and human rights in Afghanistan. I have the aspiration of
taking part in paving the road of equality in Afghanistan among all
women and men."

. . . .

I opened my eyes to the world in 1984 on a rainy spring day in the ancient city of Herat. I was my parents' first child.

But we could not stay in Herat, the Soviet occupation forced my family from our home, and we escaped to Iran, as refugees. It was there that my sister and brother were born. My parents loved us deeply, but in their hearts they also very much missed Afghanistan and our home.

My childhood years are associated with learning, and I was deeply fortunate to be able to attend school, but also as the child of an immigrant I was uneasy. I was afraid of revealing my identity to my classmates, afraid of making myself stand out, afraid that I did not belong.

When the Taliban took control, we returned to Herat. After more than a decade of fighting, it seemed like we finally would have peace. My parents did not know what was in store for them or for us. I was still a child, but I saw that even in the civilized city of Herat, the people were willing to die under the lash of bigotry and injustice rather than raise their voices, to speak out and fight back.

In my little world, all I felt was that I had fallen victim to the intolerance, terror, and violence of the Taliban. I felt powerless to fight these dark forces. But I was desperate to go to school. My mother was concerned about me going outside of the house, but I found a teacher in my neighborhood who was willing to risk teaching girls. She believed in using knowledge to fight against ignorance. That teacher patiently taught me that the world is much bigger than what I thought and that I am more powerful than I thought. She gave me the belief that I could make a difference.

That teacher who didn't have the right to teach, in a class that shouldn't exist, taught me the greatest lesson of my life: "Don't give up!"

During the Taliban times, I also thought no one could understand what was going on inside me, in my mind. But now, as a mother, I know why the lines on my mom's face were getting deeper and darker day by day. My mother suffered over my own missed childhood. She did not show her disappointment, she stayed silent on the outside, but she was burning within.

When the Taliban fell from power, I felt like a wall in front of me had been torn down. Suddenly, I was free, there was nothing blocking my footsteps forward. In 2004, I became a law student because I wanted to help distinguish right from wrong. I was thirsty to learn more. In addition to my law education, I also got a degree in leadership. I was the first female student in the leadership course. My teacher was a foreigner. Once again, like the teacher in Herat, he gave me the motivation to improve. Listening to him, I thought that maybe I could open the door for other girls to be leaders.

In 2006, in a competitive process, I won a scholarship to Germany. I was a member of the first group of girls in thirty years from the conservative society of Herat to be allowed to leave the city for an official exchange program. Germany is a developed country, so meeting students from underdeveloped Afghanistan was an unexpected surprise. But for me, the surprise was even greater. On this trip, my eyes were opened to a different world.

In 2007, I got married. Having my husband join me on the path of my turbulent life has given me more strength. Together, we traveled to the United States, where I got my master's degree at George Washington University. Seeing the U.S. up close made me want to make a difference in my country. I think the secret of the United States' development is

THAT TEACHER WHO DIDN'T HAVE THE RIGHT TO TEACH, IN A CLASS THAT SHOULDN'T EXIST, TAUGHT ME THE GREATEST LESSON OF MY LIFE: "DON'T GIVE UP!"

that the people there are able to transform their society, so that everyone in the society also has the potential and the opportunity to change him- or herself. Seeing the opportunities people in the U.S. have and wanting those for the people of Afghanistan was the thing that motivated me the most to return to my homeland.

I returned to Afghanistan in 2010, when candidates were registering for the 2010 parliamentary election, and I decided to use the opportunity to run for office and represent Herat in Afghanistan's Parliament. My husband was actually the one who suggested that I run for office, and then my father-in-law agreed. He told me, "Stay in Herat. Help women, help your province." I thought, Okay, why not? But I had no idea what a political campaign would be like. I only had one motto, based on a famous political strategy: identify yourself before your opponents do.

That election was my first practical experience in a chaotic world of politics. I had fifty-eight days of tough campaigning. During those days, I spent all my time out in the community and saw some shocking things—graveyards full of women who had died in childbirth, villages with children who had never bathed. Seeing so much poverty made me more determined to win and give these people a voice. And the encouragement I got from people while traveling through my region also gave me the passion to be their voice.

I had to break a lot of taboos to convince such a conservative society as Herat to vote for me. From the moment when I decided to run for office, I saw a huge wave of resistance from conservative society. When I was hanging up my billboards in the city, traditional people had a lot of negative reactions to them. They didn't want me to run and they continued to fight against me until the last day of my campaign. One big thing was that they didn't want me to show my face. They cut my face out of the pictures on the billboards and made many negative statements against me. Those fifty-eight days in 2010 stand out as the most stressful and tough days in my whole life.

I did not expect such enormous pressure. I will never forget the day a religious ex-MP came to my house and asked my father-in-law to get me to end my campaign. His reasoning was that it would be dishonorable and indecent if I were to work in the National Assembly. He told my father-in-law that the family's whole reputation would be ruined and that it would be a huge embarrassment if I won. After that, you can imagine how hard it was to hang posters in the city, participate in TV debates, and ask people to vote for you.

In comparison to most American candidates running for a seat in the U.S. Congress, who have an official crew of speechwriters, advisors, and secretaries, I had nobody but my husband to help with my campaign. Anytime I had an interview, he watched me and gave me feedback. Even now, anytime I have a speech, he is there. He helps me understand different points of views. He helps me to amplify my voice and enhance my skills.

I want my speeches to spread a message to the people. Women have the right of being in the society. When I was campaigning, I hoped that my words would give power to the silent majority of the province to vote for me. I wanted them to find their hopes while watching my speeches and debates.

My campaign team was all volunteer and mostly men. They were very important to my success. The biggest support was my family. As part of my campaign my husband, along with my parents and six doctors from my in-laws' family, offered free medical checks and treatment for people in different villages. People from all parts of society voted for me because they liked my opinions and my slogan: "Careful selection, responsible Parliament, and wise government."

But my campaign holds both sweet and bitter memories for me. I felt like I was giving hope to women and youth. It was like I was opening a path for them. Particularly women and girls—they were asking me to be their representative—to open up a way for them to step into politics. I really hope I can live up to this responsibility.

The people who really campaigned for me were the youth. Some I had met and others I hadn't. They persuaded their parents to vote for me. I was receiving so many phone calls from parents saying they had heard about me from their children and that they would support me.

But at the same time as I felt hope, I felt danger. I received so many threats that I had to stop the campaign toward the end. I got messages saying that the Taliban were waiting to attack me. I was restricted to going around in just one district in Herat. I had to ask for military protection. My family was also affected by the security problems. I had to take my daughter out of kindergarten because of the threat. I had to stop her school, a very hard thing for me. This is still an issue now; my friends ask me to be careful, to employ a body-guard and keep a gun in the car. But I hate such things.

When Election Day arrived, in the morning, I was thinking even if I don't get enough votes, I am the winner because struggling in such a controversy needs extraordinary bravery. At the end of Election Day I received the news that "I WON!" I got the highest number of votes among the women. That was not only the turning point of my career but my life. I became amazed when I was counting my votes because people from the religious community voted for me in addition to the youth, women, intellectuals, and professionals. I could not believe that I was able to overcome the conservative ideology of my society and could receive the religious votes—the vote of the people who were condemning women's representation in politics.

*   *   *

I have learned a lot in Parliament. We still have some big problems. The most challenging are the lack of party representation, lack of group work—being able to work together—and the lack of unification among women. Corruption is now also a part of Afghan culture, and unfortunately women have the most vulnerability toward this problem. Corruption reduces their access to justice, employment, and the basic needs of life. I think we can't stop corruption unless we bring reform to the administration system of Afghanistan.

Insecurity is still the biggest obstacle facing women and their presence in society. Even now, we have hundreds of girls' schools burned by the Taliban in certain areas of the country. Many female teachers and schoolgirls are kept home by their families because of the lack of security in the schools. Security is even a problem for the overall culture. In the last decade, Afghan people have tried to alter their culture, to make improvements for women and girls, but the lack of security prevents us from working on the issues and areas we need to.

We do have some progress. We now have the first generation of girls graduated from high school, the first generation to have uninterrupted education after decades of civil war in Afghanistan. I think this is the biggest achievement Afghan women have had. Despite the burning of girls' schools or pouring acid on the faces of schoolgirls and even poisoning them, girls make up 50 percent of students in many cities and provinces including Herat province, where it is actually at 51 percent.

I hope very much that soon the world will have a different view of Afghan women. After years of the dark regime of the Taliban, the world looked on Afghan women as victims. But I think it is important that the world look at Afghan women not as

> BUT I THINK IT IS IMPORTANT THAT THE WORLD LOOK AT AFGHAN WOMEN NOT AS VICTIMS ANYMORE BUT AS "LEADERS."

victims anymore but as "leaders." To reach that point, we very much need the Elimination of Violence Against Women law [EVAW] to be passed in Parliament. The law is the framework for that victory from an Afghan approach.

Representing my people in the Afghanistan Parliament was a great gift that people gave me in that election and it is now more than five years that I serve them proudly as one of the youngest members of the Parliament. As a woman who experienced years of limited life under the Taliban regime, representing all women and men who lived in such conditions was and always will be my highest pride.

Sometimes I think people in other countries don't realize that in this country of Afghanistan, there is a civilization. Historically and culturally, we are rich, but the Soviet Union occupation, civil war, and Taliban rule ruined that beautiful picture of civilization. I hope one day we can refresh that picture, that in maybe ten years, Afghanistan can stand on its own feet.

Afghanistan today is still not safe for female politicians at all, but I resist the fears because of the lesson I learned in my childhood: Don't give up. But even so, today, regardless of what happened yesterday, I and thousands of women like me have the right to live as the citizens of Afghanistan. That is the start of progress.

AFGHANISTAN TIMELINE

. . . .

500 B.C.—Darius I of Babylonia conquers the region.

329 B.C.—Alexander the Great conquers the region, including Afghanistan.

11th century—Mahmud of Ghazni (part of present-day Afghanistan) conquers territory and creates an empire from Iran to India. He also finishes the process begun by the Arabs in the 7th century of bringing Islam to nearly all of what will become modern-day Afghanistan.

13th century—Genghis Khan conquers Afghan territory for his empire.

1747—Ahmad Shah Durrani establishes a free and independent kingdom of Afghanistan. He rules over an empire that includes parts of modern-day India, Iran, and Central Asia. He dies in 1772. By 1792, the country falls into a civil war between two Pashtun clans, each claiming the throne. This war lasts for approximately thirty-five years.

1826—Dost Mohammad Khan ("the Great") declares himself amir and takes control of the throne. His reign unites Afghanistan under a single government.

1839–1842—First British-Afghan War begins after a mob in Kabul kills a British envoy. The war results in heavy British losses. British worry about Russian expansion south toward India.

1858—India falls under direct rule of Great Britain.

1878–1880—Second British-Afghan War begins after Afghanistan refuses a British diplomatic mission and again over concerns about Russian expansion.

1880—Abdur Rahman Khan ("Iron Amir") succeeds to the throne. He centralizes power in Kabul and is known for ruling with a firm hand.

1901—Amir Abdur Rahman dies. His son, Habibullah Khan, succeeds and presides over relatively peaceful times. Roads improve, telegraph lines link major cities, and the first secular secondary school opens in 1904. He is assassinated in 1919.

1919–1921—Third British-Afghan War. Amanullah Khan, Habibullah's son, declares total independence from Britain in 1919 as anti-British sentiment spreads.

1921—Amir Amanullah Khan begins social reforms. The first girls' school opens in Kabul. Western-style dress is encouraged and beards are outlawed.

1926—Amanullah declares Afghanistan a monarchy and names himself king.

1929—Amanullah abdicates and flees the country after his social reforms create unrest. He is deposed by Habibullah Kalakani, who reigns for nine months and reverses many reforms, including closing girls' schools, requiring women to have male escorts in public, and insisting men grow full beards. Nadir Khan deposes and executes Kalakani on November 1. Nadir is a modernist, but believes in slower change.

November 8, 1933—Nadir is assassinated and his son, Mohammed Zahir Shah, becomes king. He rules as king until ousted by a coup in 1973.

1946—Afghanistan joins the United Nations.

August 14, 1947—Pakistan as an independent nation-state is created out of a partition of Britain's India territory, after India receives its independence from Great Britain.

1953—Mohammed Daoud Khan, Zahir Shah's cousin, becomes prime minister of Afghanistan. Seeks support from Soviet Union for military and economic aid. Introduces social reforms such as abolishing *purdah*, a practice of keeping women secluded from public view. Attempted coup against the Shah of Iran.

1956—Pakistan becomes an Islamic Republic.

1959—Afghan women are no longer required to be veiled, they attend university and enter the workforce. Girls can go to the government high school in Lashkar Gah in a first step toward coeducation. Prime Minister Daoud announces that the women of the royal family will no longer wear chadris.

1963—Daoud steps down as prime minister after some in the royal family disagree with his attempts to align Afghanistan more closely with the Soviet Union. King Zahir Shah requests a new constitution and declares a constitutional monarchy.

1964—The new Afghan constitution establishes a democratic legislature and gives women the right to vote.

1973—Daoud overthrows King Zahir Shah in a military coup. He abolishes the monarchy and declares Afghanistan a republic, naming himself president. Strong ties to the Soviet Union are reinforced.

1975–1977—Daoud proposes a new constitution, which includes women's rights and other efforts to modernize the country.

1978—Daoud is overthrown and killed in a pro-Soviet coup.

February 1, 1979—Ayatollah Khomeini comes to power in Iran.

February 14, 1979—In Kabul, Ambassador Adolph Dubs of the United States is killed and the U.S. cuts off assistance to Afghanistan.

April 1, 1979—Iran becomes an Islamic Republic.

November 4, 1979—Iranians storm the U.S. Embassy in Tehran. U.S. hostage crisis begins.

December 24, 1979—The USSR invades Afghanistan.

Early 1980s—Mujahideen rebels unite against Soviet invaders and the USSR-backed Afghan army. During the Afghan-Soviet war in the 1980s, more than five million refugees flee to Pakistan and Iran.

February 15, 1989—The Soviet Union completes the withdrawal of their troops that began in May 1988 following peace accords signed in Geneva.

1989–1992—Civil war among the mujahideen.

April 16, 1992—Mujahideen fighters storm Kabul and oust President Najibullah from power. Najibullah takes refuge in the United Nations building. Civil war follows. Factions fight each other for control of Kabul.

August 1994—The first formation of the Taliban, led by Mullah Omar. From a small village near Kandahar, they begin their rise to power and start capturing provinces and territory across Afghanistan.

September 27, 1996—The Taliban take Kabul and proclaim the Islamic Emirate of Afghanistan. Major restrictions are imposed on women—they must wear burqas and face a beating for showing any skin, cannot go to school or work outside the home, and need to have a male escort in public. Music, movies, and Western-style clothes are banned, and beards become mandatory for men. The Taliban drag

Najibullah from the UN building in Kabul and publicly execute him. For the next several years, ethnic groups and the Northern Alliance—primarily mujahideen commander Ahmad Shah Masood's remaining forces—battle the Taliban for control of the country.

August 8, 1998—Al Qaeda bombs two American embassies in Africa (Nairobi, Kenya, and Dar es Salaam, Tanzania). The United States responds on August 20 with cruise missile attacks against suspected Osama bin Laden training camps in Afghanistan, missing bin Laden and his lieutenants.

September 9, 2001—Ahmad Shah Masood, the head of the Northern Alliance and a mujahideen commander still fighting the Taliban, is killed by assassins posing as journalists.

September 11, 2001—Hijackers crash four commercial airplanes in the United States killing nearly three thousand. The U.S. soon names Osama bin Laden and al Qaeda, headquartered in Afghanistan, as the prime suspects.

October 7, 2001—U.S. and British forces launch airstrikes against al Qaeda targets in Afghanistan after the Taliban do not answer calls to hand over bin Laden.

November 13, 2001—The Northern Alliance enters Kabul; the Taliban retreat southward toward Kandahar. First Lady Laura Bush delivers a radio address on November 17 to highlight the brutality of the Taliban and al Qaeda against women and children in Afghanistan.

December 7, 2001—The Taliban abandon their final stronghold in Kandahar, and surrender on December 9. Many successfully flee to sanctuary along the porous Afghan-Pakistan border and hide out in the tribal regions.

December 22, 2001—Hamid Karzai is sworn in as the leader of the interim government of Afghanistan.

August 8, 2003—NATO (North Atlantic Treaty Organization) assumes control of the International Security Force in Afghanistan, 65,000 troops from 42 countries.

January 2004—The Loya Jirga (the grand council) adopts a new constitution that calls for a president and two vice presidents.

October 9, 2004—Presidential elections are held with more than eight million votes cast. President Karzai is elected with 55 percent of the vote. He is reelected in 2009. It is the first time the Afghans have voted since 1969.

2005—Taliban insurgency regroups and launches a counteroffensive from the southern border by Pakistan.

March 29, 2005—First Lady Laura Bush makes the first of her three visits to Afghanistan. She met with then President Hamid Karzai, visited the Women's Teacher Training Institute, helped launch the American University of Afghanistan, and visited with U.S. troops. In a 2008 visit, she traveled to Bamiyan province and met with the female provincial governor and Afghan women who were training to become police officers.

September 18, 2005—The first parliamentary elections in more than thirty years take place.

2006—The American University of Afghanistan admits its first group of students, after a grant from USAID helps launch the university.

March 1, 2006—President George W. Bush makes a surprise trip to Afghanistan to inaugurate the new U.S. Embassy.

December 2, 2009—President Barack Obama announces a surge of thirty thousand additional U.S. troops to stabilize the security situation in Afghanistan.

May 2, 2011—U.S. forces kill Osama bin Laden in a raid on his safehouse in Pakistan.

September 21, 2012—U.S. troop surge in Afghanistan ends.

October 9, 2012—Pakistani teenager Malala Yousafzai, a girls' education advocate, is shot in the head by a Taliban gunman. She would go on to win the 2014 Nobel Peace Prize.

April 5, 2014—Third ever presidential elections in Afghanistan. Hamid Karzai cannot run for an additional term.

June 14, 2014—Presidential election runoff with top candidates.

September 19, 2014—Ashraf Ghani is declared the winner. He joins with the second-place vote recipient, Abdullah Abdullah, to form a national unity government as part of a power-sharing agreement. It is the first time there has been a peaceful transfer of power in Afghanistan's history.

December 2014—NATO formally ends its thirteen-year combat mission in Afghanistan.

March 19, 2015—A mob in Kabul brutally kills Farkhunda, a twenty-seven-year-old woman, after she is falsely accused of burning a Koran.

March 23, 2015—President Obama agrees to freeze U.S. troop withdrawals from Afghanistan for 2015, leaving a force of 9,800 in the country, but reiterates his promise to close all U.S. bases and consolidate the remaining troops in Kabul by the end of 2016.

September 28, 2015—Taliban forces overrun the northern city of Kunduz.

October 15, 2015—Afghan government forces, aided by U.S. air support, retake Kunduz.

October 16, 2015—President Obama announces that the U.S. troops currently stationed in Afghanistan will remain in the country until January 2017.

ACKNOWLEDGMENTS

. . . .

My deepest gratitude goes to the twenty-eight Afghan women and one man who shared their stories in these pages. Their words form the heart of this book. Their openness, honesty, bravery, and eloquence are a powerful and lasting testament to their struggles, their achievements, and their resilience. For what they have lived and their grace in telling it, I thank them from the bottom of my heart.

These women's stories could not have been told without Lyric Wallwork Winik. Lyric is a wonderful, talented writer who spent months working with the women in this book to find their voices and put their words on the page with honesty, clarity, and emotional impact.

Scribner provided a wonderfully nurturing and supportive home for this project, and at every point worked to ensure that this would be a beautiful and very-well-cared-for book. Thanks to Roz Lippel for her devotion to this project, to Susan Moldow and Nan Graham for their great support, and to Brian Belfiglio and Kyle Radler for ensuring that these stories would be shared as widely as possible. Thanks, too, to Katie Rizzo and Nancy Chen.

Emily Kropp Michel provided outstanding research support and photo compilation with great professionalism and good cheer. Jo Carmouche Shuffler produced flawless interview transcripts in record time. Katti Sheedfar offered nuanced translation, capturing the essence of words as they passed between languages.

At the George W. Bush Presidential Center, Charity Wallace, vice president of the Global Women's Initiatives, has guided the Women's Initiative with excellent vision and leadership. Her work on this project and so many others is deeply appreciated. Thanks as well to Sally McDonough at the start and Kevin Sullivan at the finish. Thanks to the Bush Center's president, Margaret Spellings, who leads by example every day. Thanks for the help of Betsy Martin. And I am deeply appreciative of my chief of staff, Caroline Hickey.

I am also particularly grateful to the following individuals who generously offered their time, assistance, and expertise on Afghanistan and the region: Ambassador Steve Steiner; Terry Neese of PEACE THROUGH BUSINESS; Christian Wistehuff of the Initiative To Educate Afghan Women; Ambassador Barbara Barrett of Project Artemis; Connie Duckworth of ARZU; Manizha Naderi of Women For Afghan Women; my White House chief of staff and the Honorable Anita McBride; and the Honorable Paula Dobriansky.

For their valuable assistance, thanks to Wynona Heim of Project Artemis; Melissa Bertenthal of ARZU; Karen Berkheimer, Karel Ford, and Sherrie Phillips of PEACE THROUGH BUSINESS; and Sarah Gesiriech, Susan Ryan, and also Alison Hendry of the Afghan Institute of Learning. Thanks to Jodie Steck and Kristen O'Hare at the George W. Bush Presidential Library and Hannah Abney at the George W. Bush Presidential Center.

Special thanks to my husband, George W. Bush, whose vision for the Bush Center is for it to be a place of learning, scholarship, and action, where ideas matter. The free exchange of ideas is a precious gift that we are both pleased to share. Thanks to my wonderful daughters, Barbara and Jenna, and to my son-in-law, Henry Hager. I am grateful for the gift of my granddaughters, Mila and Poppy, and hopeful for a better future for all the world's daughters and granddaughters.

—Mrs. Laura W. Bush

A NOTE ABOUT RESOURCES

. . . .

The individuals who share their stories in this book were located largely through the generous assistance of organizations that make up the U.S.-Afghan Women's Council, a public-private partnership housed at Georgetown University, designed to address areas of need for Afghan women and children in education, health, economic empowerment, and leadership development, under the leadership of First Ladies Laura Bush, Hillary R. Clinton, and Rula Ghani, all of whom serve together as the honorary co-chairs. Additional assistance was provided by the George W. Bush Presidential Center's Women's Initiative, through its Afghan Women's Project. Interviews were conducted by Lyric Winik primarily via Skype, often with interpreter Katti Sheedfar, as well as in person.

ORGANIZATIONS

ARZU Studio Hope. Founded in 2004 by former Goldman Sachs partner and managing director and U.S. Afghan Women's Council member Connie Duckworth, ARZU empowers Afghan women and their communities through a holistic three-pronged strategy combining fair-trade employment, education, maternal healthcare, and sustainable community development. ARZU preserves the traditional Afghan craft of rug weaving, reordering the traditional and exploitative Afghan rug trade by paying women bonuses for high-quality workmanship. ARZU weavers must agree to send their sons and daughters to school, attend literacy classes, and receive pre- and post-natal care for themselves and their babies.

The Initiative To Educate Afghan Women. An undergraduate higher education program that partners with American colleges and universities to advance the next generation of Afghan women leaders, the Initiative also provides leadership, diversity and media training, as well as academic and professional mentorship to prepare students for leadership roles in Afghanistan. Graduates of the Initiative's program now occupy senior roles in the political, economic, and social development of their homeland.

PEACE THROUGH BUSINESS. Founded by Oklahoma entrepreneur Dr. Terry Neese (founder and CEO of the Institute for Economic Empowerment of Women), PEACE THROUGH BUSINESS empowers women business owners economically, socially, and politically in both Afghanistan and Rwanda by offering a ten-week business training and mentorship program. PEACE THROUGH BUSINESS in-country graduates come to the United States where they spend a week at Business Boot Camp. They then spend seven days living and working with a female American business owner, after which they participate in an international women's economic summit. After returning to Afghanistan, they commit to mentoring other women business owners, speaking to women's organizations, and advocating for economic issues. American mentors continue to work with the women for one year via electronic communication.

Project Artemis. Located at the Thunderbird School of Global Management at Arizona State University in Glendale, Project Artemis, founded by Ambassador Barbara Barrett, trains Afghan women entrepreneurs in business skills. It provides two weeks of entrepreneurship training in the United States with materials in English and Dari, via business school classes taught by senior faculty, visits to American businesses, and personal mentoring of each woman on her business. Course topics include marketing, financial reporting, business strategy, negotiation skills, and leadership.

Women For Afghan Women. Founded in 2001, Women For Afghan Women is a women's human rights organization based across Afghanistan and in New York City. With a staff that is 99 percent Afghan, Women For Afghan Women operates legal aid centers and emergency and long-term shelters for women and children in thirteen of Afghanistan's thirty-four provinces. It is the largest shelter-providing nongovernmental organization (NGO) in Afghanistan. It also conducts human rights training to diverse groups, including law enforcement, religious leaders, and community members and advocates for women's rights.

Afghan Institute of Learning. Founded by Dr. Sakena Yacoobi, the institute was developed from refugee schools and centers for Afghans who had fled to Pakistan and was also responsible for eighty "secret" girls' schools inside Afghanistan during the time of the Taliban. Today, the Afghan Institute of Learning's mission is to provide education, training, and health services to vulnerable Afghans in order to foster self-reliance, critical-thinking skills, and community participation throughout Afghanistan and Pakistan.

Afghan Women's Business Federation. Founded by Mina Sherzoy, it promotes the welfare and rights of female workers, provides vocational and business training, and advocates for opportunities for women in Afghanistan.

Turquoise Mountain. Established in 2006 at the behest of Great Britain's HRH Prince of Wales and the then president of Afghanistan, Hamid Karzai, Turquoise Mountain seeks to revive and preserve Afghanistan's traditional crafts and arts by supporting and training local artisans in woodwork, calligraphy, miniature painting, ceramics, jewelry making, and gem cutting. In addition, Turquoise Mountain is working to restore Murad Khani, a historic area of Kabul's Old

City. Buried under garbage and without running water or utilities after decades of war, in the last ten years many of Murad Khani's historic buildings have been restored, utilities have been installed, and a health clinic and primary school have opened.

10,000 Women. The Goldman Sachs *10,000 Women* initiative is a campaign to foster economic growth by providing women entrepreneurs around the world with a business and management education and access to capital. The initiative has reached women from across fifty-six countries through a network of one hundred academic, nonprofit, and bank partners. In partnership with International Finance Corporation (IFC), *10,000 Women* launched a $600 million finance facility in 2014 to enable a hundred thousand women entrepreneurs to access capital. To date, the facility has completed sixteen transactions totaling $254 million in eleven countries.

Razia's Ray of Hope Foundation. A nonprofit organization to empower young Afghan women and girls through community-based education. Founded on the belief that education is key to positive, peaceful change for current and future generations, Razia's Ray of Hope provides young Afghan women in rural areas with the opportunity to learn and grow in a safe, nurturing environment. Its flagship project is an all-girl K–12 school that provides free, exemplary education. The foundation and its programs were begun by Afghan native Razia Jan, who, among other honors, has been named a CNN Top 10 Hero.

Fulbright Program. Founded by the late U.S. Senator J. William Fulbright in 1946 and supported by the U.S. Congress and partner governments around the world, the Fulbright Program is an international educational exchange program that offers highly competitive, merit-based grants for citizens of the United States and more than 160 other countries. Fulbright awards are granted to students, scholars, teachers, and other professionals in a wide variety of fields, with approximately eight thousand awards granted annually. It is considered one of the most prestigious awards programs in the world. Fifty-four Fulbright alumni have been recipients of Nobel Prizes and more than thirty have served as a head of state or government. As of 2014, 365,000 persons—131,000 from the United States and 234,000 from other countries—have participated in the program since its inception. More than five hundred Afghans have come to the United States on the Fulbright Foreign Student program.

Websites to learn more:

ARZU Studio Hope: arzustudiohope.org

The Initiative To Educate Afghan Women: ieaw.org

PEACE THROUGH BUSINESS: ieew.org/peace-through-business

Project Artemis: t4g.thunderbird.edu/programs/project-artemis -afghanistan

Women For Afghan Women: womenforafghanwomen.org

Afghan Institute of Learning: afghaninstituteoflearning.org

Turquoise Mountain: turquoisemountain.org

10,000 Women: goldmansachs.com/citizenship/10000women/

Razia's Ray of Hope Foundation: raziasrayofhope.org

Fulbright Program: eca.state.gov/Fulbright

U.S.-Afghan Women's Council: gucchd.georgetown.edu/USAWC

George W. Bush Presidential Center: bushcenter.org

PHOTOGRAPH CREDITS

. . . .

LIVING (p. 4), clockwise from top left
PEACE THROUGH BUSINESS
ARZU
Fakhria Ibrahimi
Fakhria Ibrahimi
Twitter photo from Zainularab Miri

LEARNING (p. 85), clockwise from top left
Women For Afghan Women
Women For Afghan Women
Fakhria Ibrahimi
Women For Afghan Women
Afghan Institute of Learning

WORKING (p. 435), clockwise from top left
Fakhria Ibrahimi
Thunderbird
Afghan Midwives Association
Fakhria Ibrahimi
Fakhria Ibrahimi
PEACE THROUGH BUSINESS

SURVIVING (p. 203), clockwise from top

Afghan Institute of Learning

Fakhria Ibrahimi

Women For Afghan Women

Afghan Institute for Learning

Afghan Institute for Learning

CHALLENGING (p. 243), clockwise from top

George W. Bush Presidential Center

Initiative To Educate Afghan Women

PEACE THROUGH BUSINESS

AP Photo/Massoud Hossaini

INDEX

· · · ·

INDEX

INDEX

INDEX